# SOCIALISM

# IN PROCESS

D1235944

# SOCIALISM
# IN PROCESS

## EDITED BY

## JUSTIN HEINZEKEHR

## & PHILIP CLAYTON

PROCESS
CENTURY
PRESS
ANOKA, MINNESOTA 2017

*Socialism in Process*
© 2017 Process Century Press

Process Century Press
RiverHouse LLC
802 River Lane
Anoka, MN 55303

Process Century Press books are published in association with the International Process Network.

Cover: Susanna Mennicke

VOLUME XIV: TOWARD ECOLOGICAL CIVILIZATION SERIES
JEANYNE B. SLETTOM, GENERAL EDITOR

ISBN 978-1-940447-27-8

Printed in the United States of America

# CONTENTS

1. Socialism in Process: Marx, Whitehead and the New American Left, 1
   *Justin Heinzekehr*

   PART ONE: REVISITING THE ALTERNATIVES:
   RESOURCES IN MARX AND WHITEHEAD

2. A Whiteheadian Approach to Rethinking Economics for the Sustainability Revolution, 19
   *Carol Frances Johnston*

3. Global Challenges and Wisdom Resources: Why Go Back to Whitehead and Marx and What Can We Learn from Them?, 39
   *Ouyang Kang*

4. Persons-in-Community in Whitehead, Smith and Marx: Exploring Marx's Concept of Class through Adam Smith's Concept of Social Order, 49
   *Mark Dibben and Cristina Neesham*

5. Organic Marxism and the Marxist Tradition, 71
   *Leslie A. Muray*

PART TWO: REINTERPRETING SOCIAL THOUGHT
FOR AN ECOLOGICAL CONTEXT

6. Commodity Fetishism and Critical Metaphysics, 85
   *Jung Mo Sung*

7. Solidarity, 99
   *Anne F. Pomeroy*

8. Alternative Values to an Extractivist Logic, 131
   *Timothy Murphy*

PART THREE: ADAPTATION AND DIVERSITY:
TOWARD A CONTEMPORARY SOCIALISM

9. Against the Insanity of Growth: Degrowth as Concrete
   Utopia, 145
   *Barbara Muraca*

10. Mariátegui and Whitehead: The Metaphysics of Local
    Marxisms, 169
    *Justin Heinzekehr*

11. Responding to Climate Change: Local Knowledge in African-
    American Communities on Maryland's Eastern Shore, 179
    *Christine D. Miller Hesed*

12. Why Movements Matter Most: A Conversation with the New
    Materialism, 203
    *Joerg Rieger*

13. Socialism for the Common Good, 227
    *Philip Clayton*

*Contributors, 249*

We live in the ending of an age. But the ending of the modern period differs from the ending of previous periods, such as the classical or the medieval. The amazing achievements of modernity make it possible, even likely, that its end will also be the end of civilization, of many species, or even of the human species. At the same time, we are living in an age of new beginnings that give promise of an ecological civilization. Its emergence is marked by a growing sense of urgency and deepening awareness that the changes must go to the roots of what has led to the current threat of catastrophe.

In June 2015, the 10th Whitehead International Conference was held in Claremont, CA. Called "Seizing an Alternative: Toward an Ecological Civilization," it claimed an organic, relational, integrated, nondual, and processive conceptuality is needed, and that Alfred North Whitehead provides this in a remarkably comprehensive and rigorous way. We proposed that he could be "the philosopher of ecological civilization." With the help of those who have come to an ecological vision in other ways, the conference explored this Whiteheadian alternative, showing how it can provide the shared vision so urgently needed.

The judgment underlying this effort is that contemporary research and scholarship is still enthralled by the 17th century view of nature articulated by Descartes and reinforced by Kant. Without freeing our minds of this objectifying and reductive understanding of the world, we are not likely to direct our actions wisely in response to the crisis to which this tradition has led us. Given the ambitious goal of replacing now dominant patterns of thought with one that would redirect us toward ecological civilization, clearly more is needed than a single conference. Fortunately, a larger platform is developing that includes the conference and looks beyond it. It is named Pando Populus (pandopopulous.com) in honor of the world's largest and oldest organism, an aspen grove.

As a continuation of the conference, and in support of the larger initiative of Pando Populus, we are publishing this series, appropriately named "Toward Ecological Civilization."

~John B. Cobb, Jr.

OTHER BOOKS IN THIS SERIES

*An Axiological Process Ethics,* Rem B. Edwards
*Panentheism and Scientific Naturalism,* David Ray Griffin
*Organic Marxism,* Philip Clayton and Justin Heinzekehr
*Theological Reminiscences,* John B. Cobb, Jr.
*Integrative Process,* Margaret Stout and Jeannine M. Love
*Replanting Ourselves in Beauty,* Jay McDaniel & Patricia Adams Farmer, eds.
*For Our Common Home,* John B. Cobb, Jr., & Ignacio Castuera, eds.
*Whitehead Word Book,* John B. Cobb, Jr.
*The Vindication of Radical Empiricism,* Michel Weber
*Intuition in Mathematics and Physics,* Ronny Desmet, ed.
*Reforming Higher Education in an Era of Ecological Crisis and Growing
    Digital Insecurity,* Chet Bowers
*Protecting Our Common, Sacred Home,* David Ray Griffin
*Educating for an Ecological Civilization,* Marcus Ford & Stephen Rowe, eds.

## ~ 1 ~

## SOCIALISM IN PROCESS:

### MARX, WHITEHEAD, AND THE
### NEW AMERICAN LEFT

*Justin Heinzekehr*

EVENTS IN THE LAST FEW YEARS have transformed the role of socialism in American culture and politics.

At the close of the twentieth century, many in the United States might have confidently assumed that socialism was an irrelevant concept of the distant Cold War past. Capitalism had shown its dominance in the fall of the Soviet Union, in the gradual liberalization of Chinese markets, in the economic boom of the 1990s. In American politics, the Democrat and Republican Parties were offering centrist and right-centrist positions, respectively; both emphasized free trade and limited government spending. There were few real alternatives available for those who desired more radical social change.

This was not particularly out of the ordinary; the United States has always been less hospitable to socialism than the rest of the world. In 1906 a German sociologist named Werner Sombart wondered, in a famous essay, "Why Is There No Socialism in the United States?" After all, under Marxist theory, the most developed capitalist country should also be the place where socialism is most likely to emerge.[1]

He concluded that the lack of American socialism is due to the fact that the working classes in the United States enjoy higher standards of living than their counterparts in Europe, greater social mobility, better integration into the political system, and a fetish-like loyalty to the Constitution.

> America is a freer and more egalitarian society than Europe. In his relationship to other people and to social institutions, and in his [sic] position in and to society . . . the American is also better-off than he would be in the contrasting European situation. For him "Liberty" and "Equality". . . are not empty ideas and vague dreams, as they are for the European work-ing class; for the most part they are realities.[2]

However, Sombart predicted that all of the factors that were prevent-ing the emergence of socialism were about to disappear. He expected socialism to become dominant in the United States within the next generation.

Obviously Sombart was mistaken on a couple levels. Although it is true that socialism has never had the same level of political prominence in the United States as it has in other parts of the world, it is also too simplistic to say that socialism has never had any signif-icant presence here. In fact, although they have often gone by other names, socialist policies, institutions, and ideologies have always existed alongside those aligned with free market capitalism. (We'll look at some of this often-forgotten heritage later in the chapter.) On the other hand, Sombart's predictions for socialism in the United States were clearly naïve, or at least very premature. It is true that the conditions for working class people changed suddenly in the next generations with the Great Depression in the 1930s. But the result was Roosevelt's New Deal, not a socialist revolution, and capitalist ideology remained dominant as the economy recovered.

In the last decade, however, the national conversation has changed drastically once again. Part of the change is due to the erosion of economic opportunity, as Sombart might have predicted.

The collapse of the real estate market in 2008 exposed the corruption and greed that had propped up the economy, and young people especially lost confidence in the efficiency and inevitability of capitalism. It is now evident that politicians have made inadequate progress in addressing the most urgent social problems of our day. Instead of the American dream, college graduates encountered a stagnant job market. Wealth disparity in the United States is worse now than it has ever been, and, despite the Paris conference of 2015, world leaders have not been able to agree on policy changes at the level required to prevent the worst consequences of climate change. It has become more and more evident that these pressing problems — climate change and environmental degradation, growing disparity of wealth, unemployment and underemployment — do not have capitalist solutions and in fact are caused by capitalist assumptions about human relationships and our relationship with the environment.

The growing disillusionment around social progress has surfaced in many visible ways: the Occupy movement, the People's Climate March, and the presidential campaigns of both Bernie Sanders and Donald Trump in 2016. Indeed, the unexpected success of Trump's campaign highlights the depth of American disillusionment, especially in the white, Midwestern working class. In one sense, Trump's victory could be seen as a victory for working class people and a wake-up call to the mainstream Democratic Party.

However, Trump's victory is deeply troubling for three reasons. First, although his campaign rhetoric emphasized solidarity with the working class against the economic elites, his stated policies would actually exacerbate the disparity of wealth in the United States. Second, although populist rhetoric is not necessarily problematic in itself, the combination of populism and inflammatory nativism threatens to undermine basic democratic values like religious pluralism and racial and gender equality. Finally, Trump's victory is an "unimaginable disaster" for our ecological future.[3] Now more than ever, we need a platform on the left that combines radical economic change, full social inclusion for racial minorities, women and LGBTQ people, and decisive action to address climate change.[4]

Luckily, we are already seeing the birth and rapid growth of a grassroots movement that aims to achieve these goals. Students on college campuses are now more likely to be involved in activism than they have since the 1960s, despite the stereotypes portraying millennials as self-centered and apathetic. Thirty-four percent of first-year students now identify as "liberal" or "far left," the largest percentage since the early 1970s.[5] This generation will likely continue to push for more liberal policies even as they age; recent studies have shown that political identities are usually formed from ages 14 to 24 and tend to be relatively stable after that point.[6] As Peter Beinart of the *Atlantic* says, "Millennials are not liberal primarily because they are young. They are liberal because their formative political experiences were the Iraq War and the Great Recession, and because they make up the most secular, most racially diverse, least nationalistic generation in American history."[7]

Still, the more cynical among us might say that these kinds of social movements have come and gone before and are not likely to result in any lasting change. Werner Sombart's 1906 prediction should make us cautious about interpreting periodic political fluctuations as radical breaks with the past. What does seem different about this leftward shift, however, is the willingness of the younger generation to be explicitly critical of the capitalist framework as a whole, and to see socialism as an attractive alternative. A recent Pew poll shows that U.S. citizens between the ages of 18 and 29 are more likely to have positive views of socialism than they are of capitalism, a threshold crossed just in the past two years.[8] A poll at the 2016 Iowa caucuses found that 43% of Democrat voters would use the term "socialist" to describe themselves (the number rises to 58% among Bernie Sanders' supporters).[9] The numbers suggest not only a desire for economic reform, but also a disillusionment with the basic economic structures that Americans have taken for granted in the past.

It remains to be seen whether or not these movements can sustain their energy and channel it to achieve substantial social change. Even if "socialism" as a term is losing some of its previous stigma, for most people in the United States a real alternative to capitalism seems to be lacking. Even if the Occupy protesters have a point about capitalist abuses, a critic might say, there is no better economic philosophy that could guide the reformulation of political institutions and social structures. Similarly, says that same critic, there are no better economic institutions and no more efficient way to structure international trade than large multinational banks that create capital and operate in a free market. The socialist state has tried and failed to regulate national economies. It is easy to criticize capitalism, but difficult to offer a constructive, practical alternative.

In contrast to these critics, the authors of this volume believe that there is a viable alternative to capitalism, for the United States and for the international economy. But for socialism to become more than a byword for left-leaning college students, we need to link action with theory. We need to connect the momentum of these grassroots movements with the socialist heritage. This is by no means to suggest that we use socialism as a body of doctrines to be used as a litmus test for those who would participate in these broad-based efforts for social change—quite the opposite. Socialism has always been a diverse movement, with many sources and many different interpretations. As Leslie Muray points out in chapter 5, Karl Marx himself considered socialism to be an evolving and adaptive movement. It is important, then, to recognize that socialism has always been pluralistic, in the United States no less than in Europe or Asia.

On the other hand, socialism has sometimes differentiated itself so much that fracturing and infighting becomes debilitating.[10] So it is significant that Bernie Sanders' campaign was able to create, quite unexpectedly, such a broad coalition organized around socialist values but incorporating a variety of ideological commitments. And although the Sanders camp could appear to be disorganized or vague at times, there are a set of shared values that bring these new "socialists" together. As a general outline of these values, we might use William Smaldone's definition:

> By socialism, I am referring to a set of related but often con-flicting political and social movements that share a particular set of ideals. Instead of a society dominated by competi-tion among individuals and groups, socialists emphasize the importance of planning, cooperation, workplace democracy, and mutual responsibility. To establish social equality, they strive to replace the capitalist economy, based on the owner-ship of private property, with one based on social or public ownership. Socialists also have aimed to build a world in which social solidarity is achieved through the realization of individual freedom and legal and social equality. As it matured into a mass movement, socialism propagated an ideal of universal human emancipation that would overcome all forms of exploitation and discrimination based on class, race, religion, or gender.[11]

In keeping with the spirit of the times, not all of our authors would agree to every point in this definition, but in general we agree on the inherent unsustainability and injustice of capitalism, the importance of class differences for social analysis, and the benefits of an economy based on the common good rather than competition.

The goal of the book, therefore, is not to present a monolithic or even completely consistent political program. Rather, we want to highlight some existing socialist theories and show how these the-ories are embedded in a specific context and respond to challenges of specific communities. We are not interested in creating or main-taining a socialist "orthodoxy," though many of us find inspiration in Marx and other classic socialist texts.[12] Rather, we hope to foster the adaptive and creative aspects that have always been a part of the socialist tradition.

This brings us to the second major goal of this book, which is to connect socialist theory to process philosophy, a school of thought that emphasizes relationship and change as the basic categories of reality rather than permanence or substance. For many of us, process philosophy, especially the version articulated by Alfred North Whitehead, helps to bring out those aspects of socialist thought which are most crucial for our day and most likely to energize activists for social change. In particular, this book highlights the role that a relational, adaptive, culturally sensitive socialism might play as an ecological alternative to capitalism. Socialists have traditionally emphasized the suffering caused by the concentration of wealth in a few hands and the growing disparity between the wealthy and the working class. We now have overwhelming evidence that the suffering of working class people around the world is exacerbated by the environmental destruction that capitalist economies require. In the twenty-first century, if we want an equitable society, we must also work towards a sustainable society.

As we think about the possibilities for a new American socialism, then, I want to first outline the different sources that American socialism has drawn on in the past, and then, more specifically, highlight the potential of a collaboration between this socialist heritage and Whitehead's process philosophy. The result would be a heterogeneous movement that nonetheless embodies the core values of socialism, emerges organically from local communities, and encourages a sustainable, just society—a "socialism in process."

## THE MANY ROOTS OF AMERICAN SOCIALISM[13]

The history of socialism in the United States is more difficult to trace than in other countries. For one thing, as we have mentioned already, socialism as an explicit political program did not take root in the United States as it did elsewhere. Although there have been Marxist movements in the United States, terms like "communism," "Marxism" or "socialism" have generally carried too negative a connotation to be used as a label for major political candidates or policies (at least until recently). However, there have also been social movements active in the United States that parallel Marxist socialism, but go by other names and take their inspiration from other sources. These too should be seen as part of the American socialist heritage. They are available as resources for emerging social movements in the United States, along with Marx himself and other Marxian philosophers.

Although Americans have always associated Marxism with atheism, there are socialist traditions in the United States that share many of Marx's concerns and yet are rooted firmly in the Christian tradition. Some have been inspired, for instance, by the book of Acts, which records the church's abolishment of private property and the distribution of goods according to need.[14] There are religious communities, like the Amish or Hutterites, who have maintained their identities in the United States since the eighteenth century and who constitute perhaps the closest thing to a permanent "communist" society anywhere in the Western world. Similar Christian values have sparked broader movements like the Social Gospel of the early twentieth century, which mobilized Protestants to advocate for affordable housing, education, and healthcare for all citizens. Although as a distinct movement the Social Gospel lasted only a short time, it had a profound effect on the American political discourse, laying the groundwork for social policies like the New Deal and women's suffrage.

The Social Gospel mainly avoided the term "socialism." However, one can also find cases where socialism was explicitly connected to the Christian ideals of social justice. Frank Zeidler, mayor of Milwaukee from 1948 to 1960, was elected as a Socialist Party candidate. He was very much influenced by his Lutheran background, and throughout his tenure encouraged cooperation between municipal and church organizations to tackle social issues like housing and race relations. After Zeidler's death in 2006, his congregation established the Zeidler Center for Public Discussion, which now holds monthly public events on issues such as immigration, gun violence, and interfaith relations.[15]

Besides the religious stream of American socialism, there is also what might be called a pragmatic stream. This would include the many publicly owned enterprises in the United States, which, paradoxically, are often supported most fervently by conservative voters and politicians. One such example is the Alaska Permanent Fund, which manages oil and mineral extraction. The natural resources are owned by the state and rented out to drilling companies. The state then pays out profits in the form of an annual dividend to each citizen, which has averaged about $1400 in the last five years.[16] We might raise questions about the environmental ethics of extracting oil in Alaska, but the fact remains that this system of public ownership and profit distribution is, almost by definition, socialist, and that it flourishes in one of our "reddest" states.[17] Similar funds exist in Texas and Wyoming, although their revenues go toward the state budget rather than being returned directly to citizens. Publicly owned utilities account for approximately 25% of the energy production in the United States, and tend to be slightly less expensive and more efficient than privately-owned utilities.[18] One of the largest of these publicly-owned operations, the Tennessee Valley Authority, was vigorously defended by local Republicans after President Barack Obama proposed its privatization in 2013.[19]

These two versions of American socialism, the religious and the pragmatic, have in common the fact that they tend not to define themselves primarily by ideology. Religious socialists might organize their actions around a set of core values, inherited from their religious tradition. Pragmatic socialists are generally focused on results rather than acting out of a political philosophy. Indeed, most people in the latter group support these socialist institutions in direct opposition to their own stated philosophies. So American socialism has never been a "pure" socialism; it has always mixed Marxist and socialist philosophies with religious values and pragmatic politics.

This ideological looseness can be a strength and a weakness. On the one hand, without connecting social action to theory, we risk missing the connections between these disparate movements. For instance, it could make it easier for religious social justice advocates to work with explicit socialist movements if they realized how similar their goals were. And it would greatly help the cause of socialism in the United States if more people realized that our economy already mixes capitalist and socialist institutions. The very fact that we haven't considered religious and pragmatic groups "socialist" gives the impression that there are fewer alternatives to capitalism than there really are.

On the other hand, the fact that these American "socialists" are not bound by preconceived ideological frameworks may encourage unlikely collaborations and hybridity that would ultimately strengthen a socialist movement. Occupy Wall Street was built on a very minimal set of principles, and it was partly because of that minimalism that it was able to mobilize such a broad group of people. The trick is to find a balance that includes careful, nuanced thinking but also enough leeway to allow for collaboration wherever possible.

## WHITEHEAD AND SOCIAL THOUGHT

In the true spirit of American socialism, then, the authors of this book have identified another potential partnership, this time between socialism and process philosophy. (Many of the essays in this volume come out of a conference session dedicated to finding connections between Karl Marx and Alfred North Whitehead, one of the major figures in process philosophy.[20]) We believe the two movements share many core concepts, and can also be enriched by the differences in their two approaches to the world. We especially hope that this collaboration will open up possibilities for social movements that link economic justice with environmental sustainability.

Like socialism, process philosophy is a diverse and evolving movement, and our authors do not necessarily agree in their interpretations of Marx or Whitehead. Yet there are a few common themes that arise when socialism and process philosophy are considered in tandem. Socialism in general, and certainly Marx's version of socialism, could be considered a type of process philosophy. Marx, for example, saw history as a dialectical movement, an evolution of human society that built continuously on the past, but also resulted in the emergence of new social structures. Whitehead held a similar conception of reality as a series of events, each one taking account of its past history, but also making a unique contribution to that history as it emerges in the present.

Whitehead helps to bring out certain aspects of Marx's writing that are sometimes underemphasized. For one, Whitehead makes a very thorough critique of Western metaphysics. One of the most dangerous ideas, according to Whitehead, is that reality is made up of discrete, independent units—substances, in other words. According to much of Western philosophy, these substances will have the same qualities no matter what context they are placed in. A rock remains a rock whether you drop it in a river, or break it apart with a hammer. In reality, Whitehead says, everything is inherently related to its environment, and its qualities are products of those relationships. If you look deeper, a rock is rock-like not because there is something inherently rock-ish about the particles that make it up, but because these particles exist in a certain configuration, a certain set of relationships. The qualities of hardness or density emerge from these relationships.

As it turns out, Western societies have tended to think about human societies as if we were a collection of individual, isolated substances rather than a community built on relationships. This kind of thinking tends to promote ideals of competition and invisible-hand economics. In fact, Marx makes a very similar claim to Whitehead when he talks about capital as a fetish (see Jung Mo Sung's chapter for more on this topic). Here Whitehead's metaphysical analysis fits nicely with Marx's socialism, and helps to clarify and expand this insight.

Given the relational nature of process philosophy, it should be no surprise that process thinkers have been highly invested in environmental theory and activism. But recent scholars like John Bellamy Foster have rediscovered Marx's own ecological contribution.[21] Both schools of thought agree that human beings depend on their relationship to the natural world, although we have been alienated from nature for various reasons. Marx emphasizes the negative role that capitalism plays in this alienation; Whitehead blames our underlying philosophy of substance. Together, both might be useful for activists struggling against the resistance of powerful politicians, corporations, and lobbyists, as well as deeply held American prejudices against social thought.

Finally, reading socialism through the lens of process philosophy helps guard against overly rigid interpretations of socialism. For instance, some have seen in Marx a mechanical and deterministic depiction of human history. Part of the problem in the United States is that "socialism" brings to mind the image of Soviet communism, the repression of creativity, individuality, and human rights. There are many disagreements about where Soviet socialism went wrong, and how much blame Marx deserves for Stalinist Russia. Some have claimed that Marx's earlier writings are more democratic and humanistic, but that his later writings emphasized determinism and materialism to the point that they encourage totalitarianism.[22] At any rate, a partnership between process and socialist philosophies helps draw out the flexibility and creativity which constitutes the best of the socialist tradition.

Because we see socialism as an adaptive, evolving tradition, we do not attempt to outline a specific program that could be applied in any context. Rather, we believe that socialism works best when it is intimately tied to particular locations and communities. Thus this book moves from general reflections on process-oriented socialism to suggestions for utilizing these resources in more specific settings. Part One considers possible resources in Marx and Whitehead for contemporary socialist movements. Part Two suggests certain adaptations that might be made within the process or socialist traditions in order to respond more fully to the environmental crisis. Part Three explores ways that ecological socialism has adapted to particular contexts and might be applied to new contexts in the future.

In the end, the goal of this book is not to return to any "original" framework or to foster a new Marxist or Whiteheadian orthodoxy.

Rather, we conceive the process and socialist traditions as existing within a constant process of reinterpretation, re-application, and revision. Reading these traditions in the context of a commitment to ecological sustainability, we discover a socialism that leads us beyond mechanical orthodoxy toward grassroots engagement. We find a process-based understanding of systems that functions not merely as an abstract description of reality, but as an effective critique of economic domination and a lever for social change.

## ENDNOTES

1   "If, as I have myself always maintained and often stated, modern Socialism follows as a necessary reaction to capitalism, the country with the most advanced capitalist development, namely the United States, would at the same time be the one providing the classic case of Socialism, and its working class would be the supporters of the most radical of Socialist movements." Werner Sombart, *Why Is There No Socialism in the United States?*, trans. Patricia Hocking and C. T. Husbands (London: Macmillan, 1976), 15–16.

2   Ibid., 108.

3   Philip Clayton, "A Trump Presidency's Impact on the Planet," The Huffington Post, November 14, 2016 <http://www.huffingtonpost.com/philip-clayton-phd/a-trump-presidencys-impac_b_12884156.html>.

4   See Bernie Sanders' post-election editorial: "Where the Democrats Go From Here," *New York Times,* November 11, 2016 <http://www.nytimes.com/2016/11/12/opinion/bernie-sanders-where-the-democrats-go-from-here.html?_r=1>.

5   Courtney Kueppers, "Today's Freshmen: Most Likely to Protest Since the 1960s," *The Chronicle of Higher Education,* February 19, 2016.

6   See Amanda Cox, "How Birth Year Influences Political Views," *New York Times,* July 7, 2014 <http://www.nytimes.com/interactive/2014/07/08/upshot/how-the-year-you-were-born-influences-your-politics.html>; Nicholas L. Danigelis, Melissa Hardy, and Stephen J. Cutler, "Population Aging, Intracohort Aging, and Sociopolitical Attitudes,"

*American Sociological Review* 72, no. 5 (October 2007): 812–30.

7   Peter Beinart, "Why America Is Moving Left," *Atlantic,* February 2016 <http://www.theatlantic.com/magazine/archive/2016/01/why-america-is-moving-left/419112/>.

8   Pew Research Center, "Little Change in Public's Response to 'Capitalism,' 'Socialism'," Pew Research Center for the People and the Press, December 28, 2011 <http://www.people-press.org/2011/12/28/little-change-in-publics-response-to-capitalism-socialism/>.

9   John McCormick and Arit John, "Anti-Wall Street Sentiment Breaks by Party Line in Iowa Poll," Bloomberg Politics, January 15, 2016 <http://www.bloomberg.com/politics/articles/2016-01-15/anti-wall-street-sentiment-breaks-by-party-line-in-iowa-poll>.

10  See, for example, the infighting and rivalry within the American socialist parties during the 2016 election cycle. Bill Scher, "Why Socialists Can't Wait for Bernie to Lose," Politico Magazine, February 4, 2016, http://www.politico.com/magazine/story/2016/02/why-socialists-cant-wait-for-bernie-to-lose-213593.

11  William Smaldone, *European Socialism: A Concise History with Documents* (Lanham, MD: Rowman & Littlefield Publishers, 2013), 2.

12  We use the broader term "socialism" rather than the more specific "Marxism" to indicate the fact that the contributors to this book do not necessarily assume Marx's writings as a framework.

13  In this section, I am especially indebted to John Cobb's opening statement at the "Organic Marxism and Ecological Civilization" conference, held in Claremont, California on April 29, 2016.

14  "All who believed were together and had all things in common; they would sell their possessions and goods and distribute the proceeds to all, as any had need." Acts 2:44 (NRSV).

15  Samuel G. Freedman, "Before Bernie Sanders, There Was Zeidler, a Religious Socialist," *New York Times,* April 1, 2016 <http://www.nytimes.com/2016/04/02/us/before-sanders-there-was-frank-zeidler-a-religious-socialist.html>.

16  From 2011 to 2015. Alaska Permanent Fund Corporation, "Annual Dividend Payouts," n.d. <http://www.apfc.org/home/Content/dividend/dividendamounts.cfm>.

17  For a discussion of the relevance of this model for other states and

countries, see K. Widerquist and M. Howard, *Exporting the Alaska Model: Adapting the Permanent Fund Dividend for Reform around the World* (New York: Palgrave Macmillan, 2016).

18  John E. Kwoka, "Public vs. Private Ownership and Economic Performance: Evidence from the U.S. Electric Power Industry" (Harvard Institute of Economic Research, 1995)< https://www.hks.harvard.edu/hepg/Papers/Kwoka_Ownership_0295.pdf>.

19  Gar Alperovitz and Thomas M. Hanna, "Socialism, American-Style," *New York Times,* July 23, 2015 <http://www.nytimes.com/2015/07/23/opinion/socialism-american-style.html>.

20  "Seizing an Alternative: Toward an Ecological Civilization," Claremont, CA, June 4-7, 2015.

21  John Bellamy Foster, *Marx's Ecology: Materialism and Nature* (New York: Monthly Review Press, 2000).

22  Dante L. Germino, *Machiavelli to Marx: Modern Western Political Thought* (Chicago: University of Chicago Press, 1972), 358.

PART ONE

# REVISITING THE ALTERNATIVES:

## Resources in Marx and Whitehead

## ❧ 2 ❧

# A WHITEHEADIAN APPROACH
# TO RETHINKING ECONOMICS

### FOR THE SUSTAINABILITY REVOLUTION

*Carol Frances Johnston*

WHEN ADAM SMITH PUBLISHED *The Wealth of Nations* in 1776, material life in Great Britain was dominated by a system that kept control of resources in the hands of a few (called mercantilism). Most believed that economics was a zero-sum game of winners and losers. Smith set out to push for more freedom and more access for more people to make their own choices about producing, selling, and buying resources and goods. He saw free markets as the most efficient way to open up that access and to improve production so that economies could grow. His ideas have succeeded brilliantly at creating maximization in the production of "goods" for sale in markets, both material and nonmaterial, and did succeed to a point in opening up participation in economic decision-making to many more people.

Along the way Smith's ideas were gradually developed into the full-blown economic model known as capitalism, and the model still succeeds brilliantly at just what it is intended to do: maximize the use of natural and human resources for the growth of economies.

However, capitalism has transformed from a theory to test and revise
into an ideology in which the soundness, and even scientific truth,
of the theory is taken for granted, and the model is being applied
across the planet regardless of actual consequences to either human
or environmental well-being.

From the very beginning, those actual consequences have been
systematically destructive of both human and natural communities,
and Smith's intent to give more access to more people has stalled.
Early on in the development of capitalism in Britain, observers noted
that the factory system was destroying the community life of the
Scottish people and damaging their health, but argued that this
damage was "worth it" because they would be materially better off.
It did not seem to occur to them to consult the people themselves
about their preferences. In fact, they complained that the people
preferred to work just long enough to earn the cash required for
taxes, then leave the factories and go back home to what observers
saw as their dire poverty. What they discounted was the importance
to the "workers" of intact, close-knit community life and their love
of nature.[1] Since then, the march of capitalism has led to the same
pattern across the world, and never are the local people who are
being forced into the market system consulted as to their own preferences and views as to what kind of "development" would be best
for them. In that sense, Smith's project to widen participation and
freedom in economic life has stalled. Many more benefit materially
than did under mercantilism, but large masses of people are still
left out of the movement to broaden effective participation and real
freedom. At the same time their access to livelihood on their own
lands has been systematically removed as they are forced to enter
the wage system.

The destruction of traditional communities has gone hand in
hand with the destruction of the natural ecosystems on which they
depend. The world has been treated as an inert thing to be mined in
every way possible for natural resources, and not as a living system.
With climate change, we have reached the level of planet-wide

damage that cannot be stopped, only ameliorated *if* the world acts to change its ways.

How are we to change our ways? Capitalism has become so powerful, and so all-encompassing, that it functions as a totalizing ideology. Changing capitalism for the sake of a healthier world is a daunting task. As Pope Francis wrote so eloquently in his encyclical, *Laudato Si'*, it is going to require the contributions of all the world's peoples, including their unique faith traditions and cultures, and especially those of indigenous peoples, to find solutions and move the world in the right direction.[2]

Alfred North Whitehead thought long and hard about the issues that underlie the trouble the world is in today, and his ideas remain among the best for illuminating the problems we have and for developing a better, healthier economics for the well-being of all life on the planet. Whitehead did not directly discuss economic theory as such, and he did not propose a developed alternative economics. However, he often used "political economy" to illustrate his analysis of Western civilization and show how philosophy was misapplied. More importantly, his "philosophy of organism," or what has become known as process-relational thought, does provide a fully developed alternative worldview and philosophy that is much more in accord with the complexity of life on this planet. Accordingly, this essay will draw on Whitehead's analysis of Western thought, especially as it is discussed in *Science and the Modern World* and *Adventures of Ideas*, developing his critique of Western thought and how it shapes global economics. Then alternative foundations for a healthier economics will be drawn from Whitehead's philosophy and suggestions presented for their use in a new economic theory for the Sustainability Revolution.[3]

## FOUNDATIONAL ASSUMPTIONS AND VALUES IN CAPITALISM

Whitehead is particularly helpful with clarifying the West's foundational assumptions about the world, and the value choices that are embedded in Western thought and so govern capitalism. In order to develop an effective alternative that leads to sustainability and genuine well-being for all, those assumptions and values need to be "uncloaked" from the perplexities of theory (to paraphrase Whitehead's term), examined, and understood, so that better and truer choices can shape a new economics of sustainability.

The first place we find Whitehead commenting on economics is when he uses it as an example of why it is dangerous to turn a deductive theory into a model and apply it without attention to consequences and without ever re-examining it to see if the embedded assumptions still hold. In *Science and the Modern World* he argues that two aspects of economic theory have had very "fatal" effects in industrialization.[4] First is the assumption that the world is like a machine, made up of inert parts. Second is the assumption that individuals are unrelated and self-existing, and therefore their social and environmental contexts (including families) can be ignored in economics.

These assumptions have led to a disconnect from human suffering and from environmental damage, and they are part of three "evils" now embedded in economics. Modern economics (1) ignores the "true relations of each organism to its environment," (2) ignores the "intrinsic worth of the environment which must be allowed its weight," and (3) suffers from "the professionalization of knowledge" which isolates areas of thinking.[5] In other words, economists think it is all right to ignore the relatedness of humans to each other and the rest of the environment because they have been trained to think of economics as a discipline in isolation from other areas of knowledge, and because they accept as givens both individualism and mechanism, with their built-in rejection of relationality. When Alfred Marshall developed neoclassical capitalism in the early twentieth century, most academic disciplines still accepted Newtonian mechanism and individualism, and the consequent assumption that entities are not inherently related. Today, both "hard" sciences such as physics and biology, and "soft" sciences such as sociology and psychology, have accepted that everything *is* inherently interrelated in a complex web of existence; they have proven the assumptions of individualism and mechanism to be wrong. But neoclassical economics still spins on, denying any need for change, and the consequences, as Whitehead claimed so long ago, are "fatal."[6]

Whitehead gives two reasons: First, individualism led to the mistake of making ethics private and individual,[7] which blinded people to the massive social injustice and sheer suffering that industrialization brings. Second, "nature" was deemed valueless and inert, and the importance of a healthy, respectful relationship between humans and nature was ignored. This oversight led to factory towns devoid of trees or growing things, air choking with pollution, and all other manner of environmental destruction that both "separated" (as if that is possible) human beings from nature and poisoned everyone. This ignoring of "the true relation of each organism to its environment" and denial of the "intrinsic worth" of the environment are genuine evils now embedded in economic theories.[8]

A third problem, which only adds to the tendency to ignore these relationships, is the fact that universities have organized the pursuit of knowledge into "disciplines" narrowly defined and pursued. This "professionalization of knowledge" has produced great efficiency in limited spheres, but lost the whole, at great cost.[9] Whitehead does not examine these consequences in the area of economics. Nevertheless, it is not difficult to apply Whitehead's analysis to economic theory. Whitehead has no problem with the development of theories: all theories must abstract from the full complexity of life to provide useful ways to focus on important patterns in that complexity. But economic theory was developed in the context of mechanism and individualism and embedded them as foundational assumptions, not to be reexamined in light of new evidence. Even worse, the economic model has been enshrined as "value-free science" and applied across the world regardless of consequences to actual human and natural communities. A few pages later Whitehead uses a modern factory as an example of a complex "organism,"[10] and advocates a holistic approach in contrast to over-abstracting economics.

## CONSEQUENCES OF THEORY IN PRACTICE:
## HOW ECONOMIES ACTUALLY WORK
## AND HOW THEY SHOULD WORK

A holistic approach to economics would look at economies as being more like living organisms than machines. Whitehead argues that economists should look to and learn from the "economies" of natural ecosystems.[11] One example he gives is the difference between a single tree trying to survive on its own and the mutual flourishing that takes place in the Brazilian rain forest,[12] where competition and cooperation are in a balance that supports the health of the whole forest as a living community. It is likely that Whitehead would have agreed with economists that it is possible to improve productivity in a way that "grows" an economy and improves material life for human beings, but he would insist that this be done by learning from nature's own creativity and working *within* that natural creativity instead of *against* it, as so much economic activity does.

To take a crucial example, modern agriculture is thoroughly industrialized. Of course Whitehead did not have industrialized agriculture in view, but his critique of economics and industrialization clearly applies. It is perhaps the most obvious example of a model that attempts to improve productivity in abstraction from nature and applies that model without consideration of nature's ways. Influenced by capitalist economic theory and the underlying power of scientific method, the industrialization of agriculture was already underway when World War II added a powerful impetus to intensify the process: millions of young men were taken out of agriculture and sent to war, so in the United States there was a great need to maximize the production of food with a minimum of labor. Consequently, machinery was applied to substitute for labor, with no thought for energy costs, and it was soon discovered that the chemicals being used in war could also be used on the land to kill weeds and insects, greatly improving production. The land began to be treated as another kind of factory, with the minimization of labor and the maximization of single crops as central goals.

For a few decades this was very effective, both in the West and, most famously, in the "Green Revolution," especially in India. Like capitalist economies more broadly, it succeeded in achieving its stated goals, but the consequences outside those narrowly chosen goals were ignored. The costs to the land and to farming communities have been enormous: massive loss of irreplaceable top soil, sterilization of remaining soil by means of chemical poisons and salinization, the removal of millions of people into teeming slums across the world, the destruction of rural cultures and communities, rising cancer rates, and a multitude of other health costs. And with every decade that passes, insects and crop diseases develop more resistance to the chemical applications. The response has been to intensify their use and to bioengineer seeds instead of looking for healthier alternatives. Yet still there are many who argue that the world must intensify this industrialization of agriculture in order to "feed the world" with a growing population, never mind the costs. The belief that industrialized agriculture is still more productive than any alternative is still very powerful, even in nations where capitalism is not the dominant form of economics.

Yet there *are* alternatives to industrializing agriculture. The growing movement called "agroecology" is proving that when science and technology are used to work *with* nature rather than *against* it, and when they are brought into genuine partnership with the millennia-old knowledge of traditional farming communities and cultures, not only do rural people benefit, but the soil is every bit as productive as it is under industrial methods. Indeed, since industrial methods deplete the fertility of the soil and chemical applications lessen steadily in effectiveness, agroecology is rapidly outpacing industrial agriculture in effectiveness. *And* the food grown is healthier to eat, the soil is actually rebuilt and sustained instead of being depleted, and farming communities are far healthier in every way. It is increasingly the case that industrial agriculture benefits only the transnational corporations that control the bio-engineered seeds and chemicals required, and the elite few who reap the profits.[13]

In *Adventures of Ideas,* Whitehead gives a lot more attention to the issue illustrated in *Science and the Modern World*—the same one raised by his example of the Brazilian rain forest—of balancing competition with cooperation. Whitehead rejects the idea of "the strife of individuals issued in the progressive realization of a harmonious society."[14] The result of implementing this idea, he argues, was that "after two generations of such industrial development, the widespread misery… aroused the public conscience."[15] Something like "industrial slavery" had been produced. Consequently many industrialized nations moved to constrain competition, "the pure doctrine of nineteenth-century liberalism,"[16] or *laissez-faire* economies. He notes (writing in the 1930s) that various ways of coordinating economies were being tried. While he does not develop this, it seems clear that Whitehead would prefer what is now called a "mixed" economy that balances free markets with oversight to ensure the common good. He would accept neither central control that stifles local initiative nor purely market-driven policies. To judge the effectiveness of any economic arrangements, he also would insist on examining the actual effects on actual people in all their relationships, including their human and natural communities,

Hints of this view can be seen in the chapter on Freedom, where Whitehead comments on the understanding of the human person that has been constructed in capitalism. He condemns outright the introduction of the idea that a corporation can be a legal "person" with limited liability. This makes into law an idea that social relationships are merely contractual—with severe consequences.[17] Far more important is the whole inherited complex of social relations, or what Whitehead calls "custom." Human persons are immersed in their environments in a web of relationships,[18] and consequently it is important to understand that human freedom is an aspect of this social context. This is the reason that it is a mistake to assume that individual freedom and social justice are contradictory. For example, unemployment tends to be considered as a social justice issue, but not an issue of individual freedom. Yet human persons cannot develop their very individuality without a social context that encourages their gifts and receives them positively. Being relegated to a condition of chronic unemployment, even with excellent welfare benefits, is a denial of freedom — of the basic human need to participate. As Whitehead puts it, "The essence of freedom is the practicality of purpose… Prometheus did not bring to mankind freedom of the press. He procured fire, which obediently to human purpose cooks and gives warmth."[19] In the American context, this means that *both* the Republican or "conservative" focus on individual freedom, apart from social equity, and the Democratic or "liberal" focus on social equity and welfare, apart from assuring freedom to develop and use individual gifts and talents, are missing crucial dimensions of human personhood and are out of balance. Both sides are trapped in individualistic thinking.[20]

This does not at all mean that Whitehead agrees with a kind of collectivist view where the individual is swallowed up by society. Not at all. Society needs individuals freely developing and freely contributing their *unique* gifts, so that they "contribute to the complex pattern of community life, each in virtue of its own peculiarity. In this way individuality gains the effectiveness which issues from coordination, and freedom obtains power necessary for its perfection."[21] While Whitehead does not go beyond this, we can see his thinking illustrated by the shift in the past decades from assembly-line uniformity and interchangeable parts (and treating people that way) to organizing workers into teams in which each member brings unique elements to the whole, including expertise in different fields and individual talents.

This brings us to "commerce," which Whitehead believes is a positive good, in that it teaches nations to use persuasion rather than coercive force. Whitehead defines commerce broadly as including "every species of interchange which proceeds by way of mutual persuasion."[22] This definition would rule out interchange that is coerced by means of human need, as when people are forced to sell their labor in order to survive and kept in inhumane and exploitative

conditions. It would be instructive to apply the definition to corporate behavior and see how much can be described as "commerce" by
Whitehead's definition. He points out that demand "may be closely
connected with some physical necessity arising out of possession
or deprivation, for example, the satisfaction of hunger or starva-
tion."[23] Capitalist economic theory does not distinguish between
basic needs and desires of all kinds (and indeed rejects every attempt
to do so), despite the repeated assertion that participation in the
market must be "free" and the assumption that it is uncoerced.[24]
This assumption should be examined and made into a criterion: if
participation is coerced, it is not a free market. For markets to be
genuinely free, workers (and not just buyers who have money) must
have real choices. One way to measure this may be to distinguish
"value" with basic needs measured differently from freely fluctuating
"desires" in the market.

    As Whitehead puts it, economic theorists emphasized "economic
laws which *should* hold," and neglected "economic procedures which
in fact *did* hold.[25] The choice to develop a deductive theory of economics was made in part for the sake of clarity and power, but it
builds in many assumptions that are not examined, including an
assumption that laborers can always return to living off the land
(despite the fact that access to common lands and resources has been
systematically removed across the world) and so have real choices and
access to alternative means of livelihood. It also neglects to include
any way to reexamine the embedded values and assumptions over
time. This clarity of theory, rigidified into dogma, ends up "cloaking
the perplexities of fact."[26] Even if the economic theorists were genuinely trying to improve conditions for all people (and it is true that
many people are materially better off), it seems clear that this clarity
of theory has not only made it possible to ignore massive injustice
done to many more people and massive damage to the environment,
but has also led to the global spread of economies modeled after the
theory that are actually systematically destroying both human and
natural communities. This is the reason it is so terribly difficult to

make headway against the patterns of destruction: economic theory, by narrowing attention and effort to the participation of individuals with money in markets, has encouraged the creation of actual economies that systematically push these destructive practices. With these economic systems in place, all attempts to change the destructive so-called "externalities" simply ameliorate, but do not stop or reverse, the damage.

One key — perhaps *the* key — to changing this dynamic of having to work against the built-in destructive effects of capitalism, is to shift economic thinking (and all thinking and practice) to learn from and work *within* the parameters of nature's own dynamic systems, instead of working *against* them.[27] Whitehead thinks that capitalism has been brilliant at recognizing the plasticity of nature and thereby initiating unprecedented economic growth. This is undeniable. However, capitalism has escaped the Malthusian dilemma of population growth, outstripping resources by three methods: "expanding Commerce, improving Technology, and utilization of Empty Regions."[28] Whitehead does not comment here on the world of issues contained in this list, including the history of colonization, the enslavement of millions, and environmental destruction. Like most of his contemporaries, he is more focused on the benefits of economic growth that utilizes non-coercive commerce and technology, and he lauds these as "Commerce developed adventurously."[29] Nevertheless, it is possible once again to apply Whitehead's own criteria to advocate for a radically different approach — one that hopefully preserves "Commerce developed adventurously" — but applies more effectively the criterion of being "non-coercive" and also incorporates Whitehead's insistence on recognizing the human embeddedness in and complete dependence on nature: that it is all right to *move* the perceived boundaries (as in shifting away from fossil fuels to solar and wind energy) to provide a better life for more people, but not to *cross* boundaries so that human health and natural systems are disrupted and endangered.[30]

## RETHINKING ECONOMICS: PROMISING CONTRIBUTIONS FROM WHITEHEAD'S PHILOSOPHICAL APPROACH

Since modern capitalism is undergirded by a philosophy of materialism and individualism, it is essential to develop a healthier, and more realistic, philosophical undergirding for a sustainable economics. This is where Whitehead is especially helpful. In *Adventures of Ideas* he devotes an entire section, titled "Cosmology," to this work.

First, twentieth-century physics upended the stable world of fixed "laws of nature" depicted by Newton. Instead of separate entities only externally related, if at all, quantum physics has shown that everything is internally and inherently related to everything else, and "natural laws" are patterns of relations that emerge over time and are discerned by a process of inductive abstraction. Since economics is based on Newtonian views, it was assumed that relationships don't really matter, and once a set of patterns for economic growth was developed, it was set as "laws" of economics that don't change. The added reality that human beliefs and cultures, and hence behaviors, are mutable patterns that can and do change is left out, and capitalism then is treated as if it were based on immutable "laws" of both nature and human behavior. Over time this has resulted in actually instilling in human cultures a pattern of behavior (individual "utility," usually wealth-maximization and consumerism) as the central driving force of human nature and behaving as if this is an essential and inevitable part of human nature.

This idea of *homo economicus*, or the "utility"-maximizing individual, strips away all relationships and makes them something an individual can choose to enter into, or not.[31] The result across the world has been the constant undermining of community cohesion and the alienation and isolation of people as individuals. Relational networks of all kinds are continuously thinned and weakened in capitalist societies, and few realize that this is built into the way capitalism works. As in nineteenth-century Scotland, the argument is still that individuals end up materially better off, so the loss of healthy family and community relations, and the alienation from nature, is worth it. Since World War II the U.S. has grown exponentially richer and richer in material wealth, but few would disagree that it has also grown poorer and poorer in relational networks of all kinds (and in virtually every corner of society, from the suburbs to the inner city, and even in rural areas devastated by the emptying out of farming communities).

Whitehead's explanation of the inherent nature of relationships makes it clear that this is just not sustainable. Human beings cannot do without dense networks of relationships, and the thinner and weaker their networks are, the unhealthier they are. Ironically, social conservatives, who are especially concerned with this thinning of relational networks (famously referred to as the loss of "family values") seem completely unaware that it is built into capitalism to ignore and even destroy communities, even though the most famous apologists for capitalism agree that this is true and are very clear about it.[32] The very insistence that individuals are to be considered as self-existent has meant that all relationships are considered to be voluntary, not essential. In actual capitalist economies, it is increasingly common to see that this is embedded in the way work life is structured. Family and community relationships are voluntary and wholly outside of work life, which takes precedence, so it's okay to have a family *on your own time and outside of work*. It is not even considered that material life is ultimately about supporting a life of healthy relationships with family, community, and nature. Increasingly, our lives are all about work, with family on the side, instead of life being about family, with work as a way to support family life. No wonder capitalist societies experience steady erosion of relational networks.

A sustainable economics, then, must first of all include in its very foundations the necessity to observe actual effects in the world and changing understandings in other fields about humanity and nature, and then revise the economic theory to improve the health of both human beings and the planet as a whole. Economics is not mathematics: it is about how human beings live an embodied life on this planet. Consequently, a balance of inductive research that looks at actual conditions and results, with judicious use of deductive theory, is essential, and so is an ongoing debate about the values and goals of economic life. To leave the question of "value" to the decisions of individuals in the market is to abandon the social obligation to discern and choose what human beings need (including a healthy measure of freedom to choose as individuals). This will be contested, but the very contest is essential to any hope of ongoing improvement.

Sustainability for humanity depends on choosing values that support long-term necessities for life on Earth. First and most urgently, this means shifting science, technology, and all the practices of living to a culture of learning *from* and working *with* the dynamic creativity of nature instead of working against it. This shift is already far enough underway to see some of the potential. Green architects are creating "living" buildings that generate more energy than they use, and doing it for less upfront cost. Biologists are developing the new science of "biomimicry," which looks for ways to improve materials by learning from living systems. Agroecology is combining the hard-earned wisdom and intricate knowledge of traditional communities with judicious applications of science and technology to improve the productivity of organic agriculture in a context that sustains whole communities and ecosystems. In fact, we know enough now to be able to declare that human societies not only *should* do this, and *must* do this for our own survival, but *can* do this, and can achieve along the way a healthier life for everyone, *and* for the planet as a whole.

Beyond sustainability, which could conceivably be achieved in ways that are manifestly unjust for the majority (at least for a time), economic theories and policies that are influenced by Whitehead would also be judged by the extent to which society is moving toward all people experiencing well-being and all species thriving in a healthy balance of interconnected cooperation and competition. Rather than *homo economicus*, I have proposed the use of *homo salutaris*—the healthy human.[33] Instead of dealing only with human individuals, totally stripped of all relations and taken in isolation, which is increasingly the actual case rather than only in theory, we need to infuse economic theory itself with attention to what makes for a healthy human being. Just raising the question leads immediately to an examination of the economic dimensions of healthy families, communities, and ecosystems, because every person lives embedded in these nested sets of relationships and suffers when they are thinned, stressed, and unhealthy. One essential criterion of this is not just that market relations are "un-coerced" but that opportunities for healthy, un-coerced *participation*—for developing and contributing one's potential—are constantly broadened in scope and quality.

A sustainable economics influenced by Whitehead would begin with the basic assumption that the world is like a living organism and all entities are inherently interrelated. It would also begin with the inductive work of learning from and in terms of nature's own creative processes. A deductive theory of economics would then be developed and experimented with, all the while studying the actual results and consequences in actual human and natural communities, with the theory being revised in light of changing circumstances and changing understandings of the adequacy of basic assumptions and value choices. Value would not be treated as uniform but take into account the value embedded in nature (living processes and creativity as well as natural "resources") and the difference in value between subsistence and preference. It might be useful to recover the original idea in economics that there are three factors of production, not just two: land as well as labor and capital. Measuring economic activity by the criteria of quality of participation as well as sustainability and sufficiency (basic needs) would be helpful, as well as evaluating the level of coercion or freedom in economic arrangements. Finally, I would add that all of this could be measured fairly adequately by making the central goal of economic growth in the health and well-being of human and natural communities, rather than growth solely in monetary transactions and production of "goods."

## CONCLUDING COMMENT: THE SUSTAINABILITY REVOLUTION AS "ADVENTURE"

For Whitehead, reality is always "becoming" and in flux. Consequently, change is inevitable and there can be no static "perfection" that lasts. Instead, human communities must pursue the "perfections" that are possible to them, or stagnate. Any civilization that achieves what is possible for it can enjoy that for a time, but inevitably things change and that cultural achievement passes away. When this happens, there can be periods of intense chaos. Whitehead believes that "quick transitions" are possible, but only when "thought has run ahead of realization."[34] The "adventure of the imagination" can make it possible to develop alternative ways of thinking and being in the world that may seem impossible now, but which can be invaluable in leading society to meet the loss of the world as it was with fresh approaches better fitted to changing circumstances: "The world dreams of things to come, and then in due season arouses itself to their realization."[35] This is the situation we are in now: the world created by capitalism is reaching a crisis unforeseen by Adam Smith and those who wished to increase participation and widen material well-being. The crisis is already causing chaos and enormous suffering, but the extent to which that can be ameliorated and the world win through to a sustainability and sufficiency for all depends very much on how we re-think right now everything we do in light of these challenges and to promote an economics that will support the Sustainability Revolution instead of undermine it.

The world needs a better worldview and philosophical approach, with a vision of a sustainable, just, participatory, and healthy world. As Pope Francis so clearly advocates, this depends on the contributions and full participation of all the world's peoples and their distinctive cultures, faiths, and wisdom, especially the indigenous peoples of the world. At the same time, the people need to see distinct *pathways* from where they live now to this better world—ways to get from here to there. As long as most people feel stuck in the way they live now—working harder and harder to keep up, inundated with information but lacking in access to real wisdom, struggling to maintain any depth of family and community ties, and often ill from stress and unhealthy food—they may see proposals for a better way to live as lovely, but unattainable and unrealistic. But when offered specific pathways to improvement in their lives, with step-by-step ways to get there, many respond positively. This is where the Sustainability Revolution becomes an "adventure" in Whitehead's sense: green architects, urban gardeners, biomimicry pioneers, zero-waste factories, LED lights replacing incandescent, solar and wind dropping in price and rising in quality to becoming competitive with fossil fuel energy, social entrepreneurs across the world encouraging the gifts and creativity of low-income communities to better their own lives in accord with their own needs and environments. The wide variety of people engaging in all these activities know they are pioneering a better, healthier world for everyone. It is satisfying, engaging, creative, and above all, adventurous work.

In all these ways, "thought" and action are "running ahead" and laying down pathways into a sustainable and just future for the world and all life on it. What an adventure it is to participate in this work!

## NOTES

1   See T. C. Smout, *A Century of the Scottish People: 1830-1950* (New Haven: Yale University Press, 1986), 66–67.

2   *Laudato Si'*, English language PDF from the Vatican Press, paragraphs 14, 63, 146, 179.

3   For a more scholarly exposition of what Whitehead had to say that is relevant to economics, see my essay, "Whitehead on Economics," in the *Handbook of Whiteheadian Process Thought*, vol. 1, ed. Michel Weber and Will Desmond (Frankfurt: Ontos Verlag, 2008).

4   Alfred North Whitehead, *Science and the Modern World* (New York: Free Press, 1967), 195.

5   Ibid., 197.

6   See, e.g., the classic essay by Lionel Robbins, "An Essay on the Nature and Significance of Economic Science," 2nd ed. (London: Macmillan, 1935), excerpted in Daniel M. Hausman, ed., *The Philosophy of Economics* (New York: Cambridge University Press, 1984).

7   Whitehead, *Science and the Modern World,* 196.

8   Ibid.

9   Ibid., 197.

10   Ibid., 200.

11   Economics missed an opportunity to get this right when Adam Smith ignored the proposal of the French Physiocrats to compare economies to the newly discovered "circulation of the blood." He had travelled in France and was aware of their work. Smith rightly rejected their focus on the land as the sole source of wealth, but along with that lost or missed the insight that material life is derived from and returns to nature and this cannot be safely ignored.

12   Whitehead, *Science and the Modern World,* 206.

13   See, e.g., the reports of the Food and Agriculture Organization of the United Nations, http://www.fao.org/about/meetings/afns/en/. Many other sources of information for agroecology and the work to prove it can be more productive as well has healthier for land, peoples, and the planet are easily found on the web.

14   Alfred North Whitehead, *Adventures of Ideas* (New York: Free Press, 1967), 33.

15   Ibid.

16   Ibid., 35.

17   Ibid., 63.

18   Ibid.

19   Ibid., 66.

20   For a well-developed alternative, see the proposal for "persons-in-community" in Herman Daly and John B. Cobb, Jr., *For the Common Good: Redirecting Economics for Community, the Environment, and a Sustainable Future* (Boston: Beacon Press, 1994).

21   Whitehead, *Adventures of Ideas,* 67.

22   Ibid., 70.

23  Ibid.

24  See, e.g., the book by Economics Nobel winner Kenneth Arrow, *Social Choice and Justice* (Cambridge: Harvard University Press, 1983).

25  Whitehead, *Adventures of Ideas,* 72.

26  Ibid.

27  Both Prince Charles and Pope Francis make this idea central in their thought. See HRH Prince Charles of Wales, *Harmony: A New Way of Looking at Our World* (Harper Perennial, 2012), and Pope Francis I, *Laudato Si'* (Vatican Press, 2015).

28  Whitehead, *Adventures of Ideas,* 77.

29  Ibid.

30  For a discussion of this issue, see the last chapter of my book, *The Wealth or Health of Nations: Transforming Capitalism from Within* (Cleveland, Pilgrim Press, 1998), esp. 113–15.

31  Mill, John Stuart, "On the Definition and Method of Political Economy," in *The Philosophy of Economics,* ed. Daniel M. Hausman, 3rd ed. (Cambridge: Cambridge University Press, 2008), 41–58. Original essay published 1836.

32  See, e.g., Peter L. Berger, *Pyramids of Sacrifice and The Capitalist Revolution* (New York: Basic Books, 1974 and 1987). Also Michael Novak, *The Spirit of Democratic Capitalism* (New York: Simon & Schuster, 1982).

33  See again my book, the last chapter, "Conclusion: The Choices for Health over Wealth of Nations," 119–21.

34  Whitehead, *Adventures of Ideas,* 278.

35  Ibid., 279.

# ❧ 3 ❧

## GLOBAL CHALLENGES AND
## WISDOM RESOURCES:

### WHY GO BACK TO WHITEHEAD AND MARX
### AND WHAT CAN WE LEARN FROM THEM?

### *Ouyang Kang*

FIRST, IT MAY BE NECESSARY TO CLARIFY why we should go back to Alfred North Whitehead and Karl Marx. Why these philosophers, and why now?

## WHY SHOULD WE GO BACK TO
## WHITEHEAD AND MARX?

The simple answer is that all nations and peoples of the world are facing new global challenges. The challenges we face in our time can be divided, philosophically speaking, into three relationships or levels: the relationship between humans and nature, between people and society, and between individuals and their own minds. While human society, on the whole, actively promotes and encourages the process of globalization, at the unconscious level we know we face extremely serious challenges.

Even speaking only of China, one can identify many conflicting value systems: globalization, modernization, new science and technology, the Western world, nationalism, market economic systems, etc. Let me describe a few of them briefly:

## TRADITIONAL CHINESE VALUES AND MODERN WESTERN VALUES

Ever since the May Fourth movement in Beijing in 1919, there has been a very strong and long-lasting debate around the conflict between Chinese values and Western values. After the beginning of the Open Door Policy in 1978 and the acceleration of modernization in China, the conflict between traditional Chinese heritage and Western modernization became even more obvious and pronounced. By definition, modernization creates new values. And because the Western world modernized itself much earlier than China, China has had to learn certain values from the West. In fact, as China modernized in the latter half of the twentieth century, there were many people who believed that modernization was equivalent to Westernization, and therefore there was a strong desire to Westernize China. Many people at this time undervalued traditional Chinese culture and history.

However, after many years of attempting to implement Western-style modernization, the Chinese people have begun to realize that Chinese modernization can only be built successfully on the ground of Chinese history and culture. China's task now is to combine traditional Chinese values with the best of Western values. There are many core elements of Western values that China should learn from: modernity, freedom, equality, justice, democracy, love, human rights, etc. There are also many traditional Chinese values that are still meaningful today, such as *Ren* (benevolence), *Yi* (righteousness), *Li* (manners), *Zhi* (wisdom), *Xin* (faith), *Zhongyong* (means), the union of Heaven and Man, the harmony of individuals and society, etc. Chinese socialist modernization should combine all meaningful values of human civilization, whether they come from the East or the West.

## MARXIST VALUES AND NON-MARXIST VALUES

In the past, the Chinese Central Committee (CCP) was committed to a specific interpretation of Marxism and asked the Chinese people to resist all kinds of thinking considered to be non-Marxist. However, since 1978, Chinese leaders and scholars have tried to overcome many previous misunderstandings of Marxism. They criticized and corrected Chairman Mao Zedong's mistakes in his later years and tried to reinterpret Marxism. In the academic world, there was a movement called "Return to Marx." People began to move beyond the misunderstandings of Marxism inherited from the former Soviet Union and began to adopt a more flexible and tolerant attitude to Marxism in general, Western interpretations of Marxism, and even non-Marxist Western ideologies. This flexibility has prompted the self-development of Marxism in contemporary China.

INDIVIDUAL VALUES AND SOCIAL VALUES

In the past, people have assumed that collectivism is the main value of Chinese culture, and individualism is the main value of Western culture. Now, many in China are realizing that, on the one hand, the individual is the foundation of society. The efforts of each individual are absolutely necessary in a market society, and each individual's needs should be protected in a just society. On the other hand, individuals can only live and act effectively as members of a group, so collective cooperation is also absolutely necessary for all individuals and for society as a whole. In the process of modernization, China needs to encourage all its people to develop and realize themselves as social individuals. (This debate between collectivism and individualism is reflected in the lively discussion of subjectivity and objectivity currently happening in the area of philosophy.)

THE VALUES OF SOCIAL EQUALITY AND
EFFICIENT ECONOMIC DEVELOPMENT

Given its Communist history, there is a long-standing tradition of egalitarianism in China. However, there were aspects of this tradition that obstructed economic development. In response, China instituted the social reforms of 1978 designed to encourage people to generate more wealth. As part of this reform, China instituted an important policy that "allowed some people to become rich earlier than others." For a while, this policy was successful in stimulating individual enthusiasm and prompting greater efficiency in economic development, but it also created many new social problems. The most dangerous one is the enlarged gap between the rich and the poor. China is now trying very hard to keep a rational balance between social equity and productive efficiency. On the one hand, the country needs to reform its labor and distribution systems in order to collect more money from the richer population and to distribute those resources to the poor. On the other hand, the country still needs to encourage able-bodied people to produce more and earn more, according to their contribution to society.

### ECONOMIC VALUES AND MORAL VALUES

In the past, China has traditionally stressed morality and justice, but neglected considerations of benefit and utility. Since 1978, however, economic development has become the central task of the whole country, but in the meantime moral education has been more or less ignored. As a result, social morality has declined to some extent. Morality has become a new social problem in China, which makes many people anxious. China is now trying to balance these two aspects: to maintain economic development and to enhance moral and political education. Our goal is to construct three kinds of civilization as part of China's social progress: material civilization, spiritual civilization, and political civilization. My university and our colleagues are actually leading a national research project to cultivate and enhance the national spirit. We hope to make a contribution to Chinese morality and to national unity.

### UNIVERSAL VALUES AND PARTICULAR VALUES

In the rapid process of modernization, people are more likely to seek a universal value that can be applied to society as a whole; but in practice modernization actually requires just as much attention to particular values. Particular values may come from different social contexts or identities: for example, different districts, different social classes, different interest groups, and different vocations. The gap between urban and rural areas, between farmers and workers, is still very big. The Chinese government has paid very close attention to the less privileged groups and less developed districts.

Corporately, we have the strong feeling that we lack enough wisdom to govern our country well, not to mention governing the planet as a whole. That is the reason we are trying to find ideas that may help us navigate these competing value systems.

## HOW DO WE GO BACK TO WHITEHEAD AND MARX?

Since 1949, Karl Marx and Marxism have always been at the center of Chinese ideology and academic studies, even if Marxism has been reinterpreted in the Return to Marx movement or the Open Door policy. But the serious challenges of modernization and globalization require us to pay attention to other wisdom traditions and intellectual resources. There are three resources that we believe to have the most potential: traditional Chinese philosophy and culture, Western philosophy and culture, and Marxism. Actually, we know that all three of these resources are absolutely necessary, and no single one of them will be enough to address the complex situation in China. We need to learn from all of them and try to pull them together.

In regards to Marxism, we need to continue the kind of reinterpretation that has already been done in China. We need to get beyond the misunderstandings that arose in the Marxism of the former Soviet Union and in Chairman Mao Zedong's understanding of Marxism in his later years, and put this new kind of Marxist theory into practice. We have done great work to re-explain and rebuild Marxism for the Chinese context, but we can still do more in this direction.

As for Alfred North Whitehead, in the past we mainly thought of him as one of the important philosophers in the modern history of Western philosophy. We (and I include myself) did not think Whitehead to be of much importance for China.

However, two events made me pay more attention to Whitehead. The first event was Dr. Lik-Kuen Tong's study and exposition of Whitehead. Dr. Tong is a professor of philosophy at Fairfield University in the United States. His doctoral dissertation was titled "Context and Reality: A Critical Interpretation of Whitehead's Philosophy of Organism."[1] Since then, he has focused on Whitehead's philosophy of Field-Being. He went on to write several important books on Whitehead, including *Between Zhouyi and Whitehead*, which were translated into Chinese and published in China. Tong has worked at Fairfield University since 1967 and established an International Institute of Field-Being at the university in 1996. He and his colleagues organized many international conferences on the topic of Field-Being in the United States, China, and other countries. Professor Tong also served as the Secretary General of the International Association of Chinese Philosophy and had a great deal of influence in that group.

The second researcher to take Whitehead to China was Professor John Cobb and his colleagues. They focused on Whitehead's process thought and established the Institute of Postmodern Studies. Introduced by my friends Professors Zhihe Wang and Meijun Fan, I visited John Cobb and David Griffin on my way back from Cuba in 2001. I delivered a lecture in Claremont and did an interview with Cobb. I learned a lot about his ideas of Whitehead's process thought and the future of international development. I went on to establish an Institute of Process Studies at Huazhong University of Science and Technology and set up some research fellowships in process studies for faculty and students.

More recently I learned from Professor Philip Clayton about his research connecting Whitehead and Marx, called "Organic Marxism." Clayton and Heinzekehr took Whitehead's philosophy of organism and applied it to a reinterpretation of Marxism.

The above examples remind me to pay more attention to Whitehead's philosophy and ideas! Reviewing Marx and Whitehead from a postmodern angle may offer us some special enlightenment.

## WHAT CAN WE LEARN FROM WHITEHEAD AND MARX?

There are many wisdom resources in history that can help us, so why should we go back to Whitehead and Marx? Why should we think that their ideas are still alive and meaningful so long after their deaths? One of the most important reasons is that, within Western philosophy and culture, these two thinkers inherited and enlarged the tradition of process thought, which philosophers had been developing from ancient Greece to Hegel.

Process thought is a very old idea in the history of human wisdom, but it is particularly well explained in Whitehead's philosophy. Because of his contribution, process philosophy has become one of the most useful research methodologies in philosophical circles today.

Karl Marx also has a very clear idea of process thought. He gives significant attention to the process of development in the natural world, human history, and individual lives. He especially insists on the progressive direction of the world and human society.

However, one also finds distinct contributions from the two of them. Marx seems mainly to use process thought as a methodology to analyze processes of evolution in nature, society, and the human spirit, seeking a rational and viable pathway for human liberation. Whitehead focuses more on process itself, developing it as a special field within philosophy, namely process philosophy. Because of the differences between their times and locations, Marx pays more attention to the practical dimensions of the social struggle and the practice of revolution, whereas Whitehead pays more attention to the theoretical construction of process philosophy.

Still, the common points between Whitehead and Marx are significant. Let me give some examples:

1.  Process consists of matter or events in temporal movement. The main reference and the main methodology for understanding the world is temporality: persistence and change through time. Though temporal methodology is familiar in the discipline of history, it has not been used so broadly in contemporary sciences,

technology, or social sciences. The importance of process thought is that it conceives of existence as a temporal situation.

2.  Processes are always concrete. Different processes have different subjects, such as matter, spirit, people, or social events, and they take place in different environments. Therefore, different processes have different statuses. There are three basic statuses: progress, stagnation, or retrogression. One of the main tasks of process studies is to find, explain, and evaluate the direction of process.

3.  The basic motivation of process is the inner contradiction of matter or event. The different kinds of contradiction prompt the movement of process and change its direction of development.

4.  Value is the most important element in process thought. Value conflicts and value choices influence the direction of a process's development.

5.  Evolution is the main direction and the main characteristic of life, human beings, and the social world.

6.  The study of process is actually the study of complexity. Both complex ideas and complex research methodologies are very important to a rational and effective study of process.

At a time when the world is torn between conflicting value systems, it is crucial that complex societies, such as China or the United States, find a way to harmonize the best elements of each system. Otherwise we run the risk of developing our economies in ways that are either too restrictive of individual freedoms and rights or too destructive of social and ecological communities. Marx and Whitehead understood that history moves forward precisely through the understanding of contradiction or complexity and through new resolutions of those contradictions. If we can really understand the wisdom of Karl Marx and Alfred North Whitehead and combine them, we may find more rational and efficient ways of developing ourselves.

## NOTES

1   Lik-Kuen Tong, "Context and Reality: A Critical Interpretation of Whitehead's Philosophy of Organism," (Ph.D dissertation, New School for Social Research, 1969).

# ⪻ 4 ⪼

## PERSON-IN-COMMUNITY IN

## WHITEHEAD, SMITH, AND MARX:

### EXPLORING MARX'S CONCEPT OF CLASS THROUGH SMITH'S CONCEPT OF SOCIAL ORDER[1]

*Cristina Neesham and Mark Dibben*

*We have one important piece of experience of the past 30 years: that is to ensure both the visible hand and the invisible hand are given full play in regulating the market forces. If you are familiar with the classic works of Adam Smith, you will know that there are two famous works of his. One is "The Wealth of Nations"; the other is the book on the morality and ethics. And "The Wealth of Nations" deals more with the invisible hand that are the market forces. And the other book deals with social equity and justice. And in the other book he wrote, he stressed the importance of… the regulatory role of the government to further distribute the wealth among the people. If in a country, most of the wealth is concentrated in the hands of the few, then this country can hardly witness harmony and stability.* ~ Chinese Premier Wen Jiabo, September 2008.[2]

IN THEIR GROUND-BREAKING WORK *Organic Marxism*, Philip Clayton and Justin Heinzekehr develop "an alternative to capitalism and ecological catastrophe" by arguing that Adam Smith, the father of capitalism, was "wrong,"[3] and that his ideas have led to the economic and social crisis of selfish free-market capitalism guided by the oft-cited idea of "the invisible hand." In this chapter we argue that there may in fact be something far more interesting in Adam Smith's economic work than laissez-faire free trade. Rather than placing the blame squarely at Smith's door, a more balanced interpretation may lead us to conclude it is more accurate to suggest those who have sought to apply his thinking to develop modern economics have been less than fair in the selective way they have applied his thought. At the very least, the result is that these applications of Smith's thought have in turn led to very recent thinking being — entirely unwittingly — somewhat one-sided.

To redress the balance a little, we will examine some of Smith's work in the *Theory of Moral Sentiments* before going on to consider how Marx himself, the father of Communism, developed his thinking from Smith's own work. First, however, we need to establish a more fundamental connection, namely the fact that Smith and Marx were, at heart, both concerned with the nature of human experience and the development of community. In this way, we build from previously published work,[4] which showed how this was a common thread in the work of not only Smith and Marx but also the other philosopher Clayton and Heinzekehr use to develop their Organic Marxism, Alfred North Whitehead.

All three philosophers share a fundamental unease with the nature and role of business, not only in economy but society as well. Indeed, each variously suggests that core societal drivers of what is good will most likely be lost to the greed of the profit motive, at the expense of human experience. However, to appreciate the links, it is necessary to delve into earlier work, at least in the case of Smith and Marx. In so doing, we are making the point that to understand Smith's *Wealth of Nations* (1776) one simply must read it through his *Theory of Moral Sentiments* (1759). After all, it is this work, not the later one, that Smith focused on in his academic career as Professor of Moral Philosophy at Glasgow, Edinburgh, and then again at Glasgow. *Wealth of Nations* was volume II, where volume I was the most important in the eyes of the philosopher himself, concerned as he was above all else with the human experience of social relations.[5] Further, to understand Marx's *Capital* (1867) one has to read it through (amongst other early work) the *Economic and Philosophic Manuscripts of 1844*. We will argue that doing this allows us both to see Smith's economic thinking in a far broader and concerned person-in-community context, and also to see Marx's understanding of class in the light of Smith's understanding of person-in-community. We start, however, with Whitehead.

## UNDERSTANDING SOCIETY IN
## WHITEHEAD, SMITH, AND MARX

As John Cobb has pointed out, the idea of person-in-community is a central aspect of Whiteheadian process thought.[6] It places the primacy of existence on the experience of individuals as actively experiencing subjects. That is, while the external relation between one entity and another may be presentationally immediate to us, what matters most is not what happens to us but rather what we make of what happens to us (the internal relation) for ourselves and others. Process thought understands that the person has a unique experience of the community; "to be constituted by participation in the same community does not mean to be identical with others constituted by that participation."[7] Person-in-community also means that "the persons who make up the community differ from one another, and as the persons who make up the community change, so does the community that they make up. Both persons and community are always in process."[8] This means that in process thought one cannot see the community as separate from the people that make it up, but equally one cannot see the individual as separate from the community of which they are a part; to place emphasis on either is to misunderstand the processual nature of reality. Each requires the other.

This allows us to appreciate that experience is the "self-enjoyment of being one among many, and of being one arising out of the composition of many";[9] interdependence, not dependence, is an ontologically given characteristic of nature. As such, the moment of experience is a self-determining, partially self-creating whole in which the present individual inevitably takes account of its past but turns it to its own use.[10] This is indeed the core point of the panexperientialist account. We can now understand that the reproduction of the social environment in which we find ourselves and of which we are a part is continually created and recreated through our ongoing experience of mutual relations.[11]

Can these ideas be found in Smith and Marx? In a recent analysis of the 2008 Global Financial Crisis in terms of Adam Smith's theory of economics, Paul Williams argues "Smith's vision for humanity is not the amoral utility maximizing hypermobile free individual but rather one in which persons strive toward an ideal of neighborliness, directed by the conscience of the impartial spectator which has been trained through prolonged relational attachment."[12] In *The Theory of Moral Sentiments*, Smith finds that the social worship of wealth and greatness, while useful as nature's "deception" to create social order and general wealth,[13] is in fact the central source of individual unhappiness:

> Are you in earnest resolved never to barter your liberty for the lordly servitude of a court, but to live free, fearless, and independent? There seems to be one way to continue in that virtuous resolution; and perhaps but one. Never enter the place from whence so few have been able to return; never come within the circle of ambition; nor ever bring yourself into comparison with those masters of the earth who have already engrossed the attention of half mankind before you.[14]

Interestingly, one finds a far more evocative explanation of the importance of the invisible hand for the distribution of goods within a community, according to the later-labelled "trickle-down effect," not in *The Wealth of Nations* but in *The Theory of Moral Sentiments*.[15] Yet even in *Wealth of Nations*, Smith emphasizes it is only conditions of natural liberty within a free society that ensure private vices, such as greed and selfishness, are transformed to produce public goods, that is, goods benefiting the whole community, beyond what was originally intended.[16] It is in these terms that Smith later discusses private prodigality and frugality, and their differently 'moralized' impact on a nation's economy.[17] If society should not interfere with the individuals' opportunities to express, pursue, and obtain the objects of their interest, the individuals themselves *are expected* to be able to convert their self-love into proper care for the furthering of their own condition. Such proper care is outside individual preferences; it refers not only to the basic skills involved in looking after oneself but also to being courageous,[18] well-informed,[19] and well-educated.[20] We suggest this represents a very different understanding of the invisible hand than might be gleaned solely from *Wealth of Nations*.

For Marx, society is the indispensable medium in which individuals organize, primarily, their material life.[21] In other words, like Adam Smith, human being (as a process or activity, as a verb in the gerund form) is expressed socially as doing and having in the context of society.[22] In the earlier Marx we find the suggestion that the solution may lie in conceiving human being as a harmonious, inter-supportive articulation between doing and having as inseparable aspects of humanness.[23] A good society should recognize human beings as socially relevant through the labor they produce rather than through the property they own. But a contrast can be made between, on the one hand, labor and property (forms of ownership) as human values and, on the other hand, commodified labor and private property (or capital) as externalized ("de-humanized") values.

Set in the context of a Whiteheadian process perspective, the similarities between Marx and Smith are readily apparent. Smith and Marx's interpretations of the roles of person in community, of human being in society, are the mirror image of each other. Smith appears to focus on the key role of society as placing an expectation on individuals that they must act selflessly as members of the community, whereas Marx appears to place the responsibility on society to recognize individual human values and turn them towards social relevance.

There is inherent freedom of choice in the process Marx describes as "rich experience," i.e., the appropriation of the world through the senses, an act of inseparable creation and ownership.[24] Rich experience is an inherent good. What Smith might describe as "self-love" is an inherent good, provided it is understood and employed in the manner Smith intended, that is as a vehicle for enriching human (socialized) experience rather than for acquiring transitory possessions.

The pursuit of profit at the expense of socially meaningful self-love and rich individual experience undermines the basis for a good society. Moreover, a system of economic transactions in which these two goods are neglected by the individuals themselves impoverishes them to an extent that, in the long run, will lead to undermining not only the moral progress of society but its material progress as well. Which is to say, like Whitehead, both Smith and Marx are concerned with understanding—each in their own way—the processual nature of person-in-community. Each philosopher is first and foremost concerned with the nature of human experience, and each in their own way appreciates the impact of that experience on the self and consequently society, and on society and consequently the self. Having demonstrated the person-in-community link between the three philosophers, we now turn to consider in particular just how Smith and Marx may be understood as singing from the self-same hymn sheet.

## MARX AND "NECESSARY CLASS CONFLICT"

Marx's political economy has been criticized on the grounds that the thesis of necessary class conflict, on which "unadulterated socialism"[25] is based, is unsubstantiated and contradicted by the very existence of the free market.[26] As a set of voluntary transactions occurring spontaneously, without third-party intervention, the free market is a system of cooperation in which two parties reach agreement without coercion, signaling that identity of interests is possible. The very act of free exchange questions the idea of necessary class conflict, defined as logical opposition of economic interests, as irrelevant to the central principles of a free-market economic system.

It is important to emphasize two points here. First, we are not seeking to demonstrate how it is possible to conceive of and practice such a system while necessary class conflict of economic interests is still present. Second, we are also not seeking to show how capitalist free-market social orders create necessary class conflict. Instead we are intending to engage in a genealogical study of Marx's concepts of class and necessary class conflict, thus laying the foundations for a new project of examining the role of class and class conflict within philosophical economic theory.

What does Marx mean by necessary class conflict? He contends that an economy in a particular social order structures relations of production in such a way that the interests of one social class (i.e., the capitalist) is by logical necessity opposed to the interests of another social class (i.e., the proletarian, or the worker):

> we have shown that the worker sinks to the level of a commodity and becomes indeed the most wretched of commodities; that the wretchedness of the worker is in inverse proportion to the power and magnitude of its production; that the necessary result of competition is the accumulation of capital in a few hands, and thus the restoration of monopoly in a more terrible form; and that finally the distinction between capitalist and land rentier, like that between the tiller of the soil and the factory worker, disappears and that the whole of society must fall apart into the two classes — the *property owners* and the propertyless *workers.*[27]

Cooperation in exchange is therefore not classless — but, for as long as property has superior social status to labor, will lead to a system that divides society into masters and slaves whose interests are, of necessity, opposed.

The genealogy of Hayek and Friedman's theories of free-market capitalism is well-documented by the authors themselves. They claim a natural affinity of their ideas with the work of Adam Smith and, in particular, with *The Wealth of Nations* (1776).[28] Less discussed (although rich documentation exists) is the genealogy of Marx's concept of necessary class conflict. This concept plays an extensive part in structuring the logic of *Capital* (1867), and there are earlier references throughout Marx's work up to this point. Going backwards, as a genealogical approach requires, we encounter the concept in *Theories of Surplus Value* (1862), *The Class Struggles in France* (1850), *Wage Labor and Capital* (1847), and *The German Ideology* (1845).

Note, however, that the above quote, clearly outlining the concept of necessary class conflict as already formed, is extracted from Marx's obscure *Economic and Philosophic Manuscripts of 1844*, a piece of work he never intended to publish and which appeared (under Engels's care) after his death. Remarkably, these *Manuscripts* are comprised of a series of notes on the classical political economists, in particular the French physiocrats (e.g., de Quesnay, Say), Adam Smith (who studied the physiocrats prior to writing *The Wealth of Nations*), David Ricardo and his school, and John Stuart Mill. In other words, the *Manuscripts* are Marx's literature review of political economy, preceding his life project of creating a political-economic system that changes the world rather than interprets it.[29]

In the following sections we use genealogical analysis to trace the conceptual progressions from Smith to Marx, as illustrated in *The Economic and Philosophic Manuscripts of 1844*. Typically, in this work, Marx starts with a reference to Smith's concept, then — often in the same paragraph — proceeds with a logical continuation of Smith's idea, sometimes revealing new implications. It is important to remember that Marx wrote his notes in German — so what we have is a posthumous translation (by "strangers") of these notes back into English.

## SMITH'S CONCEPT OF SOCIAL ORDER

In his *Manuscripts*, Marx gives full attention to a grossly overlooked part of Smith's work, namely the conclusion of Book I of *The Wealth of Nations*. From this conclusion, which is Smith's integrated account

of the existing agricultural economic system explained in terms of
a social order, Marx extracts several insights. First, three distinct
social categories are identified, based strictly on the economic outcomes they rely on: the landlord yields rent, the farmer (who owns
agricultural equipment) yields profits, and the laborer (who owns his
laboring capacities) yields wages. This economic perspective of the
social order is laid out as follows:

> The whole annual produce of the land and labour of every
> country... naturally divides itself... into three parts: the rent
> of land, the wages of labour, and the profits of stock; and
> constitutes a revenue to three different orders of people: to
> those who live by rent, to those who live by wages, and to
> those who live by profit. These are the three great, original,
> and constituent orders of every civilised society, from whose
> revenue that of every order is ultimately derived.[30]

Secondly, the interest of each of these three categories is then
analyzed in relation to what Smith calls "the general interest of the
society."[31] Accordingly, the landlord's interest is aligned with the
general interest when he uses the land to extract rent by facilitating
production:

> The interest of the first [the landlord]... is strictly and insep-
> arably connected with the general interest of the society.
> Whatever either promotes or obstructs the one, necessarily
> promotes or obstructs the other.[32]

Furthermore, the laborer's interest is also necessarily aligned with the
general interest, and Smith compassionately explains how a stagnant
or declining economy most affects the class of laborers:

> The wages of the labourer... are never so high as when the
> demand for labour is continually rising.... When this real
> wealth of the society becomes stationary, his wages are soon
> reduced to what is barely enough to enable him to bring up a
> family, or to continue the race of labourers. When the society
> declines, they fall even below this. The order of proprietors

may, perhaps, gain more by the prosperity of the society than that of labourers: but there is no order that suffers so cruelly from its decline.[33]

On the other hand, when interest is purely based on profits, as is the case with the farmer in agriculture and, by extension, the capitalist in industry, such profits can be obtained from material dysfunctions of the existing order:

> [T]he rate of profit does not, like rent and wages, rise with the prosperity and fall with the declension of the society. On the contrary, it is naturally low in rich and high in poor countries, and it is always highest in countries which are going fastest to ruin... The interest of the dealers... in any particular branch of trade or manufactures, is always... different from, and even opposite to, that of the public. To... narrow the competition, is always the interest of the dealers... but... must always be against it [the interest of the public], and can serve only to enable the dealers, by raising their profits above what they naturally would be, to levy, for their own benefit, an absurd tax upon the rest of their fellow-citizens.[34]

It is therefore Smith's economic theory of social class, as outlined above, that enables Marx to draw the following conclusion: if the worker's interest is necessarily aligned with the public interest and the capitalist's interest is necessarily contrary to it, then the worker and the capitalist are in necessary conflict.[35]

Smith's language of necessity is particularly relevant here, as it transfers into Marx's account without modifications. A theorist in search of general laws of economics, in describing economic relations Smith is strictly interested in what happens necessarily rather than contingently. From the relationship between the landlord's share and the increase in produce, through to the transformation of labor value into capital and the positioning of each "order" (class) in relation to the public interest—Smith's discourse invariably applies categorical terms (such as "necessarily," "naturally," "every," "never," "must") to the characterization of these relationships.[36] Smith's conclusion about the nature of the capitalist's interests is also categorical: "[merchants are] an order of men whose interest is never...the same with that of the public, who have generally an interest to deceive and even oppress the public, and who accordingly have, upon many occasions, both deceived and oppressed it."[37] The implications of Smith's thesis about social classes for political economy have been correctly observed by Arrighi, who provides a compelling reading of Smith on this issue:

> The interests of the first two orders (or social classes, as we would call them today), argues Smith...coincide with the general social interest because the real value of both rents and wages tend to rise with the economic expansion and to fall with the economic decline of society. The interests of profit earners, in contrast...clash with the general social interest, because they always involve a widening of the market and a narrowing of the competition.[38]

The idea of logical opposition of interests between capitalists and laborers (in particular) is present in this interpretation as well—and this encourages us to argue that it remains perhaps the most coherent interpretation of Smith's text that is currently available.

Arrighi also identifies the point where Marx's concept of necessary class conflict departs from Smith's concept of opposing class interests: while Smith examines division of labor within the context of market transactions, Marx scrutinizes the insides of the (increasingly larger) industrial organization, where the "social" division of labor becomes "technical."[39] This change of context also produces an important shift from the class-based opposition of interests identified by Smith through theoretical analysis to Marx's observations of actual conflicts occurring in the industrial organizations of his time:

In these abodes, Marx discovers that technical and organizational change originate, not just in the competition among capitalists and in the emergence of new specialized branches of trade and production, as Smith has already theorized, but also in the incessant conflict between capital and labor over wages and working conditions.[40]

While we note that Marx has extended the concept of conflict from a theoretical level (understood by Smith as logical opposition) to a practical one (now understood as concrete manifestation of class struggle as an outcome of the dialectics of history), it is also clear that Marx's concept of necessary class conflict (theoretically defined) originates in Smith's theory of social order as articulated in *The Wealth of Nations*. Note, in particular, that at the time *The Economic and Philosophic Manuscripts* were written, dialectical necessity was not fully articulated in Marx's own writings. Therefore, at this stage, it is reasonable to assume that Marx, too, is speaking of nothing else but Smith's logical opposition of class interests.

## MARX'S ANALYSIS OF SMITH

The continuity and progression of Smith's economic theory of social order into Marx's conception of class is clear. Moreover, it is made clear by Marx himself, when he suggests that the conclusion he draws about the two conflicting classes, as quoted above, is "on the basis of political economy itself, in its own words."[41] This observation comes at the end of Marx's analysis of Smith's chapter. It is on this basis that Marx evaluates Smith's main contribution to reside precisely in formulating economic wealth in terms of labor and in placing the necessary class conflict between the profit-maker and the wage-earner at the center of the social and political dynamics of the capitalist economic system:

> It was likewise a great and logical advance of modern English political economy, that, whilst elevating *labour* to the position of its *sole* principle, it should at the same time expound with complete clarity the *inverse* relation between wages and interest on capital, and the fact that the capitalist could only gain by pressing down wages, and vice versa... the worker and the capitalist doing-down each other, is shown to be the *normal* relationship.[42]

Importantly, Marx distinguishes Smith from all predecessors and contemporaries for his "enlightened political economy, which has discovered within private property the *subjective essence* of wealth"[43] by relating it to labor as its central source of value. This is how Smith himself proposes to redefine the wealth of a nation:

> The liberal reward of labour, therefore, as it is the necessary effect, so it is the natural symptom of increasing national wealth. The scanty maintenance of the labouring poor, on the other hand, is the natural symptom that things are at a stand, and their starving condition that they are going fast backwards.[44]

> Indeed, the most prominent claim that unifies the five volumes of Smith's work is that the wealth of a nation should be measured neither by the amount of gold in the treasury, nor by the amount of land it can render to agriculture—but by the prosperity of the wage earner as the most disadvantaged in the social order. It is this perspective that leads Marx to agree with Engels in considering Smith "the Luther of political economy."[45]

Marx's reading of Smith also helps us understand some important historical details of Smith's context. Little attention is now being paid to the fact that Smith's main argument in *The Wealth of Nations* was built as a critique of the mercantile system. Moreover, in identifying Smith's theory of labor, Marx observes how Ricardo and his school further develop the path forged by Smith in the analysis of industry and trade, and how in the process they emphasize private property over labor and objectify the status of the laborer in ways that Smith did not subscribe to. Marx takes note of how Smith's original humanism is lost in this transition.[46] He blames Ricardo for this loss, and considers "McCullogh and Mill more guilty than Ricardo."[47] The charge is laying out the laws of private property without understanding the human (subjective) dimension of labor as a more complex factor than a commodity, producing human value beyond economic value. Whereas in Smith we repeatedly find considerations of the human and social condition of the laboring poor—all the way to Book V (which is entirely about regulation) — in Ricardo and subsequent political economists such considerations disappear.

We can therefore conclude that Marx's concept of class is logically and genealogically derived, without significant changes, from Smith's concept of "order of society."[48] And, consequently, we are entitled to ask: what justifies appeal to Adam Smith's work to support a capitalist ideology of organization as applied in management studies today, when a genealogical analysis clearly indicates that a labour ideology of organization can make (at least) an equally legitimate claim? Hence, it is a question of crucial historical importance to elucidate why economic theorists have chosen to put the full weight of Smith's contribution on one mention of self-interest (on p. 39) and one mention of the invisible hand (on p. 331) instead of his political-economic account of social classes. Smith develops a theory of social order whose implications have not been sufficiently explored. This theory has its moral foundations in *The Theory of Moral Sentiments* and finds economic expression in *The Wealth of Nations*. It also constitutes the most coherent foundation for the argument that the two works are an integral part of the same philosophy.

## IMPLICATIONS FOR UNDERSTANDING ETHICAL ACTION: FROM THINKING TO DOING

We have shown how both Adam Smith and Karl Marx expressed considerable and near-identical concerns regarding the experience of people in economic society. We have also shown how, despite very different ontological premises, these concerns are discernible in the metaphysics of A. N. Whitehead and can be found in the concept of person-in-community. Along with Smith and Marx, Whitehead lamented the trends in business he witnessed:

> The modern salesmanship associated with mass production ... the determined attempt to force completely finished and standardised products upon the buyers ... is producing a more deep-seated reason for the insecurity of trade. We are

witnessing a determined attempt to canalise the aesthetic enjoyments of the population...But all intensity of enjoyment, sustained with the strength of individual character, arises from the individual taste diversifying the stream of uniformity. Destroy individuality and you are left with a vacancy of aesthetic feeling, drifting this way and that, with vague satisfactions and vague discontents.[49]

The striving for goodness through individual novelty allows us to return to more fundamental questions related to the global crisis and the place of management and economics therein—and hence the possible role of an Organic Marxism in the development of an Ecological Civilization. The potential for reassessing the role of economics in the development of the good society concerns the extent to which business corporations are capable of addressing themselves to an ecologically ethical civilization. In Smith's system of natural liberty, the driver of social authority is the market *with* important qualifiers from government,[50] while social authority beyond legislation is performed by appeal to self-interest. In Marx's advanced communist order, whatever remains of social authority is exercised solely at the level of civil society, through appeal to collective consciousness. For Whitehead, the market of potentials is garnered by the self-interested occasion for its own use in the drive towards conscious knowing of collective feeling.

This integration of market and society in process thought allows the philosopher Arran Gare to suggest ethics itself needs to be transformed so as to be centrally concerned with the virtues required to develop and sustain desirable social forms.[51] This involves an axiological repositioning, in terms of what are taken to be the problems of ethics and how moral philosophy is understood.[52] To address global problems, Gare suggests ethics must concern itself with the virtues required to develop and sustain an ecologically aware democracy of individual action. From an inherently processual perspective, organizations of people must be able to re-orientate away from the needs of the market towards a more natural and genuinely free orientation concerned with the common good.[53] Developing these virtues involves the revival of a feeling of mutual responsibility for creating a better world. Such ethics, Gare suggests, must not only provide guidance for action but also offer people a sense of their place and role in history, in nature and in inspiring the vision to motivate work geared for a better world.[54]

As a consequence of what Smith, Marx, and Whitehead have emphasized in relation to individual behavior, in addressing the need for an "organic way forwards, there is a core requirement for management to reconnect with the feelings of workers and with the feelings of society in general, rather than remaining irrevocably wedded to the profiteering demands and peer pressures of the stock market, to the detriment of all other values."[55] As the renowned Austrian and Marshallian economist Brian J. Loasby rightly suggests, economics (and with it, we argue, management as the activity of putting economics *into practice*) — "should begin with the individual, [but unlike *Homo economicus*] it must be a social individual, because the individual does not exist apart [from her] relationships with others."[56]

## STRIPPING THE SUBJECT OUT

This chapter has considered the fundamental process principle of person-in-community as seen in the work of A. N. Whitehead as well as in Adam Smith and Karl Marx. It has employed a genealogical approach to document the argument that Smith's political economy is what we may call archetypal, in that it contains the seeds of both capital and labor ideology. It is a contingency of history, we argue, that Smith's theory has been captured to serve the former and not the latter. Since, as Williams argues, "Smith differs from modern proponents of utilitarian economic orthodoxy,"[57] this is particularly unfortunate. It has become clear to us today that Friedman and Hayek appealed to Smith's work in an attempt to found neoliberal ideas of the free market on a theoretical and cultural tradition of comparable weight and standing with social contractarianism (its main rival at the time[58]). About five decades after the event, given that the tradition of anti-socialist neoliberal thinking (stimulated by a long Cold War and its aftermath) has indeed been established, it would be most appropriate to credit Friedman and Hayek themselves with founding this tradition — thus freeing Adam Smith from erroneous attributions, in particular with regard to class-based economic relations, labor versus capital as sources of value, and the role of regulation in free markets.

Marx and Smith both correctly insisted that we cannot have a meaningful understanding of justice and equality without considering the distribution of both labor and material wealth created via social activity, including physical, intellectual, and cultural labor. Along with Whitehead, they both saw, in addition, that human beings are rich in the diversity of their talents, interests, and needs, and that man is more than a machine of consumption; the idolatry of money and things had no place within their respective visions. That idolatry impoverishes humanity. We must temper and modify the notion that either Marx or Smith were primary concerned with distribution of material wealth, for this ignores their appreciation of the richer dimensions and relations within the human. They both insisted that we cannot meaningfully and sincerely talk of social justice, social order, harmony, or stability in abstraction from the distribution of labor and wealth together.[59]

Like Whitehead and Marx, therefore, Smith represents commonsense thinking that takes serious account of the subjective side of reality; when we focus on the subjective side of his philosophy, as Marx did and as we have in the foregoing discussion, person-in-community is obvious.[60] Interestingly, a similar genealogical analysis can be applied to examine the appropriation of Marx's political economy into Lenin's (1902/1973) theory of communism.[61] Furthermore, in "really existing socialism,"[62] we note a substitution of capital for labor in the social hierarchy of economic relations, while similar master-slave relations are maintained. Whitehead's emphasis on the active subject over the modern science project's subsequent emphasis on the passive object has been crucial in providing the means by which to comprehend what Smith's and Marx's first interpreters separately seem to have done to both these philosophers' original ideas — and with what consequences.

## CONCLUSION

Hence, in the context of an economic theory of the social order, Marx's project can be rephrased to read: owners of political decision-making power have always (re)interpreted the master-slave relation, in various ways, to give political advantage to the social and economic attributes of their own class; the point is to transcend it. Both Smith's and Marx's political economies contain the seeds of such transcendence. In short, Marx adopted his concept of class from Smith's concept of social order; Smith and Marx are indeed singing from the same hymn-sheet. Yet each and every further development of these archetypal theories by their separate commentators — or, to pursue the choral metaphor, orchestrators — has led to a *tragic subversion* of the original project.

We therefore suggest *applications* of Organic Marxism — the powerful combination of Marx and Whitehead intended to derive an alternative to orthodox understandings of capitalism that may thereby help discern a way towards an Ecological Civilization — to economies, as "leadership in building new" forms of civilization and order[63] might benefit not from rejecting Adam Smith as "wrong" *per se*. For, like Whitehead and Marx, Smith was most concerned as a philosopher with the social nature of human experience. Instead, applications of Organic Marxism might usefully look to read and perhaps indeed incorporate not just Smith's *Theory of Moral Sentiments*, but even his *Wealth of Nations* treatise — when that work itself is understood more completely through the lens of his broader moral philosophy. As Marx realized very early on, and Premier Wen Jiabo noted on CNN, there is much good to be found there for the project at hand.

## NOTES

1    A later version of this paper, focused on management, is published as Cristina Neesham and Mark Dibben, "Class Conflict and Social Order in Smith and Marx: The Relevance of Social Philosophy to Business Management," in *Philosophy of Management* 15, no.2 (2016): 121–33. The authors are grateful for the copyright permissions contained therein.

2    Speaking on CNN at the time of the Global Financial Crisis that engulfed many Western capitalist liberal market economies, and in response to a question concerning the apparent contradiction of a *socialist* market economy. Quoted in Paul Williams, "A Visible Hand: Contemporary Lessons from Adam Smith," in *Adam Smith as Theologian*, ed. Paul Oslington (New York: Routledge, 2011), 133.

3    Philip Clayton and Justin Heinzekehr, *Organic Marxism: An Alternative to Capitalism and Ecological Catastrophe* (Claremont: Process Century Press, 2015), 216.

4    Cristina Neesham and Mark Dibben, "The Social Value of Business: Lessons from Political Economy and Process Philosophy," in *Applied Ethics: Remembering Patrick Primeaux,* ed. Michael Schwartz and Howard Harris (Bingley: Emerald Group Publishing, 2012), 63–83.

5    Christopher J. Berry et al., ed., *The Oxford Handbook of Adam Smith* (Oxford: Oxford University Press, 2013). For a more specific theological treatment, see Oslington, *Adam Smith as Theologian.* We are grateful to Dr. John Quiring of the Center for Process Studies for indicating this remarkable book to us.

6    John B. Cobb, Jr., "Person-In-Community: Whiteheadian Insights into Community and Institution," *Organisation Studies* 28, no. 4 (2007): 567–88.

7    Ibid., 578.

8    Ibid.

9    Alfred North Whitehead, *Process and Reality,* corr. ed. (New York: Free Press, 1978), 220.

10   See also Mark Dibben, "Exploring Whitehead's Understanding of Organizations: Moving beyond the Organising Experience of Individual Managers," *Philosophy of Management* 7, no. 2 (2009): 13–24.

11  Michael Halewood, "Introduction to Special Section on A. N. Whitehead" *Theory, Culture and Society* 25, no. 4 (2008): 1–14. Also Michael Halewood and Mike Michael, "Being a Sociologist and Becoming a Whiteheadian: Concrescing Methodological Tactics," *Theory, Culture and Society* 25, no. 4 (2008): 31–56 and Michael Halewood, "Sociology, Societies and Sociality," in *Applied Process Thought*, vol. 2, ed. Mark Dibben & R. Newton (Frankfurt: Ontos Verlag, 2009), 293–317.

12  Williams, "A Visible Hand," 137.

13  Adam Smith, *The Theory of Moral Sentiments*, ed. Knud Haakonssen (Cambridge: Cambridge University Press, 2002), 214–15.

14  Ibid., 69.

15  Ibid., 215–16.

16  Adam Smith, *An Inquiry into the Nature and Causes of the Wealth of Nations,* ed. Edwin Cannan, vol. 1 (Chicago: University of Chicago Press, 1976), 477–78.

17  Ibid., 360.

18  Adam Smith, *An Inquiry into the Nature and Causes of the Wealth of Nations,* ed. Edwin Cannan, vol. 2 (Chicago: University of Chicago Press, 1976), 296.

19  Ibid., 282.

20  Ibid., 305.

21  Karl Marx and Friedrich Engels, *Collected Works,* vol. 3 (London: Lawrence and Wishart, 1975), 298.

22  Ibid., 275–79.

23  Ibid., 283–84.

24  Marx and Engels, *Collected Works,* 301–02.

25  Milton Friedman, "The Social Responsibility of Business is to Increase Its Profits," *New York Times*, 13 September 1970.

26  Friedrich von Hayek, *The Road to Serfdom* (London: Routledge, 1944); Willem Keizer, "Hayek's Critique of Socialism," in *Hayek, Co-ordination and Evolution,* ed. Jack Birner and Rudy Van Zijp (London: Routledge, 2002), 207–31.

27  Karl Marx, *The Economic and Philosophic Manuscripts of 1844* (New

York: Prometheus Books, 1988), 69.

28  Milton Friedman, *Capitalism and Freedom* (Chicago: University of Chicago Press, 1962); Friedrich von Hayek, *The Constitution of Liberty* (London: Routledge, 1966).

29  Karl Marx, *The German Ideology* (New York: International Publishers, 2004).

30  Smith, *Wealth of Nations,* 178.

31  Ibid.

32  Ibid.

33  Ibid.

34  Ibid., 179.

35  Marx, *Economic and Philosophic Manuscripts,* 69.

36  Smith, *Wealth of Nations,* 177–79.

37  Ibid., 179.

38  Giovanni Arrighi, *Adam Smith in Beijing: Lineages of the Twenty-first Century* (London: Verso, 2007), 47.

39  Ibid., 77–78.

40  Ibid., 78.

41  Marx, *Economic and Philosophic Manuscripts,* 69.

42  Ibid., 87.

43  Ibid., 93.

44  Smith, *Wealth of Nations,* 82.

45  Marx, *Economic and Philosophic Manuscripts,* 94.

46  Ibid., 94.

47  Ibid., 174.

48  Smith, *Wealth of Nations,* 177.

49  Alfred North Whitehead, *Whitehead's American Essays in Social Philosophy,* ed. Helen M. Johnson (New York: Harper and Brothers, 1959), 72–73.

50  Williams, "A Visible Hand."

51  Arran Gare, "Process Philosophy and Ecological Ethics," in *Applied*

*Process Thought,* vol. 1, ed. Mark Dibben and Thomas Kelly (Frankfurt: Ontos Verlag, 2008), 361–80.

52   Rob Macklin et al., "Process Ethics and Business: Applying Process Thought to Enact Critiques of Mind/Body Dualism in Organizations," *Process Studies* 43, no. 2 (2014): 61–86.

53   Mark Dibben, *A Process Philosophy of Management* (Anoka, MN: Process Century Press, forthcoming).

54   Gare, "Process Philosophy"; Dibben, *A Process Philosophy of Management.*

55   Dibben, *A Process Philosophy of Management.*

56   Brian Loasby, "The Ubiquity of Organisation," *Organisation Studies* 28, no. 11: (2007), 1752.

57   Williams, "A Visible Hand," 137.

58   This rivalry is illustrated in the publication of *Hayek's Law, Legislation and Liberty* (London: Routledge, 1973; Vol. 1 was first published in 1971 and Vol. 2 in 1972), at about the same time as John Rawls's *Theory of Justice* (Cambridge: Harvard University Press, 1971).

59   We are grateful to Ronald Preston Phipps for pointing this out in conversation.

60   We are grateful to John B. Cobb, Jr., for pointing this out in conversation, and for this section's subheading.

61   Vladimir Lenin, *What Is to be Done? Burning Questions of Our Movement* (Peking: Foreign Languages Press, 1973), 50–160.

62   Ferenc Feher et al., *Dictatorship over Needs: An Analysis of Soviet Societies* (London: Blackwell, 1984).

63   Clayton and Heinzekehr, 243; for an alternative rendering in terms of a "Post-Marxist Speculative Naturalism," see Arran Gare, *The Philosophical Foundations of Ecological Civilization: A Manifesto for the Future* (London: Routledge, 2017).

# ❧ 5 ❧

## ORGANIC MARXISM AND THE

## MARXIST TRADITION

### *Leslie A. Muray*

PROCESS THOUGHT, like any other discipline, is a dynamic, historical movement that, even as it is profoundly shaped by the past, responds creatively or destructively to the challenges of the present. This perspective provides a helpful way of understanding developments in Marxism, in particular Organic Marxism. From this perspective, the history of Marxism can be seen as a constant attempt to define itself, to find itself in the face of ever new challenges. In doing so, Marxism has all too often tightened the boundaries of its self-definition. Marxism could have been open to new influences and made creative responses to them. Instead, as all movements and traditions do at times, Marxism excommunicated, tortured, and executed its "heretics."

Even when the campaign against "heretics" was not bloody (as in the Social Democratic debates between Bernstein and Kautsky regarding "revolution or reform" or the Bolshevik-Menshevik debates prior to the Bolshevik Revolution), "orthodoxy" or "correct teaching" was narrowly defined. This orthodoxy was considered the

71

"authentic" core of the Marxist tradition, thus in effect "essentializing" select aspects of that tradition and "excommunicating" competing alternatives.

Thus, for example, the dominant form of Marxism as propounded by Soviet ideology essentialized the "scientific socialism" of the later Marx (with its proclivity toward economic determinism) and anathemized the humanistic works of "young Marx" (with its focus on freedom and creativity). In similar fashion, Western Marxists and critical Marxist dissidents of the former Soviet bloc privileged and essentialized the writings of the young Marx and used them to critique both capitalism and what they euphemistically called "already existing socialism" (the "Praxis Circle" in the former Yugoslavia, or "the Budapest Circle" consisting mostly of former students of György Lukács in Hungary). Others did something similar in identifying "authentic" Marxism with the young Marx and seeing the later Marx in continuity with the earlier. While significant arguments were advanced at times, the discussion was all too often colored by polemics and what seemed to be an arbitrary designation of the essence of Marxism.

In their *Organic Marxism: An Alternative to Capitalism and Ecological Catastrophe*, which I consider to be the best and most creative book about Marxism, Philip Clayton and Justin Heinzekehr resolve all of the dogmatic debates within Marxism in one big swoop. They maintain that "one must... engage in a careful process of sorting through the legacy of Karl Marx's work in order to establish what a viable Marxism will mean in the twenty-first century."[1] They advocate, to use David Ray Griffin's phrase, a "constructive postmodern" form of Marxism that "calls for a number of important revisions of and updates of classical Marxist thought and practice."[2]

The first of these revisions, they claim, is that "Marxism is not a universal predictive science." To them, the social determinism and the desire to predict the advent of a universal revolution and utopia is a feature of European modernism that needs to be abandoned. Secondly, "Marxists do not need to insist only on state ownership, state-run businesses, and the abolition of market forces."[3] They point out that most socio-politico-economic systems are hybrids of various systems. Some aspects of the global economic systems may bear a resemblance to those of Marx's day but others may not. We need to deal with those discrepancies in creative and novel ways. Third, Marxism, which was never meant to be a purely theoretical dispute, needs a radical blending of theory and practice in order to correct the imbalances of the past. Fourth, Marxism is not a superfluous label for arbitrary policies governments impose. It is all too easy for Marxism to become empty sloganeering. The authors maintain that "by contrast, updated Marxist analyses of the dynamics of wealth and power can help leaders to modify unjust systems and to implement wise policies."[4] Fifth, "a vibrant, living Marxism cannot be 'one size fits all.'" This means that, instead of a universal theory applicable at all times and in all places, "the only useful Marxism for our time will be a *postmodern* Marxism, which means that it will exist only as adapted to a particular time and place: this nation, this culture, this language and history, these particular needs of these particular people." This means that Clayton and Heinzekehr seek "*a culturally embedded Marxism*; a set of core commitments that take different forms as they are applied in different political and economic contexts."[5]

Thus, we have been presented with a form of Marxism that is "organic" to a particular society and culture. It is also "organic" in seeking to promote an "ecological civilization," one that promotes humans as part of non-human nature and offers sustainable ways of living in harmony with non-human nature. We shall return to this in my treatment of alienation later in the chapter.

In developing the notion of Organic Marxism, Clayton and Heinzekehr cover the entire range of the history of the Marxist tradition. As important as the past is (a theme to which I shall return), their focus is on the problems of the present. To overcome the injustices and exploitation of the global market economy, they develop the notion that human rights are categorized as "blue," "red" and "green" rights. Blue rights are the typical rights espoused by liberal democracies, red rights are economic rights, and green rights are rights to a clean and sustainable environment, not only for present but future generations as well. The authors want to see the institutionalization of these three kinds of rights. In the case of economic rights, this entails going beyond Western European models of social democracy to entering economic activity around distributive justice in pursuit of the common good, maximizing efficacious participation in the decisions that affect peoples' lives.[6]

Clayton and Heinzekehr assert that Organic Marxism is a form of Open Marxism. What they mean by Open Marxism is the open-endedness, creativity, and interrelatedness of systems in constructive postmodern orientations in the sciences, philosophy, economics, and political theory. They see Open Marxism as a means to draw out the parallels between Organic Marxism, process philosophy, and traditional Chinese thought. They point out in a very helpful way how both Marx and Whitehead sought to get away from "either/ or" ways of thinking in favor of "both/and" thinking that is quite compatible with traditional Chinese modes of thought.[7]

## ISSUES

There are two issues that I would like to raise, at the risk of engaging in Marxist scholasticism. One of these has to do with Clayton and Heinzekehr's critique of the determinist trajectory of much of the Marxist tradition. While I totally agree with their argument, I would like to point out that there is another dimension to the problem. As ex-Marxist philosopher Nicholas Berdyaev has pointed out, there is not only an economic determinist tradition in Marxism but also a "voluntarist" trajectory. For Berdyaev, this voluntarism is most readily apparent in Lenin's emphasis on the revolutionary practice of a vanguard whose subjective agency supersedes and is independent of economic laws. He writes that "economism was the denial of the integration of revolutionary outlook and of revolutionary action." Furthermore, he maintains that "to this trust in elemental impulses

Lenin opposed the consciousness of a revolutionary minority which was called to take control of the general process."[8] Thus, both the determinist and voluntarist trajectories in Marxism provide a philosophical backdrop for oppressive practices.[9]

Secondly, our two authors speak fondly of the "Return to Marx" movement both in China and in the West (as in the works of Anne Fairchild Pomeroy). This movement refers to engagement with the works of Marx without references to later Marxists such as Kautsky, Lenin, Mao, etc. While I have considerable sympathy for this movement (at times there is significant tension between Marx and later theoreticians, such as Marx and Lenin on the role of the Party and dictatorship of the proletariat), I cannot help but wonder if this can truly be accomplished. What I mean is that later interpretations have become such a part of the Marxist corpus that, even if we have not studied them or have deliberately ignored them, they still influence our interpretations. Their thought has become part of us, as though by osmosis.

Let me bring in both Whitehead and Marx to make my point. For Whitehead, a moment of experience, an actual occasion "prehends" the past. It cannot help but prehend the past. That is to say, it "internalizes" the past. It internalizes not only its own past but the past of the entire universe. Moreover, since even in human beings 91% of our psychic life is subconscious, most of our prehensions are at a subconscious level.

Marx says something very similar when he writes: "Men make their history but not as they please; they do not make it under circumstances chosen by themselves but under circumstances directly encountered, given and transmitted from the past."[10] We are profoundly shaped by the past even as we grasp for the possibilities of the future.

## THE LATENT POSSIBILITIES OF THE PAST

I have raised the foregoing issues not as an opponent but as an enthusiastic supporter of the further development of Organic Marxism.

In the next two sections, I hope to build collegially on the work of Clayton and Heinzekehr by focusing on a Whiteheadian concept in the first instance, a Marxist in the second.

In the first instance, I would like to return to the Whiteheadian notion of prehension. As we have seen, momentary experiences cannot help but prehend the past. As they do so, at times they become aware of possibilities in the past that were either forgotten, neglected, or buried that are now quite relevant to the present. Although I would advance the notion very carefully and cautiously, I would argue that *by analogy* philosophical/religious traditions need to look back on their past in an inclusive way and find forgotten, neglected, buried trajectories latent for realization in the present. For example, without superimposing European models on China, a study of the Marxist tradition and its connection to anarchism could be fruitful in the contemporary rediscovery of local, sustainable, organic agriculture and the participatory modes of organizing those local communities. Perhaps more importantly, this approach can enhance efforts to retrieve the traditional philosophical traditions of China, an effort that is very significant for the creation of an "ecological civilization."

Practically speaking, this would mean that hierarchicalism following the model of filial piety would not be considered "essential" to Confucianism. Rather, the revival of Confucianism would mean focusing on self-cultivation for being a citizen of an "ecological civilization." In similar fashion, a revival of Daoism would focus on living in harmony with the non-human nature and its rhythms. It would encourage simplicity and celebrate the local. A revival of Chinese Buddhism(s) would entail those practices that enhance a sense of kinship with all creatures and cultivate compassion for all sentient beings.

## THE MARXIST THEORY OF ALIENATION

At this point, I turn to the Marxist theory of alienation as a complementary piece to Organic Marxism. I shall examine the theory and then explore briefly its contemporary relevance.

Marx's theory of alienation is inseparably intertwined with his anthropology. According to that anthropology, the most fundamental characteristic of being human is the capacity for creativity and freedom. That creativity and freedom is expressed in work.

However, on account of the advent of private property, at least in the sense of the private ownership of large scale units of production, work as an expression of the fundamental human capacity for creativity and freedom is distorted; it is alienated. Alienation from our human creativity and freedom takes three forms. The first form of alienation is from the product of labor. Since the product of labor belongs not to its creator, the worker, but to the owner of the means of production, the creator is separated and estranged from her/his creation. For workers, labor is the fulfillment of the goals of someone else rather than their own projects.

The second form is alienation from the act of labor. As people work for others, they are told when to work, how to work, etc. Not only are aims and production dictated but so are means and methods as well. In other words, rather than being in harmony with the "inner" integrity of one's creativity, workers surrender that creative freedom and internalize an external authority.

The third form is alienation from species-life. To Marx, borrowing from Ludwig Feuerbach, species-life is the social-individual dimension of human existence. Since some own the means of the production and others do not, a sharp class division between oppressor and oppressed develops, leading to the class struggle that alienates humans from each other and from their basic "nature" as social beings. Moreover, there is antagonism between the oppressed on account of the competition for jobs, especially during times of economic recession.[11]

While alienation is a characteristic of all societies that have private property, such as slave economies or feudalism, for Marx alienation took a particularly acute expression under the conditions of the capitalism that he knew. One can readily acknowledge the ameliorative reforms that have been taken since his time and yet admit the contemporary relevance of the theory of alienation: the high percentages of people interviewed complaining about the lack of fulfillment in work in the United States; the fact that, quite aside from the growing number of women working and embarking on professional careers, it takes two adults working full time to maintain a household with a comfortable standard of living; the fact that both spouses are working increasingly longer hours—until fairly recently for less "real" earned income.

Marx and his philosophical descendants are ambiguous about the means for overcoming alienation. It involves, in Hegelian fashion, "the negation of the negation," alienating oneself and fellow members of the oppressed class(es) from alienation and overthrowing the sources of that alienation. How that is done, whether violently or peacefully, was one of the systematic ambiguities of Marx's thought. There is certainly much in Marx's thought that is in tension with the later totalitarian trajectories of Marxism. Suffice it to say that there is a dimension to Marx's thought that suggests (as does the thought of such later Marxists as those of Yugoslav Praxis Circle and some contemporary Green political theorists) that alienation is transformed when people have a real sense of participating in the decisions that affect their lives.

## MARXISM AND ANTHROPOCENTRISM

Both Marx and Engels attempted to situate human beings in the non-human natural world. Both had some familiarity with Darwin. Engels' response to Darwin was to apply the notion of the dialectic, the very concept of dialectical materialism to reality, human and non-human, as a whole. In his *Dialectics of Nature,* Engels asserts that there is a dialectical movement in the non-human natural world, suggestive of a creativity and dynamism contradictory to modernity's mechanistic view of nature.[12]

There is another side to Marx and Engels (and the Marxist tradition as a whole), however, namely its own anthropocentrism. In

Marx, for example, human labor is the connecting link between humanity and the non-human natural world. Thus, while humans are situated in the non-human natural world, it is readily apparent that what is important is human labor and that the non-human natural world is important only as the stage on which the human drama is played out. In other words, the non-human natural world is only of instrumental value and not of intrinsic value.

Roger Garaudy has described Marx's idea of human labor as "the humanization of nature." With this term, Garaudy is attempting to capture Marx's attempt to do justice to both the continuities and discontinuities between humans and the non-human natural world, but the very words "humanization of nature" are suggestive of anthropocentrism and an instrumentalist view of the non-human natural world.[13]

Although Engels attempts to situate humans in the natural world, it is no less apparent in his thought that what was really important is human activity, with the non-human natural world of importance only in terms of its relationship to human beings, not in terms of the intrinsic value of the constituent parts.[14] Moreover, while fully acknowledging both the voluntaristic and deterministic sides of Marxist thought, given the historical proclivity of dialectical traditions to be deterministic, as, for example, the outcome of history being predetermined (the kingdom of freedom in both Hegelianism and Marxism, becoming communism in the latter), it is questionable in my mind as to whether Marxism can provide a consistent and coherent understanding of a non-mechanistic and non-deterministic view of nature. Certainly, the dominant tradition in Marxism, both in terms of its intellectual history as well as its socio-politico-economic practice, like most of the Western tradition, has been anthropocentric. Such anthropocentrism is not only itself alienating in a most fundamental sense but also expressive of what to me is the most basic form of alienation, namely alienation from the non-human natural world, from the Earth, and from the cosmos itself. This most basic alienation from the universe is at the root of all other forms of alienation—from ourselves, from our fellow creatures, human and non-human, and from the sacred. And it is all of these interrelated forms of alienation that Organic Marxism is seeking to transform.[15]

## CONCLUSION

A final question I need to ask on behalf of and addressed to all proponents of Organic Marxism: is it still Marxist? Marxism can be described as many things—philosophy, economic theory, ideology. For Marx himself, Marxism was pre-eminently a critical philosophy. This meant that nothing, not even Marxism, was beyond question. Like Whitehead, Marx thought that there was no finality to his thought. Rather, like Whitehead, he saw it as an opening to further "adventures of ideas" and creative transformations.[16] In this, Organic Marxism is in line with the best of the Marxist tradition(s).

## NOTES

1    Philip Clayton and Justin Heinzekehr, *Organic Marxism: An Alternative to Capitalism and Ecological Catastrophe* (Claremont, CA: Process Century Press, 2014), 6.

2    Ibid.

3    Ibid.

4    Ibid., 8.

5    Ibid.

6    Ibid., 100–38.

7    Ibid., 155–75.

8    Nikolai Berdyaev, *The Origin of Russian Communism* (Ann Arbor: University of Michigan Press, 1966), 121.

9    Ibid., 121, 123ff, 127.

10   Karl Marx, *The Eighteenth Brumaire of Louis Bonaparte* (New York: International Publishers, 1991), 15.

11  Karl Marx, *Economic and Philosophical Manuscripts of 1844* (New York: Prometheus Books, 1988), 69–84.

12  Leslie A. Muray, "A Comparison of the Concept of Freedom in the Thought of Roger Garaudy and Daniel Day Williams" (Ph.D dissertation, Claremont Graduate School, 1982), 63–67.

13  Roger Garaudy, *Karl Marx: The Evolution of His Thought,* trans. Nan Aptheker (New York: International Publishers, 1964), 84.

14  Frederick Engels, *Dialectics of Nature,* trans. Clement Dutt (New York: International Publishers, 1960), 18–19, 279–96.

15  I need to acknowledge the thorough and creative work of John Bellamy Foster and other Ecological Marxists at the *Monthly Review,* as well as the work of Wang Zhihe, Director of the China Project at the Center for Process Studies, Claremont, California, in seeking to retrieve "the Ecological Marx." See for example Foster's *Marx's Ecology: Materialism and Nature* (New York: Monthly Review Press, 2000). As much I appreciate their endeavors, I remain unconvinced. I still see Marx as attempting to situate humans in the non-human natural world but still winding up with an anthropocentric view of the relationship between humans and non-humans. This is where process thought/constructive postmodernism can be a resource for the creation of a creatively transformed Organic Marxism.

16  Karl Marx, *Writings of the Young Marx on Philosophy,* ed. Loyd Easton and Kurt Guddat (New York: Doubleday, 1967), 414ff.

# PART TWO

# REINTERPRETING
# SOCIAL THOUGHT

For an Ecological Context

## 🦅 6 🦅

# COMMODITY FETISHISM AND
# CRITICAL METAPHYSICS

*Jung Mo Sung*

I s it still relevant to discuss Marxism nowadays? After all, it has been a while since the dissolution of the socialist bloc. New philosophies and social theories seem to have buried Marxism as a philosophical and social theory for our time. It is obvious that many of Marx's analyses refer to his specific economic and political moment, and the capitalism we face today is very different than the capitalism of the nineteenth century. However, there are human and social themes that abide for centuries; therefore, we can still find relevant contributions in Marx's thought.

In order to establish a dialogue between Marx's thinking and process philosophy, I would like to make some reflections prompted by an affirmation in the book *Organic Marxism*:

> As Organic Marxists, we blame this capitalist view of justice both for worker inequalities and for the growing environmental catastrophe. We now know that the planet itself cannot sustain the payouts that the capitalist system provides to the world's wealthiest one percent, nor the

lifestyle of consumption and waste that they buy with their wealth. With Marx, we advocate a system that brings the distribution of resources into harmony with what people actually need to survive, not with their unlimited desires.[1]

In general, I agree with this affirmation. However, I do think there are points that deserve to be explored and deepened. That is the goal of this chapter.

## ENVIRONMENT SUSTAINABILITY AND SOCIAL INEQUALITY

The authors point out two fundamental problems with the current globalization system: the growing economic inequality and the environmental crisis. However, by stating that the capitalist process of accumulation of wealth and lifestyle based on overconsumption is unsustainable for our planet, the focus is reduced to the environmental crisis.

Even if it is done unconsciously, the death and suffering of hundreds of millions of the poor and marginalized people of the system take secondary importance. I know the authors do not underestimate this death and suffering, but there is a tendency of environmental thinking to prioritize the environmental crisis over inequality and social exclusion. Even more than simply placing the matter in second place, I think there is an underlying theoretical issue that makes social matters lose their importance in the environmental debate. In other words, the hegemonic way of thinking about the environmental crisis does not enable the articulation of the environmental crisis and the social crisis together. That is why social issues come up in the debate, but fade away over the course of the argument.

There is no doubt the poor will be damaged the most when the environmental crisis becomes catastrophic. However, the solution of the environmental crisis on its own will not solve the problems caused by the great social inequality and exclusion that we see in the world today. The goal to achieve environmental sustainability within the global capitalist system does not presuppose nor demand the solution to the social problem of the poor and outcast.

The theme of environmental sustainability has become important in the Western world since the Rome Club document, *Limits to Growth*,[2] alerted us to the impossibility of granting to the worldwide population the standard of consumption and lifestyle of the rich countries. That is, it presented the notion of the limitation of nature against the modern myth of progress and of unlimited economic growth.

All of this means that before the twentieth century humankind hadn't faced the conflict between the myth of unlimited economic growth and the limits of the environmental system. However, the exploitation and domination of social groups and peoples have existed for thousands of years. The dominion of the Roman Empire, as well as the slavery, colonization, and exploitation of the Americas, Africa, Asia, and Oceania, and other great social systems of oppression and exploitation, have existed without causing any significant environmental crisis that would pose a threat to the sustainability of the system. In other words, inequality and social exploitation exist prior to the environmental crisis, and the latter can be solved without addressing social issues. To address those issues, it is not enough to pursue new, less-polluting technologies, a decrease of total pollution emission, or a decrease of non-essential, non-recyclable goods. In fact, in a cold and inhumane calculation, the death of a couple of billion people of the lowest tiers of the world society would solve the problem of environmental sustainability.

It is obvious that nobody in their right state of mind proposes such an extreme solution, but it is a reminder that we should not lose track of the social crisis, and that we will find a solution to the environmental *and* the social crisis in the economic logic that is the root cause of both.

## NEEDS AND UNLIMITED DESIRE

In the text quoted above, after pointing out the process of accumulation and wealth concentration, Clayton and Heinzekehr propose as an alternative "a system that brings the distribution of resources into harmony with what people actually need to survive, not with their unlimited desires." At first sight, we would agree with the proposition of a new economic social system, in which there would be a fundamental rule of distribution of commodities according to the real necessities of survival and not to unlimited desires.

In order to better understand what this new alternative proposition means, one must analyze the relation between wealth, needs, and unlimited desire in capitalism. As our goal is to establish a dialogue between process thought and Marx, let us examine one of Marx's famous quotes:

> The wealth of those societies in which the capitalist mode of production prevails, presents itself as "an immense accumulation of commodities," its unit being a single commodity. Our investigation must therefore begin with the analysis of a commodity.

> A commodity is, in the first place, an object outside us, a thing that by its properties satisfies human wants [*Bedürfnisse*] of some sort or another. The nature of such wants, whether, for instance, they spring from the stomach or from fancy [*Phantasie*], makes no difference.[3]

For those who are familiar with Whitehead's thinking, the notion of commodity as "substance" stands out right away. In capitalism, the individual commodity is seen as the elemental form of the structure of wealth in capitalism. Moreover, a commodity is seen as an external object, independent from human being, whose qualities are capable of satisfying any type of human needs. Marx's analysis of the commodity shows that his view is not in accordance with the substantialist view.

On this point, process thinking has a lot to contribute to the overcoming of a metaphysics based on the notion of substance in favor of a metaphysics based on the notion of process and relations. However, I think there is a need to go beyond this overcoming. For the mere substitution of a relational or processual view for a substantial view of commodities and wealth is not enough to comprehend why a capitalist logic of accumulation endangers the environment we live in and casts away so many people from the benefits of society. Moreover, it does not explain why the great part of the world's population dreams of becoming beneficiaries of the market system and satisfying their desires by the consumption of commodities.

We need to understand the relation between the production of wealth by the collection of commodities and the satisfaction of human desires, which are unlimited by nature. Humans are beings of needs and desires, and desire knows no limits. We are beings capable of thinking the infinite, of desiring the infinite, and of desiring infinitely. One of desire's characteristics is precisely the fact that it does not acknowledge or accept limits. All of us desire the fulfillment of our desires. It wouldn't be a desire otherwise.

The notion of "unlimited desire" does not appear in Marx's writings, but it does in *Organic Marxism*. The authors of this book contrast the satisfaction of real needs with the satisfaction of unlimited desires. In fact, they reject the attempt to satisfy unlimited desires. For if desires are unlimited, they cannot be completely fulfilled. This distinction between need and desire is very common in Marxist thought, as in other anti-capitalist groups. However, Marx himself doesn't make this distinction. He says: "A commodity is, in the first place, an object outside us, a thing that by its properties satisfies human wants [*Bedürfnisse*] of some sort or another. The nature of such wants, whether, for instance, they spring from the stomach or from fancy [*Phantasie*], makes no difference."[4]

Marx gives examples of two types of "wants" or needs: the need that comes from the stomach, organic survival needs, and the need that comes from "fancy" or "imagination." We will not discuss here which term better translates the word *Phantasie* and what Marx meant by it; both translations convey a sense of limitlessness. On the other hand, Marx uses the word "want" and not "desire." However, the need that comes from *Phantasie* is unlimited, and so, in this sense, we can make a link with the notion of unlimited desire. The footnote that refers to the need that comes from *Phantasie* states: "Desire implies want; it is the appetite of the mind, and as natural as hunger to the body... The greatest number (of things) have their value from supplying the wants of the mind."[5]

Therefore, we can assume that the notion of need from imagination or *Phantasie* has a relation to what we say today about unlimited desire. In fact, even nowadays, there is a relation between need and desire. We human beings need more than material goods to survive. We need to feel that it is worthy to live. We must satisfy our need for others to recognize us as human beings.

This need of being recognized by other people is also an organic need. We are organic beings who feel that the body needs recognition. The complete lack of this recognition may lead us to depression or even suicide. However, it is an organic need of a different type than the need of material goods such as food, air, shelter. It is what is commonly named as need or desire to "be" or to "have being." This need or desire to "be more" or to "have more being" knows no limits, for "being" is not a substance to acquire and keep in a safe, or something that wears out or makes us feel overwhelmed. We will never have enough being.

The issue is how each society, in each historical moment, establishes the method and criteria for a person to acquire "being," which is what Hegel called "the struggle for recognition." In capitalism, the satisfaction of this need for recognition, or the unlimited desire of being, happens by the acquisition, consumption, and accumulation of wealth in the form of collection of commodities. For example, when someone feels a bit down, diminished in their personhood, a very common piece of advice given to them is to "go shop in the mall." Shopping seems like good medicine for this feeling of low self-esteem. We feel better when we buy something or simply admire the beautiful brands on display, feeding our dream of one day buying them.

In the old days, in pre-capitalist societies, when a person felt down, they used to go to a sacred place, usually a temple, to be in contact with the sacred forces in order to feel purer and stronger, so they would recover by acquiring the "being" that they lacked. Nowadays, the place to be in contact with the sacred forces, which give back "being," are no longer churches but the shopping malls, "real" or "virtual." That is why many shopping malls have an architecture reminiscent of temples, cathedrals, or other sacred places.

*Galleria Vittorio Emanuele II, shopping mall in Milan, Italy*[6]

Insofar as the desire of being has no limits, the desire of buying-to-achieve-being also has no limits. Capitalism presents itself as the way to unlimited economic growth capable of satisfying unlimited human desires. In this sense, the danger of the environmental crisis by the surplus of production and consumption is an inherent result of the capitalist logic and its promise. This is one of the reasons why a great part of the American right wing does not want to let go of the capitalist dream and denies that the environmental crisis is due to human action. And, so, they attack proposals to decrease the emission of polluting gases and consumption as something that is against the American dream. As the scientific arguments about the environmental crisis are accepted, one needs to acknowledge the impossibility of the fulfillment of the promises of capitalism for unlimited economic growth to satisfy unlimited human desires.

We may say that one of the causes of the environmental crisis is the "spiritual way of capitalism" that yearns for fullness by the unlimited accumulation of wealth in the form of commodities.

The next question is, why do people see in commodities and wealth the main and only way to satisfy this need (desire of being) that exists in all human beings? In order to answer this question, we need to go beyond the critique of the substantial view of commodities. I think Marx's concept of fetish is fundamental here.

## FETISHISM AND THE SOURCE OF "BEING"

Marx states:

> A commodity appears, at first sight, a very trivial thing, and easily understood. Its analysis shows that it is, in reality, a very queer thing, abounding in metaphysical subtleties and theological niceties... A commodity is therefore a mysterious thing, simply because in it the social character of men's labour appears to them as an objective character stamped upon the product of that labour; because the relation of the producers to the sum total of their own labour is presented to them as a social relation, existing not between themselves, but between the products of their labour... There it is a definite social relation between men, that assumes, in their eyes, the fantastic form of a relation between things... This I call the Fetishism which attaches itself to the products of labour, so soon as they are produced as commodities, and which is therefore inseparable from the production of commodities.[7]

Before we analyze Marx's text, it is important to remind ourselves that we human beings aren't isolated, autonomous individuals who satisfy the desire of being by acquiring "being" in any substantial sense. We are human beings in relation with other human beings and with other beings of our environment. However, the important fact is that we are born desiring to "be," but without knowing how to acquire this "being." Evolution has not bestowed a strong instinct upon us that would guide us automatically to this "being" that we so desire. We need to learn the way of "being more." The first step is to find someone that already has "being" and learn from him or her what makes him or her have this "being." This person becomes the model of human being that we want to imitate. Therefore, we start to desire the things and qualities that this model desires, has, and continues to accumulate.

We imitate the desire of our model of human being in the hope of having the things and characteristics that he or she has; he or she will recognize us as also having this "being." As we are recognized, we feel and know that we have a bit of this desired being. We "are" as we are recognized by the other people that we have recognized as possessors of "being." Therefore, the desire of being appears materially as the desire of being recognized as human beings by other human beings. And so, we desire the things or characteristics desired by the people we desire to be recognized by.

In capitalism, these desired things that seem to promise the "being" that we desire are called commodities. This is what we experience in our daily lives. People dream of buying the newest brands. There are those who spend hours or even days in line to be the first ones to purchase new models of desired commodities (e.g., the release of new iPhones). This is not explainable without understanding the metaphysical characteristics of these commodities, their fetishist characteristic. In these commodities, there is a promise of being that a person from the distant past would not understand at all. This person from the past would look for this religious characteristic in a religious object, but not in a useful product for everyday life. So, in the same way, a person who spends hours in line for the iPhone does not understand how someone could not see the "magic" of the iPhone and prefer an outdated religious object.

This magic-religious view of commodity, the fetishism of commodity, is not a result only of effective advertising and capitalist ideology. To Marx, as we saw on the quote above, "the mysterious character of the commodity-form consists therefore simply in the fact that the commodity reflects the social characteristics of men's own labor." This worldview and the human relations reflect, as in a mirror, the social relations that we have in work and in the Market.

In the market capitalist system, the workers have no direct access to the means of production necessary to produce the goods to support one's own life and one's family. One has to sell one's own labor, which is seen here as a commodity, for those capitalists who own the means of production. In this purchase and sale agreement, the workers sell their labor force and receive money (which is seen as a commodity) in the form of a salary. Therefore, the social relation between employee and employer is intermediated by a relation of exchange of two commodities. The businessperson who buys the labor force has to sell the commodity produced in the consumers' market. If this commodity does not find a consumer willing to buy it in exchange of the consumer's money, the worker will lose his or her job and the means of sustaining the family. So, the life of the worker depends on the relation that this commodity will have in the market.

We no longer have social relations between people, but between commodities, which bring people along behind them. As Marx says, the social relations of production made by humans appear now as social relations between commodities. People depend on their commodity to establish or not establish their relation to the market world. This inversion between subject, human producer, and the produced object, which becomes the subject of the relation, is what Marx calls fetishism.

The inversion that we described is not easily observed nor perceived by economic agents. As I said, the fetish of the commodity "reflects" or, in other words, it is a reflection of the relations of production. In addition, this reflection has a role more important than it might seem at first sight. When someone wants to see oneself, one can only do it by the reflection of a mirror or another reflecting surface. It is by the reflected image that we see ourselves. It is only by the image reflected in the fetish of the commodity that one sees oneself as participant in and agent of economic and social relations. In that way, we realize our economic and social relations by the logic of the fetishism of the commodity and we feel that the fetishized relation in the market economy, in which the subject becomes object and the object subject, is something normal, as reality should be. We feel at home in this inverted relation.

As the market logic invades all aspects of personal and social life, people yearn to satisfy their desire of being by accumulation and conspicuous consumption. For these represent an envied lifestyle and high standard that are recognized by other worthy human beings. All of it creates fascination for the commodity and for capitalism. Due to this fascination, people can sacrifice all the rest—the life of the poor and of nature—in the name of the market and the accumulation of capital.

In a world like this, the opposition commonly placed between "having" and "being" makes no sense. For the "having" has become the only way to achieve being. Whoever has, is; whoever doesn't have, is not. The being that a person looks for to feel more human is not in the people or the direct human relation, but in the commodities of luxury that we desire to buy.

In addition, the admiration and jealousy that these luxury commodities provoke in other people, a way of recognition, proves empirically that the mysterious source of humankind is not in the people but in the commodity. That is why Marx says, "In order, therefore, to find an analogy, we must have recourse to the mist-enveloped regions of the religious world."[8] Capitalism has become a kind of everyday religion.

As an expression of this religious characteristic of capitalism, I would like to quote a statement that sums up the "good news" of capitalism in a "secular" speech, but with a deeply religious content. To Fukuyama, "good news has come" with the liberal capitalist system;

"technology makes possible the limitless accumulation of wealth, and thus the satisfaction of an ever-expanding set of human desires."[9]

Unlimited accumulation of wealth to satisfy unlimited desires of consumers has become the "ultimate concern" (Paul Tillich) of the capitalist system and meaning of human life. The search for unlimited accumulation can only be achieved by the accumulation of wealth in the hands of a few, denying the limits of sustainability of the environmental system. Inasmuch as we do not change the ultimate concern that drives our global society, it is not possible to solve the twin crises, social and environmental.

## ALTERNATIVE SOCIETY

The illusion of unlimited economic growth to satisfy all desires can only be overcome by a critique of the commodity fetish and the metaphysical denial of the limits of nature and the human condition. To that end, process philosophy, with its critique of the substantialist view of reality—substance as the ultimate foundation of society—and its proposal of a processual and relational view of reality, can make great contributions to the debate and to the elaboration of an alternative society. However, I think that the substitution of a processual view for a substantialist view is not sufficient to the critique of commodity fetishism. One must also unveil the inversion that occurs in the process of production, distribution, and consumption of commodity, the process that inverts the relation between subject and object. In other words, we need a metaphysical critique that is capable of criticizing substantialist metaphysics and, at the same time, the inversions made by commodity fetishism and market relations.

The problem is that, as Marx says, the fetishization of the commodity is not a product of consciousness, of the mind, but it is a reflection of the system of economic production focused on the market, and on market relations. At first sight, the solution would be to end market relations, as was attempted before in some countries where communist revolutions took place. However, in economies of great scale, as in contemporary societies, it is not possible to end market relations. That would demand a central planning system with total control of the decisions within the economic system, which in the mid-term would be inefficient and incapable of satisfying the needs of society.

On the other hand, the neoliberal solution to make the "free market" the only decisive principle and the coordinating mechanism of the economic-social system is not sustainable, least of all fair. The social and environmental crises are proof of that.

Therefore, we need to think of an alternative where these three subsystems cohabit in a relation of tension: (a) a market economy; (b) a socio-political democratic system capable of establishing limits to the accumulation of wealth and of directing the economy to maintain conditions of social and environmental sustainability; and (c) a civil society with a strong cultural and educational system capable of valorizing the search for "being" in the mutual recognition of social and human relations, limiting the social effects of commodities. All of this demands a valorization and stimulation of social movements in the political and cultural realms. If there is not a constant active participation of a significant part of society, it is very difficult to contain and control the fetishizing logic of the market system.

Furthermore, we need to overcome the modern myth of unlimited humankind and help individuals and the collective population learn to recognize and accept human limits, while recognizing that we are beings capable of desiring unlimitedly. In this matter, religious and spiritual traditions can make a fundamental contribution. A humanizing spirituality is one that helps us find a way of "living well" in the insurmountable tension between infinite desire — whose maximum expression is the desire for God — and the recognition of the limits of human condition. We are beings with limits that can think and desire the infinite, the unlimited. The critique of fetish is a critique that allows us to overcome the illusion of satisfying infinite desire with unlimited accumulation. In this matter, Marx is still very useful and enlightening to us.

## NOTES

1   Philip Clayton and Justin Heinzekehr, *Organic Marxism: An Alternative to Capitalism and Ecological Catastrophe* (Claremont, CA: Process Century Press, 2014), 201.

2   Donella Meadows et al., *The Limits to Growth* (New York: Universe Books, 1972).

3   Karl Marx, *Capital: A Critique of Political Economy,* vol. 1, trans. Samuel Moore and Edward Aveling (Moscow: Progress Publishers, 1887), 29 (https://www.marxists.org/archive/marx/works/download/pdf/Capital-Volume-I.pdf).

4   Ibid.

5   Ibid., 55. Marx is quoting Nicholas Barbon's "A Discourse on Coining the New Money Lighter" (1696).

6   Paul Bica, "Galleria Vittorio Emanuele," Digital Image. Flickr. May 24, 2014 (https://www.flickr.com/photos/dexxus/14133651758. License from Creative Commons: https://creativecommons.org/licenses/by/2.0/legalcode).

7   Marx, *Capital,* 49.

8   Ibid., 50.

9   Francis Fukuyama, *The End of History and the Last Man* (New York: Free Press, 1992), xiv.

$\approx 7 \approx$

# SOLIDARITY

## Anne F. Pomeroy

*Finally, there is deity, which is that factor in the universe whereby there is importance, value, and ideal beyond the actual.... We owe to the sense of deity the obviousness of the many actualities of the world, and the obviousness of the unity of the world for the preservation of values realized and for the transition to ideals beyond realized fact.*

\- Whitehead, *Modes of Thought*

THE PRECEDING CHAPTERS have painted a bleak picture of the contemporary reality which is the productive process of capitalism.[1] The metaphysical and ontological structure provided by process philosophy as the philosophy of internal relations most appropriate to an articulation of Marx's analysis renders the labor theory of value into a statement regarding the usurpation, exploitation, and misdirection of the most essential feature of human processive production: the human self-determined creation of novelty.

Capitalism, as the valorization of value, depends absolutely upon the creativity of the human being as productive of novelty above and

beyond mere self-reproduction, but by transferring the creative production of labor to commodity value, it reduces creative labor to mere
reproduction. Thus, within the processive, productive activity of capitalism, the human being is alienated from her essential nature and
activity. Labor is merely reproduced, like a thing, valued only by the
direct physical transmission of inherited past. The forward thrust of
present time as infused with future time is minimized as the creative
activity of present flows into the already constituted commodity value.

Thus capitalism itself appears as a form of lived misplaced concreteness in which human beings are literally ruled by abstractions,
particularly the abstraction of value. As we labor within capitalism,
we allow our very being/becoming to be dominated by the reiterative
inheritance; we allow ourselves to be constituted by past value and
thereby misplace our concrete processive activity in abstract commodity value. In this, we have alienated not only our own being but
the creative unfolding of the processive universe itself. Capitalism's
productive process is processive production increasingly commodified, individuality increasingly generalized, intensity increasingly
reduced to repetition, creativity increasingly stifled, the concrete
increasingly "valued" merely by and as abstract value. Capitalism is
a process whereby we live (survive) by misplacing abstract commodity value for the achievements of "value" of the creative individuals.

As such, capitalism is essentially antithetical to process itself. By
"devaluing" the human creativity in the present, by "valuing" human
life according to the commodity value of its labor power—its value
as product of past labor, its money value—capitalism stagnates process, turning the adventures of novel becoming into the anaesthesia
of repetition.[2]

Where the "value" of processive creativity is actively displaced
into the physically reiterative value of the commodity, where the present act of creativity is "valued" merely by how it can increase commodity value (and increase itself as commodity value), there external
relations alone achieve an affirmation of status. Where the unique
self-relating, self-constituting of each occasion of experience as just

this achieved and achieving valuation is misplaced in abstract value, there internal relations are de-valued. The necessary internal bonds that are the very fabric of processive reality are "forgotten."[3] Each individual occasion is seen not as absolutely dependent upon and constituted by its relations to all other occasions, but as autonomous and independent: a value achieved, stagnant, simply located. Within capitalism, any moment of any labor, any commodity is, as a value, just like any other: just another dollar amount waiting to be realized. Each concrete occasion, as a relational achievement, is recognized only through the lens of its abstraction as a mere individual alongside others—none is irreplaceable, and each concrete occasion is mediated and brought into relation only when it functions as abstraction.

Within capitalism, valorization is only possible when concrete relations are abstracted from the actual social context. In fact, because the capital-relation is only possible when the relata are so abstracted, it becomes quite easy and natural, within this form of social relations, to hold out individualism, autonomy, independence, and competition as ideals. Strictly speaking, within capitalism, these ideals may be the only lures to any novelty at all; they certainly appear to be the primary lures. Where the abstraction of our lived experience makes creative novelty as an achievement of self impossible; where the creativity of human life is purchased, redirected, and ossified in commodity value; there creative novelty as a quantitative achievement of status through increased "possession" of property values may be the only goad to advancement. This is a paltry substitute indeed for the creativity of the self-determined individual-in-relation. And it is one which operates at cross purposes because absolutely independent achievement is, in a processive universe, a contradiction in terms. This is the irony of poverty as property.

We do not seem to be occupying a place of great comfort regarding the "progress" of humanity at present. Our abstractions appear to be in the process of burying us.

> [I]n the nineteenth century, when society was undergoing transformation into the manufacturing system, the bad

effects of these doctrines [substantial independence and mechanism] have been very fatal. The doctrine of minds, as independent substances, leads directly not merely to private worlds of experience, but also to private worlds of morals. The moral intuitions can be held to apply only to the strictly private world of psychological experience. Accordingly, self-respect, and the making the most of your own individual opportunities, together constituted the efficient morality of the leaders among the industrialists of that period. The western world is now suffering from the limited moral outlook of the three previous generations.[4]

In regard to the aesthetic needs of civilised society the reactions of science have so far been unfortunate. Its materialist basis has directed attention to things as opposed to values. The antithesis is a false one, if taken in a concrete sense. But it is valid at the abstract level of ordinary thought. This misplaced emphasis coalesced with the abstractions of political economy, which are in fact the abstractions in terms of which commercial affairs are carried on. Thus all thought concerned with social organisation expressed itself in terms of material things and of capital. Ultimate values were excluded.[5]

It might be all too tempting at this point to give in to a form of despair and contradiction, which has plagued so much recent critical and radical thought. The difficulty is this: if we are actually involved in a form of life that recreates ourselves and our world as primarily commodified, drastically reduces our creative abilities, occupies and preoccupies the time in which we could have the leisure to reflect, turns that present creative temporality into stagnant reiterative value, etc., then (1) how is it possible to think the critique which we are presently articulating and (2) what will be the mechanism whereby this self-generating spiral towards alienated, abstract being is reversed? Can we be the authors of our downfall and salvation simultaneously, or have we, in thinking the critique of capitalism, undermined that critique itself?

Two related tasks must be accomplished by any critical project that desires and deserves serious consideration. First, it must account for the possibility of its own standpoint in the situation of which it provides a critique (i.e., there can be no "view from nowhere"). And second, it can only accomplish this first task by way of making the emergence of the critique internal to the situation being critiqued. In other words, in our case, the increasingly prevalent lived abstractions of capitalism must provide the envisionment beyond capitalism whereby its critique is made possible.

The social practices by which the concreteness of creative human processive production is misplaced by the abstractions of the capitalistic productive process are possible precisely because human persons are creative in a way that goes beyond the primarily reiterative social processive being of things. This creativity is the source, the only source, of the surplus value with which such things become endowed in capitalism. But this creativity itself is made possible because of the unique role that specifically human consciousness plays in the self-creative activity which is the processive being of the *human* being. The domination by consciousness, and the specific functions which human consciousness performs, allows for maximal adaptability through the creative production of novelty.

But the role of consciousness is to go beyond the mere physical reiteration of inherited data. Its role is to entertain the elements of that data in novel combinations, to detach the formal elements such that they can be entertained in new aesthetic contrastive combinations. In other words, human consciousness abstracts. But isn't abstraction precisely the function which we have been criticizing within capitalism? Wasn't it the practices of abstracting from concrete use-values to general exchange-values for the sake of commodity exchange, and the application of this original abstraction to the human being from whose concrete creative essence was further abstracted her mere reproduction, which began the spiral of commodification?

The critique of misplaced concreteness, whether in thought or in practice, is the critique of "mistaking the abstract for the concrete."[6]

In other words, it is the critique of a certain functional use of or role played by abstraction, and it designates this use to be both misleading and destructive. But the misuse of the abstractive tool does not necessitate its elimination except as regards that particular use. After all, the abstractive function is itself the source of novelty. It is no more than an "omission of part of the truth,"[7] and we engage in such omission all the time. In fact, processive valuation requires such selective omission, and human perception absolutely depends upon it. Therefore, when abstraction is employed, there is no reason why it must, in and of itself, misplace itself for concreteness. It is an abstraction from concreteness, to be sure, but not necessarily a mistaken designation of the nature of the concrete. Therefore, as unfortunate as misplacing concreteness can be in thought, as devastating and destructive as it is in capitalistic practice, so also abstraction can serve more fortunate and constructive purposes.

> Thus a fortunate use of abstractions is of the essence of upward evolution. But there is no necessity of such good use....
>
> It is interesting to note that in the entertainment of abstractions there is always present a preservative instinct aiming at the renewal of connection, which is the reverse of abstraction. This reverse process, partly instinctive and partly conscious, is wisdom of that higher life made possible by abstraction.[8]

In other words, abstraction itself can uncover the necessity of relationality—they are dialectically linked. It will be the purpose of this chapter to seek out this "fortunate use of abstractions" as the critical and constructive tool. We need to find our way to the abstractions that seem to goad us to realizations and self-discovery and the desire for higher experience. We need to discover the abstractions that lure us to the intensity of experience that will constitute our upward evolution. We need to uncover "[t]he factor in human life provocative of a noble discontent [which] is the gradual emergence into prominence of a sense of criticism, founded upon appreciations of beauty, and of intellectual distinction, and of duty."[9]

## ETERNAL OBJECTS

In order to understand how the abstractive ability functions in human being/becoming, we need first to gain a clearer picture of the conceptual operations specific to human consciousness. However, human consciousness is the highly complex functioning of embedded nexūs. In other words, by the time we reach the macrocosmic scale wherein our discussion can focus upon the phenomena of human consciousness, we are already operating at a level of extreme social complexity. Once again, in order to discern in what ways a processive philosophy can inform us regarding the operations of such complex conceptual activity, it is necessary to begin at the metaphysical level: to construct the social macrocosmic from the atomistic-relational microcosmic. We need to briefly review, therefore, the ontological intersection of these two levels.

In Whitehead's scheme of the phases of concrescence, a distinction is made between the primary phase of physical inheritance and the secondary and subsequent phases of conceptual valuation. Domination in any given entity or society of entities by the physical or conceptual poles will alter the functional ontological designation of that entity or society or nexus. A complex, enduring society whose regnant nexus is dominated by high-level conceptual activity is productive of greater novelty than one dominated by physical inheritance. Living societies are marked by the originality of their responses to environmental alterations. Human beings, of course, display the predominance of extremely complex mentality, which allows for maximal novelty of creativity amidst the levels of processive ontological beings.

Thus, it is the dialectical bipolarity of the actual entity on the metaphysical level that allows us to functionally distinguish physical activity from conceptual activity. Each occasion of concrescence has a primary phase consisting of physical feeling, which is conformal or causal and embodies "the reproductive character of nature,"[10] and secondary phases of conceptual valuation.[11] These phases and their functions are absolutely concomitant in the concrescence. There can be no conceptual (subjective) valuation without a real causal (objective) ingression of the actual world, but likewise a physical feeling without conceptual valuation would grind processive creativity into dumb repetition.[12] However, while both poles, as operative in their respective phases of concrescence, are always present in every occasion of experience, the schema still allows for the emphasis or domination of one or the other of the poles and for increasing levels of complex operation as we build up from the microcosmic to the macrocosmic—from the processive atoms-in-relation to societies of such atoms.

From this processive schema, several features emerge that are of particular importance to our discussion of human consciousness and to our discovery of fortunate abstractions. If the physical feelings of the primary phase are reproductive and conformal, if "[i]n the conformal feelings, the *how* of feeling reproduces what is felt,"[13] then, even though the novel actual entity is the effect, it is (at this phase) novel in terms of being the newly emergent actuality *reproducing* the data of its actual world under *its* spacio-temporal perspective. In the phase of conformal feeling alone there is only perspectival novelty but not yet the novelty of decisive valuation. Such novelty emerges only byway of the phases of conceptual valuation.[14]

The difference between the conformal and conceptual feelings has to do with the "diverse modes of ingression of the eternal objects involved."[15]

> A simple physical feeling enjoys a characteristic which has been variously described as "re-enaction," "reproduction," and "conformation." This characteristic can be more accurately explained in terms of the eternal objects involved. There are eternal objects determinant of the definiteness of the objective datum which is the "cause," and eternal objects determinant of the definiteness of the subjective form belonging to the "effect." When there is re-enaction there is one eternal object with two-way functioning, namely, as partial determinant of the objective datum, and as partial determinant of the subjective form. In this two-way rôle,

the eternal object is functioning relationally between the initial data on the one hand and the concrescent subject on the other.[16]

[On the other hand, a] conceptual feeling is feeling an eternal object in the primary metaphysical character of being an "object," that is to say, feeling its *capacity* for being a realized determinant of process...The subjective form of a conceptual feeling has the character of a "valuation."[17]

Therefore, the conformal feelings are those by which there is a reproduction of the past occasion as superject in the present occasion as subject. Such conformal, physical feelings constitute the element of the experience whereby there is real transmission of feelings from one occasion to another, whereby the many actualities functioning as objective data become the novel entity, and whereby there is extension and solidarity in the processive universe.[18] The conceptual feelings, on the other hand, introduce the valuative operations of the mental pole upon this inherited data. The novelty emergent in conformal feelings is the mere novelty of the entity's primary constitutive phase as a perspectival reproduction of the data; the novelty emergent in conceptual feelings involves the introduction of self-determined evaluation. The perspectival novelty of the primary phase is how *all* processive being produces novelty or is a novel configuration of the data despite a weak or negligible operation of the mental pole, but when the secondary phases achieve heightened operation, we can account for that novelty that constitutes creative environmental adaptability and the higher levels of experience.

The differences of the operation of the eternal objects in the respective feelings amount to this: in the first phase there is dative ingression to which the physical feeling of the emergent entity conforms. The eternal objects in this case are re-enacted in the intensive patterns derived from the actual world. They transmit directly the character that they achieved as that data. They are still clothed in their objective forms. (I suspect that this is how there is a feeling on the part of the experiencing subject of the dative ingression as the real imposition of the "other.") In the conceptual feelings, however, the eternal objects derived from the physical feelings are entertained as separable from the actualities from which they are ingressed. The eternal objects become free of their dative determinations and become available as pure potentials. In other words, the eternal objects functioning in the first mode of ingression are forms of the definiteness of the data physically felt as objective; in the second mode, the eternal objects are forms of potential definiteness conceptually felt as possibilities for the subjective valuation.

Additionally, there are two phases to the operations of the mental pole. In the first, there is a conceptual reproduction of the physical pole. This is the operation that Whitehead calls conceptual valuation.[19] The eternal objects reproduced apart from the patterned realizations imposed by their dative origins become available for the concrescing actuality's subsequent conceptual operations whereby it will become as *this* patterned contrast. They become freed of their dative constitution and offered as pure potentialities for the self-determination. The eternal objects are thus abstracted from their actual origins. "A conceptual prehension is a direct vision . . . of some possibility as to how actualities *may* be *definite*. There is no reference to particular actualities, or to any particular actual world."[20] The eternal objects truly serve here as "pure potentials for the specific determination of fact."[21] They serve as forms abstracted from actual definiteness, available as potential for definiteness. It is, therefore, the eternal objects as actually ingressed in contrastive patterns (aesthetic valuations) and as potentials for ingression in contrastive patterns, which lend to the processive universe both its formal continuity and simultaneously its formal malleability. The detachment of the formal elements of a reproductive actual physical prehension by means of the conceptual pole allows for free self-creation by the subject from out of its actual world.

In the second phase of the operation of the conceptual pole there is conceptual reversion "by which the subsequent enrichment of subjective forms, both in qualitative pattern, and in intensity through contrast, is made possible by the positive conceptual prehension of relevant alternatives."[22] Here the eternal objects, now as subjective forms, are placed into contrasts and contrasts of contrasts, etc. By virtue of conceptual reversion "novelty enters the world."[23]

To sum up:

> Eternal objects express *how* the predecessor-phase is absorbed into the successor-phase without limitation of itself, but with additions necessary for the determination of an actual unity in the form of individual satisfaction... The *how* of the limitations, and the *how* of the additions, are alike the *realization* of eternal objects in the constitution of the actual entity in question. An eternal object in abstraction from any one particular actual entity is a potentiality for ingression into actual entities. In its ingression into any one actual entity, either as relevant or as irrelevant, it retains its potentiality of indefinite diversity of modes of ingression, a potential indetermination rendered determinate in this instance.... Potentiality becomes reality; and yet retains its message of alternatives which the actual entity has avoided. In the constitution of an actual entity: — whatever component is red, might have been green; and whatever component is loved, might have been coldly esteemed.[24]

The conceptual phases of the concrescence are still a long way from human consciousness, but we have located, at the metaphysical level, the account of how actuality itself provides the formal elements which, as detachable from that actuality, become available for novel arrangement and the valuational contrasts which provide formal (and finally actual) alternatives.

## FROM HUMAN CONSCIOUSNESS TO RADICAL CONSCIOUSNESS

Reconstructing some sort of theory of human consciousness from *Process and Reality* is no small task, but the construction of such a theory is absolutely necessary if we are to provide some kind of viable notion of subjective praxical agency in capitalist society and to locate the methods of "fortunate abstraction" that might be available to provide both vision and productive practice beyond our present form of social relations.[25] I have laid out Whitehead's basic scheme regarding the microcosmic conceptual operation and its relation to formal possibilities in order to show that process metaphysics is able to ground potentiality as emergent from actuality (and vice versa), and novelty as emergent from the inheritance of a settled past.[26] Since, "[c]onceptual feelings and simple causal feelings constitute the two main species of 'primary' feelings" and "[a]ll other feelings of whatever complexity arise out of a process of integration which starts with a phase of these primary feelings,"[27] these metaphysical elements constitute our starting point. By supplementing these metaphysical foundations with some of the material on consciousness, extension, and higher experience, I hope to be able to provide, at very least, the kind of preliminary groundwork which will push us over the hump of internal inconsistency threatening the critical project. I will show how the formal elements, provided by capitalism itself, make its critique by human consciousness possible.

"Consciousness," Whitehead tells us, "is not necessarily involved in the subjective forms of either [physical or conceptual] type of prehension."[28] This means that although the concrescence of all actual entities involves the operation of both physical and conceptual poles, not all occasions exhibit consciousness. This is because consciousness does not emerge in the first mode of conceptual feeling: conceptual valuation. Thus, consciousness emerges in subsequent modes and "arises when a synthetic feeling integrates physical and conceptual feelings." Such integration involves a kind of recollection of or reflection upon the physical feeling, but "the abstract element in the concrete fact is exactly what provokes our consciousness."[29] There appears to be, therefore, both reflective and comparative operations within consciousness or, more appropriately, we could say that consciousness is that conceptual activity whereby there is a re-collection of the physical feelings and a reflection upon that datum in a comparative contrast with its inherent formal potentiality.

> In [conscious] awareness actuality, as a process in fact, is integrated with the potentialities which illustrate *either* what it is and might not be, *or* what it is not and might be. In other words, there is no consciousness without reference to definiteness, affirmation, and negation. Also affirmation involves its contrast with negation, and negation involves its contrast with affirmation. Further, affirmation and negation are alike meaningless apart from reference to the definiteness of particular actualities. Consciousness is how we feel the affirmation-negation contrast. Conceptual feeling is the feeling of an unqualified negation; that is to say, it is the feeling of a definite eternal object with the definite extrusion of any particular realization. Consciousness requires that the objective datum should involve (as one side of a contrast) a qualified negative determined to some definite situation.[30]

Thus, within consciousness, propositions are operative. Propositions are hybrid entities "between pure potentialities and actualities."[31] They are the entertainment of eternal objects as applicable to a certain definiteness or actuality. Thus it is that a proposition must be conformal (true) or non-conformal (false).

When a conformal proposition is admitted into feeling, the reaction to the datum has simply resulted in the conformation of feeling to fact:

> When a non-conformal proposition is admitted into feeling, the reaction to the datum has resulted in the synthesis of fact with the alternative potentiality of the complex predicate. A novelty has emerged into creation.[32]

This point is particularly important. It is by way of non-conformal propositions admitted into feeling that novelty enters the processive universe. This is why the Category of Conceptual Reversion is "the category by which novelty enters the world."[33] This is why Whitehead says that "in the real world it is more important that a proposition be interesting than that it be true."[34]

We can see why this would be the case, particularly with the high-level operations of human conceptualization: the entertainment of non-conformal propositions is the consideration of alternative possibilities in reference to the given actuality. By way of the entertainment of non-conformal propositions, our "interest" in the actuality is generated. By way of the entertainment of non-conformal propositions we ask ourselves, "what if it were otherwise?"

> The triumph of consciousness comes with the negative intuitive judgement. In this case there is a conscious feeling of what might be, and is not. The feeling directly concerns the definite negative prehensions enjoyed by its subject. It is the feeling of absence, and it feels this absence as produced by the definite exclusiveness of what is really present.[35]

Such consideration generates our interest not just in a merely contemplative manner but, because of our conscious reflection on our own role in the generation of process as its "producers" and because of the dialectical character of processive being, the consideration generates our *active* interest. "The ideals cherished in the souls of men enter into the character of their actions."[36] The non-conformal propositions lure us to our own creative novelty as our potential (and actual) creation of novelty. "A propositional feeling is a lure to creative emergence in the transcendent future."[37] It is the way in which the actuality given in present activity becomes infused with the potentiality of the future emergent from the given.

We note here again the statement of the materialist principle. The eternal objects within the actuality of physical inheritance are given as the datum of the experience. Yet that very datum as emergent from and given to dialectical being (bipolar actuality) contains the possibility of its own transcendence. Through conceptual reversion, through the entertainment of propositions, novel combinations of the potentiality and actuality of the given are entertained. The data is inherently value-laden in several ways: as already this achievement of value (subject), as potentially any of the perspectival achievements of value from it (superject), and as all the potential valuations of this data open to any given perspectival entity in process (superject of that subjective becoming). Thus the future already infuses the present as its potentiality, and the present is already a realization of the offerings of the past. The present already contains its possible futures, and the past can be found in the present, which is one of its achieved values.

With human consciousness, we have burst the boundaries of novel entertainment and, therefore, creativity. Human consciousness with its high-level operations of intellect, imagination, judgement, etc., appears to occupy the pinnacle of conceptual development by a social nexus in this processive universe. And it is precisely this adept, malleable, explosive, conscious conceptuality of the human being which makes her creativity reach such heights of novelty. In particular, this intellect allows our effusive entertainment of those non-conformal propositions that result in novelty.

The materialist principle stated above and the notion of human consciousness emergent from the processive viewpoint give the critical project its internal consistency. Because the formal possibilities (as eternal objects) are given in the data that are the actual world, and because they are detachable from the actuality in which they are given; because the operation of the conceptual pole can involve entertainment of contrasts, conceptual reversion, and the feeling of non-conformal propositions; and because human consciousness involves the best-developed and most complex forms of conceptuality, we are able to entertain the possibility of the actualization of what is "not yet" in the present but potential to it by virtue of its specific content. But more than this, human being in particular does, and indeed must, entertain the "not yet." According to the process view, this is what we are: maximally creative beings. And such novelty emerges from the entertainment of alternatives. Any social practice, any form of social relations that seeks to quell our physical/conceptual entertainment of possibilities, must necessarily fail because it will be presenting to us, as the very beings we are, the possibility of its being other than the case. We are the being that entertains the "other." Human consciousness is anticipatory consciousness.

Capitalism is not merely a form of social relations but is also the datum out of which we are invited to construct our processive future. It gives us the physical inheritance of the content of its social relations. Through its practices we are reproduced as capitalist labor, but simultaneous with this inherited content it gives us the forms of that content. And so capitalism provides the notion of private property, but simultaneous with that we receive the detachability of the forms and the entertainment of the non-conformal proposition: the possibility of property as not private. It gives us the freedom to sell our labor and the possibility of not selling our labor. It gives us wealth in the hands of the few and the possibility of wealth in the hands of many. It gives us wealth as commodity value and the possibility of wealth as not-commodity "value." It gives us domination and exploitation and the possibilities of our freedom from domination and exploitation. In fact, I would maintain, that the more capitalism becomes itself, the more obvious these conceptual reversions are for consciousness.

Lest this sound too idealistic, let me make perfectly clear that the possibilities of which I speak are not simple possibilities presented to practice. It is most certainly not that easy. They are non-conformal propositions whose entertainment is made possible by the social reality of the practice of capitalism. However, at the same time, they are lures for feeling, and therefore the entertainment of the possibilities inherent in the actuality serves, even if slightly or very slowly, to alter the becoming of the entity. Not only do "propositions grow with the creative advance of the world,"[38] but the creative advance of the world grows with propositions. And this would explain why Marx insisted that the demystification of the formal structure of the capitalist form of social relations was vital to the revolutionary effort. Such demystification makes the formal possibilities inherent in the structure leap forth in consciousness. It is also why the media manipulation of public consciousness has become such an important part of the operation and continuation of capitalism as a social-economic system.

If capitalism, in its very development, produces the possibilities of thinking beyond it, if in fact the further development of capitalism over time merely serves to make its formal structure more visible and thus more accessible to conscious conceptual reversion, then it is absolutely necessary for the continuation of capitalism that those whose personal interests are served by capitalism dominate the public consciousness. If human beings, by their very nature, entertain formal possibilities given in their inherited actuality as detachable from that reality, then it is in the capitalist's interest to control either the presented actuality or the formal characteristics of that actuality or both.

Attempts at such control by capitalist-owned and operated media can and do occur in numerous ways. The media can co-opt the formal possibilities in its own conceptual frameworks as Marcuse says happens with political and social assimilation,[39] or they can present the social reality as already meeting the needs of anticipatory consciousness as occurs with the spectrality of advertising, or they can simply control the availability and content of information as occurs with "brainwashing under freedom" and the "manufacture of consent."[40] In this day and age of the expansion of U.S. capitalism's imperialist adventures, it is therefore not surprising that mainstream and alternative media sources are increasingly owned by large corporations and that such control of information has reached an almost frenzied pitch. The good news from the process standpoint is that such control must necessarily be, in the long run, unsuccessful. It can only serve to goad the increase of its presented alternatives: the more clearly it states what is the case, the more clearly we are able to think about how that case could be otherwise. It exposes itself in its repetition.

Human consciousness cannot help but engage in conceptual reversion in the form of the entertainment of the "not yet" and the "other than actual." This functional consciousness is our very nature; it is what we do and how we become from our dative origination.

All processive being is dialectical and could not be without being dialectical. Dumb physical reiteration without conceptual operation would mean absolute spatial and temporal reiteration. In other words, it would mean no spatial or temporal extension — it would mean the absence of process, because it would mean the absence of all change and thus the absence of all being. For there to be change there must be conceptual operation, even if it involves the reiteration of the physical feeling as under a specific spatio-temporal perspective. Being is dialectical. What makes the human being unique is that we think dialectically. We think the other and thereby we think being. And I mean this quite literally. Our dialectical conceptual operation makes it possible that we both think what might (will) be and in that thinking, because there is no conceptual operation abstracted from physical feeling, we become as that thinking being. By thinking dialectically, by entertaining potentiality in the way we do, we think (and become) novelty: new being, new material relations, new social relations. We turn and overturn reality. Human consciousness, as anticipatory consciousness, is dialectical consciousness.

In relation to capitalism, dialectical thinking is anti-capitalistic thought in several ways. As already pointed out, it is thought that engages in the entertainment of the non-conformal propositions. Taking the "facts" of capitalism, human consciousness entertains their dialectical overcoming. But additionally, and on a deeper level, dialectical thinking is anti-capitalistic. Capitalism involves a reification of the past, but dialectical thinking is always necessarily oriented to the potentiality of the future: non-conformal propositions entertain the "not yet." Capitalism reproduces labor as primarily reiterative, but dialectical thinking explodes in novelty: the entertainment of potentiality is the hallmark of human productive novelty. Capitalism reduces use value to exchange value and re-presents all exchange values as money, but dialectical thinking serves to multiply the possibilities of realizing alternative "values": contrasts elicit depth.

It will be said that this is idealistic, impracticable, that we should buckle down and be realistic. But we need to look very carefully at what realism is according to the position we have been holding. On a processive view, to ascribe to realism is to ascribe to a repetition of the past. It is to allow what will be to be dictated by what has been. It is to relegate process and progress to the dustbin of dead data. It is, therefore, the height of capitalist ideology.[41] There is, in fact, no lack of realism in the ideal since the ideal can, on the process view, only arise from the datum provided as formally entertained. In a sense, therefore, it already "is."

When we are told to be realistic, to give up on the vision of the ideal, we are being asked to wrench the efficacy of future possibility out of the present. We are being asked to kill the present. But more insulting yet, we are asked to leave the sweatshops as they are, to leave the teenagers working in the Nike factories in Indonesia, to leave the streets of the South Bronx as they are, to leave the children who live in and on the garbage dumps of the Philippines or Guatemala as they are, to leave injustice as it is. We are being asked to turn away from the likes of Harriet Tubman or Gandhi, Rosa Parks, Zapatista Commandante Marcos, or Daniel Berrigan; they are crazy idealists. But if these ask too much, then realism is a view towards nowhere. We are told that our ideals are currently impossible to realize but this misses the role of the ideal in human consciousness entirely.

> Impracticable ideals are a program for reform. Such a program is not to be criticized by immediate possibilities. Progress consists in modifying the laws of nature so that the Republic on Earth may conform to that Society to be discerned ideally by the divination of Wisdom.[42]

Such ideals may be impracticable, at present, but are most certainly practical. We stand with Kant, who meant by the practical "everything that is possible through freedom."[43]

So capitalism is destructive to the essence of the human being because it is non-dialectical, but because it is non-dialectical it is also anti-processive. It is felt as alienation because it is anti-humanism. It is felt as alienation because it is anti-processive and so also it is the negation of being, which is processive, dialectical, and mediated by productive subjectivity. But human consciousness, as anticipatory consciousness and as dialectical consciousness, is also therefore radical consciousness: anti-capitalistic consciousness, the union of thinking and being, the union of the ideal and real. This is true humanism.

There is one more conclusion to be drawn from this line of thought. If dialectical consciousness is consciousness of being as becoming; and if processive being itself is the real unity in difference of the physical and conceptual, of being and becoming, of subject and superject, etc.; then processive thought itself is dialectical thought and is, therefore, radical thought. A philosophy of internal relations like process philosophy is already radical, anticipatory, dialectical consciousness. Process thought itself is an articulation of the conceptual revolution necessary to the real reversion of capitalism in practice.

What Marx perhaps failed to realize was that the conceptual scheme of internal relations underlying his use of terminology, his conceptual categories, his use of the dialectics, his limits and extensions of abstraction, and his envisionment of a communist future, was already revolutionary, and was just as revolutionary as the critique of capitalism that was based upon it as its ultimate articulation. Process philosophy, a philosophy of internal relations, is already radical consciousness because it is necessarily dialectical and thus anti-capitalistic consciousness. Perhaps Marx's purpose in the early writings was to articulate this revolutionary conceptual groundwork, but perhaps also he overestimated the public's understanding of the Hegelian dialectic from the start. Perhaps his purpose in the proposed ethics was to come full circle and articulate these revolutionary grounds of the critique of capitalism as also grounding the possibility of human being (and being human) finally realized. We see, therefore, that abstractions need not be misplaced for the concrete. We see that abstractions may indeed be fortunate. "The idea is a prophecy which procures its own fulfillment... Plato's idea.... has a creative power, making possible its own approach to realization."[44]

## BEYOND CAPITALISM

But given that process thought is revolutionary thought, and contains the potential alternatives to capitalist social relations, the next question becomes: what exactly are those alternatives? We have, in a sense, already provided the answer. To think beyond capitalism is to think dialectically; to think dialectically is to think processively. Therefore, the process framework is the beyond of capitalism. The inner logic and tendency of capitalism is to maximize profits by maximizing surplus labor time, to minimize reproductive time for the productive human being, and to maximize time for production above and beyond reproduction (novelty). By way of process thought we understand that the development of the forces of production given in capitalism can lead to a maximization of the creative ability of the human being. By way of process thought we understand creative novelty as the processive becoming of the individual in community. Thus, maximization of surplus labor time in capitalism is, in and of itself, the potentiality of the creative social-self. Capitalism offers up its own solution.

> Although limited by its very nature, [capitalism] strives towards the universal development of the forces of production, and thus becomes the presupposition of a new mode of production, which is founded not on the development of the forces of production for the purpose of reproducing or at most expanding a given condition, but where the free, unobstructed, progressive and universal development of the forces of production is itself the presupposition of society...[45]

> [The] antithetical form [of capitalism] is itself fleeting, and produces the real conditions of its own suspension. The result is: the tendentially and potentially general development of the forces of production — of wealth as such — as a basis.[46]

The beyond of capitalism, provided by the data of capitalism itself, is the possibility of fully processive being understood as such.

Carol Gould provides a particularly clear articulation of the three historical stages of production described by Marx in the *Grundrisse*. (1) In the stage of pre-capitalist formations, she says, the form of social relations is one of "personal dependence" characterized by "internal relations that are concretely particular" and are "relations of inequality" among members of a "community." (2) In the stage of capitalism, she says, the form of social relations is one of "personal independence based on objective dependence" characterized by "external relations that are abstractly universal" and are "relations of formal equality" between individuals with mere "external sociality." (3) In the stage of communal society, the form of social relations is one of "free social individuality" characterized by "internal relations that are concretely universal" and are "relations of concrete equality" between "communal individuals."[47] What is striking here is the final description. It is the description of full communism. It is also, I believe, nothing more than a description of processive being.

Actual entities are "free social individuals." Each entity emerges out of its given actual world and therefore is always already a social individual; yet that entity is a self-creative valuation of that data and therefore free from any deterministic coercion by the data. The actual world is the social context that provides the opportunity for the self-creation that that emergent entity is. The "internal relations are concretely universal" because each entity is constituted by its internal relations to all other entities. The aesthetic patterning of those relations is the entity's concreteness and those self-same relations project the entity beyond itself as objectively immortal. The unity of the universal and particular (the eternal objects and the actual entities) make internal relations (as being/becoming) possible. Finally, the relations of these "communal individuals" (individuals that, for their very individuality, depend upon their relational community) are relations of "concrete equality" because each individual is as "valuable" an achievement in the processive universe as any other.[48] But their achievements of "value" are absolutely concretely related to their relational configurations of data and aim. "Each according to her needs, each according to her ability."

Marx's description of communism is a description of processive human being that knows and realizes itself as such. There is no antithesis between the social and the individual because processive human being is aware that she arises from her social nexus: that she is a configuration of and contribution to that nexus. And so the community is the opportunity for the "all-round development of the individual,"[49] and each individual adds to the character of the community. The interest of the community is to allow maximal intensity of development to each of its constitutive members. Only in this way does the community itself reach the heights of its creative potential. The harmonization of ends between the social individuals, the eradication of conflicting tendencies, is absolutely in the interest of each individual because her potential to realize her developmental intensity depends absolutely upon the social environment out of which her development proceeds. Dative conflict requires elimination from feeling; dative harmony allows for greater inclusion, greater and more intense contrasts.

> Each serves the other in order to serve himself; each makes use of the other, reciprocally, as his means. Now both things are contained in the consciousness of the two individuals: (1) that each arrives at his end only in so far as he serves the other as a means; (2) that each becomes means for the other (being for another) only as end in himself (being for self); (3) that the reciprocity in which each is at the same time means and end, and attains his end only in so far as he becomes a means, and becomes a means only in so far as he posits himself as end, that each thus posits himself as being for another, in so far as he is being for self, and the other as being for him, in so far as he is being for himself—*that this reciprocity is a necessary fact, presupposed as natural precondition for exchange.*[50] [italics mine]

> Only in community [with others has each] individual the means of cultivating his gifts in all directions; only in the community, therefore, is personal freedom possible.[51]

The realization of our processive being is a realization of the thoroughgoing relationality of the processive universe. It is the realization that the achievement of each processive occasion of experience effects the becoming of all others. It is the realization that each individual accomplished intensity shoots through the fabric of processive being as an impulse lights up a neural net. It is the realization that the individual achievement can become only out of the entire network of previous relations and that it will become as part of that expanding network. As the individual is constituted by its internal relations of the totality, so also the totality is the extensive relation of all individual achievements. Thinking beyond capitalism is realizing that a social totality claiming to achieve human emancipation by way of the re-routing of creative novelty into reproduction is no "achievement" at all. Thinking beyond capitalism is realizing that the social totality achieves only as its individuals achieve *themselves*.

> Freedom means that within each type the requisite coördination should be possible without the destruction of the general ends of the whole community. Indeed, one general end is that these variously coördinated groups should contribute to the complex pattern of community life, each in virtue of its own peculiarity. In this way individuality gains the effectiveness which issues from coördination, and freedom obtains power necessary for its perfection.[52]

This is Marx's notion of real wealth.

> [W]hen the limited bourgeois form is stripped away, what is wealth other than.... [t]he full development of human mastery over the forces of nature, those of so-called nature as well as of humanity's own nature? The absolute working-out of his creative potentialities, with no presupposition other than the previous historic development.[53]

If thinking the beyond of capitalism is thinking process and we, as human beings, are processive beings, then thinking the beyond of capitalism is thinking the human essence. Anticipatory consciousness, dialectical consciousness, radical consciousness, is self-consciousness. Thinking the beyond of capitalism is an act of conscious self-appropriation and self-affirmation. It is the affirmation of the human being as processive, as a creative subject/superject of process. Therefore, to think the beyond of capitalism is to think of myself as the processive agent of that beyond; it is the appropriation of my own productive being as the source of that beyond. It is my self-awareness of my radical praxical being.

I understand myself as an intimate liaison of all processive being. I affirm myself as the creative source of the novelty of future process. I have authentically appropriated my own being.

> The basis as the possibility of the universal development of the individual, and the real development of the individuals from this basis as a constant suspension of its *barrier*, which is recognized as a barrier, not taken for a *sacred limit*. Not an ideal or imagined universality of the individual, but the universality of his real and ideal relations. Hence also the grasping of his own history as a *process*, and the recognition of nature (equally present as practical power over nature) as his real body. The process of development itself posited and known as the presupposition of the same.[54]

> [W]ith the positing of the activity of individuals as immediately general or *social* activity, the objective moments of production are stripped of this form of alienation; they are thereby posited as property, as the organic social body within which the individuals reproduce themselves as individuals, but as social individuals.[55]

Because the human being is that being that produces effusive novelty, self-appropriation is the appropriation of my productive-processive being and my understanding of that being as my "ownmost" possibility in, of, and for the world. This is the first step to becoming and being the beyond of capitalism.

So also, self-affirmation and self-appropriation are real freedom. To affirm my processive being is to understand myself as a subject of process, in process, and for process. To understand myself as a processive subject is to understand that I create myself from the relational totality of my actual world, that what I am is my active self-relation to and of that totality. It is also, then, to understand that I am a thoroughly and absolutely unique perspective on that totality: no other individual can be this particular here and now. My creative self-relation cannot therefore be the equivalent of any other. And so, understanding myself as a processive being is understanding that I cannot *be* wage labor. Because my creative stance is *unique*, it cannot *belong* to anyone else. Understanding myself as a processive subject is, therefore, a re-appropriation of my creative potential as *mine*. It is a freeing of myself for myself and, by extension, for others. Self-affirmation is self-appropriation as real freedom. This is the true content of class consciousness and the reason why the proletariat (wage labor) is the universal class. They are the ultimate representation of the universal human bondage occurring within capitalism; their essential poverty is capital's private property. Therefore, class consciousness is human consciousness — the consciousness of this bondage (capitalism's bondage of the human essence and human potential) is the key to real freedom. The liberation from wage labor (the liberation of the proletariat) is, therefore, the liberation of all human life for itself.

Furthermore, since this transformation is carried out by individuals in social relations and this is a social activity, the conditions for this individual self-transcendence are themselves social conditions. Thus for Marx, freedom as the process of self-realization is the origination of novel possibilities, acting on which the social individual creates and recreates him or herself constantly as a self-transcendent being.[56]

We do not require capitalism's value as the medium of exchange. We are the medium of exchange — we are the mediators of the relationality of the universe. When we understand ourselves as such, when we appropriate ourselves, our own creative essence, we free ourselves for the world. We achieve ourselves as "free social individuals."[57]

When we think of freedom, we are apt to confine ourselves to freedom of thought, freedom of the press, freedom for religious opinions. Then the limitations to freedom are conceived as wholly arising from the antagonisms of our fellow men. This is a thorough mistake. The massive habits of physical nature, its iron laws, determine the scene for the sufferings of men. Birth and death, heat, cold, hunger, separation, disease, the general impracticability of purpose, all bring their quota to imprison the souls of women and of men. Our experiences do not keep step with our hopes. The Platonic Eros, which is the soul stirring itself to life and motion, is maimed. *The essence of freedom is the practicability of purpose. Mankind has chiefly suffered from the frustration of its prevalent purposes, even such as belong to the very definition of its species.*[58] [italics mine]

Those purposes, which belong to "the very definition of" the human "species," are, of course, creativity itself. The beyond of capitalism frees ourselves for ourselves.

What Marx calls full communism is a realization of processive solidarity: the absolute concomitance of the social and the individual. Since processive thought is already radical, anti-capitalistic thought, the real overcoming of capitalism is the actualization in human social relations of process. "Only at this stage does self-activity coincide with material life, which corresponds to the development of individuals into complete individuals."[59] It is the actualization of our essential being; but this essence does not reduce us to commonality; it frees us for the full development of our individuality. It is the actualization of our absolute difference from each other, but such difference does not separate us from one another because it arises as our gift to one another. It is actualization of our uniqueness, but such uniqueness is not self-centered because each achievement is a relational-ization of and for the whole. "The many become one, and are increased by one."[60] Such easy dichotomies are to be actually overcome.

> *Communism*... as the real *appropriation of the human* essence by and for man; communism therefore as the complete return of man to himself as a *social* (i.e., human) being—a

return become conscious, and accomplished within the entire wealth of previous development. This communism, as fully-developed naturalism, equals humanism, and as fully-developed humanism equals naturalism; it is the *genuine* resolution of the conflict between man and nature and between man and man — the true resolution of the strife between existence and essence, between objectification and self-confirmation, between freedom and necessity, between the individual and the species. Communism is the riddle of history solved, and it knows itself to be this solution.[61]

A genuine dialectical unity is achieved finally for human life; and because we are beings-in-relation to one another, this is not just self-appropriation and self-affirmation as freedom for myself, but the freedom which I gain by appropriating my own creative ability is also an act of freeing others. Only when I feel the solidarity of myself and all others will I really feel the suffering of the other as (necessarily) my suffering.

We do not yet live such being-in-solidarity. Real solidarity as process in actuality is not yet, but it is real as the potential future of the present and, as such, the entertainment of the non-conformal proposition of full communism, of social solidarity, is a lure for feeling. "The entire movement of history is, therefore, both its *actual* act of genesis (the birth act of its empirical existence) and also for its thinking consciousness, the *comprehended* and *known* process of its *coming-to-be*."[62] And so in the present we live the future only as the not-yet-potential and in that know ourselves to be the processive agents of this coming-to-be. As we think processively, as we think dialectically, we are thinking beyond capitalism; in thinking beyond capitalism we are affirming ourselves; in affirming ourselves we are freeing ourselves for this potential. "*Communism* is the necessary pattern and the dynamic principle of the immediate future." "[W]e characterize *communism* itself because of its character as negation of the negation, as the appropriation of the human essence which mediates itself with itself through the negation of private property."[63]

And so, in the present, we strive to speak of the not-yet. We struggle and stumble, our tongues are tied, and our minds battle with this thought, which is our real freedom and our real possibility. We need to speak in metaphors in order to speak through all the one-sided conceptualizations that crowd our consciousness. We find it so difficult to think dialectically, we find it so difficult to express the character of processive reality, because we live still in tension with these articulations. We find it difficult to say what is not yet actual, but we hint and try and find ourselves on the brink of saying but not yet being able to say clearly. When we live process, we will no longer need to say it. True social solidarity would be a true revolution in consciousness and thus an ability to conceptualize in entirely novel ways. It would not, therefore, constitute an ideal endpoint but the starting point of a new epochal processive adventure of becoming anew. Not the end of history but its true beginning.

And, in the final analysis, it is possible that we cannot characterize full communism except to speak of it as the realization of dialectical and processive being. It is possible that, in keeping with the truly dialectical nature of processive being, actually living process, actually uniting our essence with our existence, will necessarily mean already thinking beyond that actuality, but this time with our windows of potentiality wide open and our potential for novelty limited only by the possibilities given in our actuality and not by imposed scarcity. Lived solidarity may well constitute a real evolutionary leap.

> Religion is founded on the concurrence of three allied concepts in one moment of self-consciousness, concepts whose separate relationships to fact and whose mutual relations to each other are only to be settled jointly by some direct intuition into the ultimate character of the universe. These concepts are:
>
> 1. That of the value of an individual for itself.
> 2. That of the value of the diverse individuals of the world for each other.

3.  That of the value of the objective world which is a com-
    munity derivative from the interrelations of its compo-
    nent individuals, and also necessary for the existence of
    each of these individuals.[64]

Dialectical consciousness, processive consciousness, radical consciousness, self-consciousness and self-appropriation as real freedom,
are all instances of the concurrence in thought and in potential actuality of these three concepts. Therefore, full communism may be the
realization in consciousness and in actuality of the sacred character
of the universe. The absolute end is the "evocation of intensities."[65]
Real solidarity as lived process, and lived process as the freedom of
the human being to creativity bounded only by the data, might be
our conceptual *noesis* with the boundlessness of the primordial graded
envisionment: the realization of the sacred character of the universe
and that realization as the appropriation of our role in its creation.

According to Isaac Luria's Kabbalist doctrine of *Tikkun*, the
breaking of the "vessels" of God's attributes scattered divine sparks
in fragments throughout the material world. The task of healing these
broken vessels, an enterprise in which "man and God are partners,"
reestablishes the "harmonious condition of the world" not as a res-
toration, but "as something new."[66]

## NOTES

1   Reprinted with slight modifications by permission from *Marx and
    Whitehead: Process, Dialectics, and the Critique of Capitalism* by
    Anne Fairchild Pomeroy, the State University of New York Press
    ©2004, State University of New York. All rights reserved.

2   Regarding the value of the human being as measured in money, the
    money fetish, and the inversions produced by that fetish, see Karl
    Marx, *The Economic and Philosophic Manuscripts of 1844* (New York:
    Prometheus Books, 1988), 136–41. Of particular interest is Marx's
    descriptions of money as "[t]he overturning and confounding of
    all human and natural qualities, the fraternization of impossibil-
    ities — the *divine* power of money — lies in its *character* as men's

estranged, alienating and self-disposing *species-nature*. Money is the alienated *ability* of mankind" (Ibid., 139). Money is able to invert the world and turn everything into its opposite precisely because it is itself the alienated ability of mankind: the initial inversion of essence from which the other inversions flow. Regarding the contrast between adventures and anaesthesia, see Alfred North Whitehead, *Adventures of Ideas*, esp. 252–98.

3   It might be an interesting and fruitful project to pursue the notion of our forgetfulness of being which appears in Heidegger's texts through this more radical interpretation. It might be claimed that such forgetfulness is a direct function of our alienated and alienating social practices — that such forgetfulness is a kind of existential ideology, a philosophical symptom of the reduction of essential human capacity to inessential commodity value which is the very life and 'being' of capitalism. As a function of carrying out social relations which are primarily external relations (value as the mediator of human relations), we pull ourselves away from (alienate ourselves from) the internal relations which are necessarily the *being* and *creativity* of the processive universe. For examples of Heidegger's views on our forgetfulness of being see Martin Heidegger, *An Introduction to Metaphysics*, trans. Ralph Manheim (New Haven and London: Yale University Press, 1959); *Early Greek Thinking: The Dawn of Western Philosophy*, trans. David Farrell Krell and Frank A. Capuzzi (San Francisco: Harper & Row, Publishers, 1975); *Poetry, Language, Thought*, trans. Albert Hofstadter (New York: Harper & Row, Publishers, 1971).

4   Alfred North Whitehead, *Science and the Modern World* (New York: Free Press, 1967), 195–96.

5   Ibid., 202–03. Of course, according to the philosophy of internal relations, we need to see views of substantial independence, mechanism, private morals, psychologism, the dichotomy between facts and values, etc. as expressions of capitalism's form of social relations. They are various manifestations of the same alienated productive activity.

6   Ibid., 51.

7   Alfred North Whitehead, *Modes of Thought* (New York: Free Press, 1968), 138.

8    Ibid., 123–24.

9    Whitehead, *Adventures of Ideas*, 11.

10   Alfred North Whitehead, *Process and Reality,* corr. ed. (New York: Free Press, 1978), 238.

11   Ibid., 236–38.

12   The concomitance of physical and mental poles in the Whitehead-ian schema should remind the reader of the concomitance of intu-itions and concepts in the Kantian scheme, expressed in the famous phrase, "Thoughts without content are empty, intuitions without concepts are blind." See Immanuel Kant, *Critique of Pure Reason* (Indianapolis: Hackett, 1996), 107. The difference, of course, is that Whitehead moves the interdependence of the features of inher-ited data and organization of that data to the metaphysical level to account for permanence and change as they appear in the fabric of our experience.

13   Whitehead, *Process and Reality,* 164.

14   It should be noted that the discussion here of the abstracted phase of conformal feeling is not meant to imply that such a phase could, in the concrete, ever occur "alone." The concrete becoming of an actual entity is always dipolar and atemporal. This discussion is for purposes of analytic clarity only. It is a discussion which can only occur within the genetic division.

15   Ibid., 163.

16   Ibid., 238.

17   Ibid., 239–40.

18   For a superb treatment of these notions see Jorge Luis Nobo, *White-head's Metaphysics of Extension and Solidarity* (Albany: State Uni-versity of New York Press, 1986).

19   Whitehead, *Process and Reality,* 248.

20   Ibid., 33.

21   Ibid., 22.

22   Ibid., 249.

23   Ibid.

24   Ibid., 149.

25　I am deeply indebted to Russel Kleinbach's work in *Marx Via Process* wherein he delineates a Whiteheadian theory of human consciousness and explicates its importance for understanding a Marxian theory of freedom.

26　In this regard see also my discussion on dialectical materialism: Anne Fairchild Pomeroy, *Marx and Whitehead* (Albany: State University of New York Press, 2004), 43–61.

27　Whitehead, *Process and Reality*, 239.

28　Ibid., 23.

29　Ibid., 241–43.

30　Ibid., 243.

31　Ibid., 185–86.

32　Ibid., 186–87.

33　Ibid., 249.

34　Ibid., 259.

35　Ibid., 273.

36　Whitehead, *Adventures of Ideas*, 42.

37　Whitehead, *Process and Reality*, 263.

38　Ibid., 188.

39　See Herbert Marcuse, *One-Dimensional Man*, 2nd ed. (Boston: Beacon Press, 1991), 19–34.

40　See Noam Chomsky, *The Chomsky Reader*, ed. James Peck (New York: Pantheon Books, 1987), 121–36. The notion of "the manufacture of consent" was, Chomsky points out, coined by Walter Lippmann to indicate a "revolution" in "the practice of democracy" (136). Needless to say, what Lippmann saw as a great advance, Chomsky sees as fundamentally antithetical to freedom.

41　See Pomeroy, *Marx and Whitehead*, 107–25.

42　Whitehead, *Adventures of Ideas*, 42.

43　Kant, *Critique of Pure Reason*, 732.

44　Whitehead, *Adventures of Ideas*, 42.

45　Karl Marx, *Grundrisse* (London; New York: Penguin, 1993), 540.

46  Ibid., 541–42.

47  Carol Gould, *Marx's Social Ontology: Individuality and Communality in Marx's Theory of Social Reality* (Cambridge, MA: MIT Press, 1980), 4–5.

48  Ibid.

49  Karl Marx and Friedrich Engels, *The German Ideology* (New York: International Publishers, 2004), 31.

50  Marx, *Grundrisse,* 243–44.

51  Marx and Engels, *German Ideology,* 83.

52  Whitehead, *Adventures of Ideas,* 67.

53  Marx, *Grundrisse,* 488.

54  Ibid., 542.

55  Ibid., 832.

56  Ibid., 109.

57  See Roslyn Bologh, *Dialectical Phenomenology: Marx's Method* (Abingdon: Routledge, 2010), 92.

58  Whitehead, *Adventures of Ideas,* 66.

59  Marx and Engels, *German Ideology,* 93.

60  Whitehead, *Process and Reality,* 21.

61  Marx, *Economic and Philosophical Manuscripts,* 102–03.

62  Ibid., 102.

63  Ibid., 123.

64  Alfred North Whitehead, *Religion in the Making* (Cambridge: Cambridge University Press, 2011), 48.

65  Whitehead, *Process and Reality,* 105.

66  Susan Buck-Morss, *The Dialectics of Seeing: Walter Benjamin and the Arcades Project* (Cambridge, MA; London: The MIT Press, 1991), 235. The quotations within Buck-Morss's text come from Gershom Scholem, *The Messianic Idea in Judaism, and Other Essays in Jewish Spirituality* (New York: Schocken Books, 1971), 46, 13.

## ぎ 8 ぎ

# ALTERNATIVE VALUES TO AN

# EXTRACTIVIST LOGIC

*Timothy Murphy*

A S WE APPROACH THE POINT AT WHICH IT BECOMES
impossible to prevent the full effect of climate disruption, it is
critical to examine the grounding for this planetary crisis. The very
logic of exponentially increasing extraction, expressed by capitalism's unconditional demand for growing profits, embodies a twisted
understanding of that all-important question: what is valuable? What
we value drastically shapes our efforts and energies. This chapter will
describe the theory of value in process thought. It will show complementary insights from neo-Marxists Michael Hardt and Antonio
Negri as it relates to their critique of Empire. This organic Marxist
framework provides an alternative theory of value to the current
dominant paradigm.

Process thought is at its root a theory of value. In their compelling book, *Organic Marxism*, Philip Clayton and Justin Heinzekehr
identify aesthetic values as one of the four major parts of process
thought.[1] They define the world as a network of values. How things
are valuable is, at the same time, inextricably linked to how they are

interconnected. In this way, process thought circumvents and transcends the binary debates that ensnare many thinkers.

Much theorizing has been done over competing notions of value. The primary options have left us trapped in models that do not help us avoid the pit of ecological destruction. In fact, they drive us towards that abyss. These options are instrumental value and intrinsic value.

Under the framework of instrumental value, things are valuable to the extent that others can use them for their own purposes. They are a resource to utilize for some other end. Fossil fuel extraction inherently displays an instrumentalist logic. Things are not valuable for themselves but only in how they can be used for the sake of profit. Coal, oil, and natural gas, which power much of our economic epoch's growth and industry, become necessary evils as a foundation for growing economies and lifting people from poverty. They are a means to an end.

Instrumentalist logic even finds its way into ecological arguments. It says that we must preserve at-risk ecosystems because there are many plant and animal species we have not yet discovered. Who knows what treasures they may hold for future medical or scientific usage? It asks us to conserve species and habitats because other creatures may be useful to us in the future. The implication here is that if there is no obvious usage for us, there is no value in those creatures or environments. Instrumental value on its own, especially when viewed through an anthropocentric lens, makes planetary problems worse.

The main alternative is affirming intrinsic value. In this way of thinking, things are valuable for their own sake, for their very act of existing, and not for the usage they may have for others. In many ways, this is a notable improvement. A redwood tree is not valuable because it can produce so many foot-pounds of pulp for industrial paper manufacture, or wood for new homes, but for its sheer majesty. A person has intrinsic worth, and rights, irrespective of how others may benefit from their exploitation. Other ecological ethicists go further and say that there are communal intrinsic values, such as the value of a species or an ecosystem, or the intrinsic value of biodiversity.

While this perspective may be an improvement over instrumental value on its own, an immediate problem arises. Intrinsic value does not explain how things are valuable for each other. Without this corrective, whatever units one declares as intrinsically valuable — whether individuals, species, or ecosystems — are opaque in value to each other. Its implications are towards autonomy and isolation, a world consisting of so many intrinsically valuable entities that are in no way connected to each other. They are valuable but separate.

It is here that I see process thought as rescuing us from these binary options. As process philosopher Brian Henning has so helpfully explained, "[S]elf-value is always intertwined with the value of others and with the value of the whole."[2] Process weaves together notions of instrumental and intrinsic value into an ecological ethic. This is because *the way* that entities form and interrelate with each other is also the way that they achieve value.

Value comes from the combination of what Alfred North Whitehead calls intensity and harmony. Intensity and harmony are expressions of the process of becoming and how value is formed through that process. There are two sides to every event: how much feeling of others it holds in its constitution, and how these feelings are integrated together. The former is intensity and the latter is harmony. For Henning, "the creative process of the universe itself... aim[s] at achieving the most harmonious, inclusive, and complex whole possible."[3] This is how value is created.

Entities or events that can integrate seemingly divergent elements into a related whole become a contrast. Intensity and harmony go together. The contrast of many elements together in a related event leads to a more intense value-experience. Harmonization happens as an activity of growing together or concrescence. Whitehead brilliantly summarizes his view of value and actuality:

> Everything has some value for itself, for others, and for the whole. This characterizes the meaning of actuality... We have no right to deface the value experience which is the very essence of the universe. Existence, in its own nature, is the upholding of value intensity... [N]o unit can separate itself from the others, and from the whole. And yet each unit exists in its own right. It upholds value intensity with the universe. Everything that in any sense exists has two sides, namely, its individual self and its signification in the universe.[4]

By this, Whitehead demonstrates the inseparability of all actualities, whether past or present, from the creation of values for themselves and for others — their mutually intrinsic *and* instrumental value. Note that this interpretation does not restrict instrumental value to human interests. It is a valid relationship for all planetary creatures. The value produced in one actuality allows for greater potentials to be realized in its environment. Likewise, being part of a complex environment filled with value-events allows for the entity in that context to express greater value in its own self-enjoyment. A rich, healthy environment is beneficial for the individual's self-enjoyment within that environment, which is itself constituted by the innumerable individuals benefiting from one another's existence.[5]

Charles Birch and John Cobb follow this paradigm and add to it, affirming that it is critical to incorporate intrinsic value, which they believe should be "measured by richness of feeling and capacity for richness of feeling."[6] In effect, all things have value for themselves, because they all have a measure of agency and subjectivity, however slight.[7] From electrons to human beings, existence is part of a holistic continuum. There are no objects that are not also subjects. This is what Whitehead himself called his reformed subjectivist principle, which declares: "apart from the experiences of subjects there is nothing, nothing, nothing, bare nothingness."[8]

In promoting value, Birch and Cobb describe subjectivity and self-creation as the ground for richness of experience. Value can only arise from free decisions. In Henning's complementary reading of process philosophy, there are no facts in isolation of values, and no values in isolation of facts; there are only fact-values.[9] No entity is ever static; it is a value process of intensity and harmonization. To be a value for oneself inherently means that one is also a value for others.

In being subjects, entities have intrinsic value for themselves, but in being objects felt by others they have instrumental value in those other entities' self-creation. This is what it means to say that the way things are interconnected is the means by which they have value for themselves, for others, and for the whole world.

When discussing value, process theorists generally direct themselves more towards the "natural" world and less towards inter-human relations. However, socialist theory has emphasized this latter component to a much greater extent. We can see a complementary pattern with the neo-Marxist theorists Michael Hardt and Antonio Negri.

Hardt and Negri are relevant insofar as they express a version of Marxist theory indebted to process thought. They blend Marxism with Gilles Deleuze's immanent version of process thought. (Deleuze himself was greatly appreciative of Whitehead's work.) The philosopher Roland Faber has persuasively demonstrated the overlap and influence of Whitehead upon Deleuze's more immanent process philosophy.[10] In effect, as we work to fuse ecological thinking through postmodernity and Marxism, we already have two Marxist theorists indebted to process-oriented ways of thinking about transforming society.

The key notions of Hardt and Negri's thinking as they pertain to value are the multitude, the biopolitical, and Empire. Hardt and Negri's notion of the multitude replaces the function of the proletariat in Marxist discourse. While the latter was generally conceived of as industrial workers, the former includes potentially everyone on the planet. Hardt and Negri reject classic Marxist descriptions of a single working class grounded in male industrial labor as the engine of socialist transformation, for there is "no political priority among the forms of labor."[11] Another way to say this is that while the multitude becomes a postmodern proletariat, the latter is defined as "all those who are subordinated to, exploited by, and produced under the rule of capital."[12]

This shift is made possible through their reinterpretation of production. For them, the multitude is engaged in the social production of life itself, called the biopolitical, for labor is increasingly a production of services and relationships as much as physical goods. In this way, it is "immaterial" in product, which spreads as the normative image for all labor to follow, just as the industrial line was the key norm in earlier eras. Said another way, the biopolitical is the network of life that produces itself. Thus, "the divisions between the economic, the social, and the cultural tend to blur."[13] The biopolitical is inherently productive, because it is always creating value through singularities in a mutually connected web.[14] Notice the strong parallel here with a process theory of value. The multitude, like the value-facts of process, is not a transcendent universalism but an immanent universalism that grows out of the productive relationships between distinct communities. Hardt and Negri wish to avoid transcendentalizing the immanently productive biopolitical. They suggest that, unlike in the past, the conditions are ripe "for the various types of labor to communicate, collaborate, and become common" against capitalism's regime.[15]

Instead of adding value, transnational economic globalization as Empire is more like a vampire that extracts the surplus from this production process for its own perpetuation as biopower.[16] It values only that which it can extract for profit from these immanent relationships of production. Throughout this process, class exploitation and stratifications endure with inequalities becoming more severe through the "mandate of flexibility and mobility" of work. Such deregulation allows for more work and exploitation while keeping wages low.[17] While there are different types of production, the ideal-type has shifted away from industrial models of order and towards affective forms of labor that are flexible and communicative. This shift in production does not make it automatically less exploitative, for Empire maintains the segmentations between groups of working people through maintaining conflict via "the constant fear of poverty and anxiety over the future."[18]

By showing that the multitude is involved in production, Hardt and Negri explain how the multitude and even unemployed persons are actual agents. Everyone is laboring in the form of producing life and relationships and can thus be an agent of change against globalizing Empire. There are in fact two forms of multitude: there is the multitude as it actually exists and engages in the production of all social life and relationships, and there is the political project of the becoming multitude, free from Empire, which remains a real potential not yet actualized. The multitude consists of a diverse set of social locations and experiences that, while not identical, exist in a potential web of communication across differences. The existence of the multitude simply makes revolution *possible* rather than inevitable.[19] This complements the open, nondeterministic future so central to process thought and Organic Marxism. There can be a planetary counter-globalization movement of many singularities communicating on a common matrix, but it is also possible that they may be sublated into yet another regime of Empire. The ontological multitude that produces social life exists, but it is an open question whether a historical multitude will develop and cast off Empire for their dream of a grassroots democracy of direct participation.

In spite of the obvious resonances between process thought and Hardt and Negri, it is important to acknowledge that the latter do not explicitly identify themselves as ecological Marxists. Throughout their seminal trilogy, however, they address the connections between capitalist extraction and ecological damage. For example, they recognize how our economic system promotes ecological devastation and seeks to privatize what they call the "commons" for personal profit, such as building dams on rivers or appropriating indigenous knowledge of the earth for corporate profit.[20] Likewise, corporations claim ownership to the genes of seeds, thus contributing to a sense of their bare instrumental value.[21]

One further corrective is that while Hardt and Negri emphasize how Empire's logic works immanently, others have rightly pointed that there is a value-driven transcendence that motivates Empire and its institutional support. This value-ideal drives people to sacrifice even when the advantages of doing so are not readily available to them. It is the *"ethos"* of Empire, its ultimate notion of what is valuable and what is worth sacrificing in pursuit of these values.[22] Empire requires that people be actively incorporated into it and want its worldview as their own.[23] This phenomenon is faith in the market or "market fundamentalism [that] plays a central role in the global capitalist system."[24] This new Empire attempts to attract through soft power and form mimetic desires within the subordinated, with the goal of perpetual growth via the process of accumulation and consumption, and unending war upon those who resist this attraction.[25]

Analogous to the insights of the best of process thought and Hardt and Negri, ecological civilization as expressed by Organic Marxism starts with the actual living conditions and problems of a context. Larger patterns and interconnections can and will emerge from there, but one must not jump prematurely to any universals. Starting with universals that are applied to various contexts is the opposite of what is being suggested. It is not enough to understand the harm done through extractivist values of late capitalism and why a process-socialist alternative is needed. Following Marx, we know the point is not merely to understand the world, but to change it.

Hardt and Negri's multitude can act anywhere that profit-extractivist models rear their heads, including localized actions, for "each struggle remains singular and tied to its local conditions but at the same time is immersed in the common web."[26] Allow me to give but one real-life example: the environmental justice organization Communities for a Better Environment (CBE). CBE organizes in the primarily Latinx neighborhoods of Huntington Park and Wilmington in the Los Angeles region, as well as Richmond in the Bay Area of California. Its members fight against refineries and toxic pollutants in their neighborhoods. Their methods include community organizing in low-income communities of color to build power to influence decisions affecting them, legal work like lawsuits in fights against industries and regulators, research in understanding where environmental problems are happening, and savvy use of media and communications to complement the rest of their work.[27] Through this combination, they have succeeded in stopping oil refinery expansion in Richmond, CA; strengthened flaring regulations in the port community of Wilmington, CA; won settlements for contaminated areas impacted by toxic gasoline additives; and achieved environmental justice policy recommendations from the California EPA, among other victories over the years.[28]

Their members know that their lives matter, that *they are valuable*, even if protecting them is not profitable for businesses. Their communities' access to "clean air, water and soil and to a healthy, safe, livable community are intrinsic[ally]" valuable.[29] Meanwhile, they understand that by organizing together and improving air quality in their communities, they improve life for people fighting for environmental justice in Riverside County, because air currents drive pollutants from their neighborhoods eastward, where they are trapped in the Inland Empire. Like Whitehead's mutual affirmation of instrumental and intrinsic value, CBE's struggle expresses their value for themselves and for others. They recognize that their fight is both local and extends across the planet, partnering with regional, statewide, and national environmental justice allies like the California Environmental Justice Alliance, Climate Justice Alliance, and the Indigenous Environmental Network.[30] Like Hardt and Negri, they see their work as part of an interwoven network of singularities in common struggle. Because environmental exploitation is happening across the planet, the multitude can attack a particular expression of Empire wherever it may appear—there is no single target.

CBE community members make their stand in their location as part of the multitude's broader resistance. Across the planet, they can inspire other emulating actions that are relevant to those specific settings. With their commitment to equity, ecological justice, democracy, and economic justice, they show that another world is possible.

Process philosopher Roland Faber notes that when rethinking value, "the political consequence, then, is not the preservation of humanity and the struggle for its survival *per se*, but the *diversification of its environment in order to allow for the most creative openness for novelty that does not exclude humanity but does not center around humanity, either.*"[31] Ecological civilization will value things for themselves, for others, and for the whole. It must not make this argument only on behalf of humans, but for *the whole life network*. We do not affirm the network of life merely for its own sake or for our own, but for its related mutual benefit and flourishing. As Clayton and Heinzekehr write, "[H]umanity becomes responsible to consider not only human interests but also the interests of other species as inherently valuable as well."[32] We otherwise fall into a paternalistic or narcissistic relationship with the rest of the planet. Process and Marxist resources clearly offer an alternative to transglobal capitalism's logic of extraction. While using distinct theoretical resources, these traditions offer an interrelated frame for articulating what is valuable. In doing so, they offer alternative values against the logic of extraction where all entities are valuable for themselves, for each other, and for the whole world.

## NOTES

1   Philip Clayton and Justin Heinzekehr, *Organic Marxism: An Alternative to Capitalism and Ecological Catastrophe* (Claremont, CA: Process Century Press, 2014), 163.

2   Brian G. Henning, *The Ethics of Creativity: Beauty, Morality, and Nature in a Processive Cosmos* (Pittsburgh: University of Pittsburgh Press, 2005), 62.

3   Ibid., 3.

4   Alfred North Whitehead, *Modes of Thought* (New York: Free Press, 1968), 111.

5 See Henning, *Ethics of Creativity*, 52–64 on the ecstatic interpretation of Whitehead's thought, which argues that intrinsic value persists beyond the concrescence of an entity even as it also acts instrumentally in influencing other entities.

6 Charles Birch and John B. Cobb, Jr., *The Liberation of Life: From the Cell to the Community* (Denton, TX: Environmental Ethics Books, 1990), 205.

7 Ibid., 2.

8 Alfred North Whitehead, *Process and Reality*, corr. ed. (New York: Free Press, 1978), 167.

9 Henning, *Ethics* 4.

10 Roland Faber, "De-Ontologizing God: Levinas, Deleuze, and Whitehead," in *Process and Difference: Between Cosmological and Poststructuralist Postmodernisms*, ed. Catherine Keller and Anne Daniell (Albany: State University of New York Press, 2002), 215.

11 Michael Hardt and Antonio Negri, *Multitude: War and Democracy in the Age of Empire* (New York: Penguin Press, 2004), 106.

12 Michael Hardt and Antonio Negri, *Empire* (Cambridge: Harvard University Press, 2000), 256.

13 Hardt and Negri, *Multitude*, 224.

14 For more on their concept of the biopolitical as it relates to immaterial labor, see Hardt and Negri, *Multitude*, 108–115.

15 Ibid., 107.

16 This is not unlike Whitehead's recognition that evil draws upon and destroys the value upon which it depends. See Alfred North Whitehead, *Religion in the Making* (Cambridge: Cambridge University Press, 2011), 82–84. T

17 Hardt and Negri, *Empire*, 338.

18 Ibid., 339.

19 Hardt and Negri, *Multitude*, 340. See also Michael Hardt and Antonio Negri, *Commonwealth* (Cambridge: Harvard University Press, 2009), 344, where they write: "[T]he parallel coordination among the revolutionary struggles of singularities is possible, but it is by no means immediate or spontaneous."

20  Hardt and Negri, *Multitude,* 282–84. See also Hardt and Negri, *Commonwealth,* viii.

21  Hardt and Negri, *Multitude,* 112–13.

22  Néstor Míguez, Joerg Rieger, and Jung Mo Sung, *Beyond the Spirit of Empire: Theology and Politics in a New Key* (London: SCM Press, 2009), 1.

23  Ibid., 19.

24  Ibid., 84.

25  Ibid., 89.

26  Hardt and Negri, *Multitude,* 217.

27  Communities for a Better Environment, "How We Create Change" (http://www.cbecal.org/issues/how-we-create-change/).

28  Communities for a Better Environment, "Victories!" (http://www.cbecal.org/about/victories/).

29  Communities for a Better Environment, "Environmental Justice," (http://www.cbecal.org/issues/environmental-justice/).

30  Communities for a Better Environment, "Movement-Building" (http://www.cbecal.org/about/movement-building/).

31  Roland Faber, "Ecotheology, Ecoprocess, and Ecotheosis: A Theopoetical Intervention," *Salzburger Theologische Zeitschrift* 12 (2008): 89.

32  Clayton and Heinzekehr, *Organic Marxism,* 200-01.

# PART THREE

# ADAPTATION AND DIVERSITY

Toward a Contemporary Socialism

# AGAINST THE INSANITY OF GROWTH:

## DEGROWTH AS CONCRETE UTOPIA

### Barbara Muraca

F OR A LONG TIME ECONOMIC GROWTH has been essential for the stabilization of modern, industrialized societies.[1] Now, from a means to guarantee prosperity it has turned into a goal of its own. Far from going "green" at all, growth at any cost increases the pressure on the environment, dramatically exacerbates social inequalities, and erodes the basis of democracy. A radical social-ecological transformation is needed instead, in which the addiction to growth loses its grip and real democracy, autonomy, and solidarity are strengthened within the collectively negotiated biophysical conditions for our life on Earth. New social movements, social experiments, and innovative practices all over the world embody radical alternatives to the dominant imaginary, which is colonized by growth.

The Degrowth movement that originated in Europe at the end of the 1990s under the headline of "degrowth for ecological sustainability and social equity" has been increasingly influential as a platform for fruitful alliances between different social and environmental movements worldwide. Degrowth can play the role of a "concrete utopia" that radically challenges the imaginary dimension of modern growth-societies while fostering some of its increasingly dishonored promises, such as securing well-being, social justice, and democracy.

Following Bloch, Whitehead, and more recent works in utopian studies, I claim that Degrowth can work as a concrete utopia that anticipates possibilities for realization hidden in the folds of the actual world, enhancing them with militant optimism. Concrete utopias have both a prefigurative and a performative power: they envision alternative imaginaries by opening spaces for subversive collective practices that are already hidden in the contradiction of the present. Social experiments and new social movements create spaces in which alternative ways of conceiving needs, desires, and their satisfaction are experienced and tested. By provisionally suspending the pervasive impact of dominant societal imaginaries, social experiments can crack open the established understanding of what is considered to be real and give room to alternative practices of common living.

## CRACKS IN THE FAIRY TALE OF GROWTH: THE
## END OF THE PROMISE OF PROSPERITY

Economic growth has played a crucial role in stabilizing modern industrialized societies by guaranteeing employment, social mobility, and tax revenue, thus allowing them to finance their quest for prosperity. For the developed nations, growth was always coupled with the promise of prosperity for present and future generations. As long as the pie as a whole continued to grow, governments could by and large avoid social conflicts and unpopular measures to redistribute wealth. In this way, steady growth has produced for a long time social peace, political stability, and a so-called legitimation of outputs within the social democracies of modern Western societies.[2]

We have now reached a point at which the magic of growth is losing more and more of its power, even if there are many who still do not want to acknowledge this fact. The still common belief in countries of the Global North that the future will be better and our children will have a better life has been significantly shaken in the last decades. Similarly, the myth that one's performance and service will be the basis for climbing the social ladder gradually fizzled during the financial crisis. Instead, more and more people now recognize that the increasing pressure to perform only leads to ever-increasing stress and even harsher competition. In the race against everyone else, it's been a long time since people believed that they could really get further ahead (or better, climb higher); the goal of the race now is simply to maintain the status quo. Similarly, it's been a long time since continuing growth guaranteed full employment, at least not the kind of full employment that makes possible a dignified life.

As a result, the younger generation, especially in Europe, finds itself living among the debris of broken promises in an epoch of gradual collapse. For a long time they have been feeling a vague sense of discomfort, recognizing that something is really broken in the logic of growth. The limitations and constraints that are imposed on them for the sake of this goal just don't seem justified any longer. If growth was once a means to guarantee wealth and a good quality of life, now it has turned into a goal of its own, to which even the quality of life has to be sacrificed. More and more people are now heading out on the search for alternative practices, ones that no longer force them to live under the constraints of the present system.

## THE GROWTH-MACHINE IS LIKE A CRAZY BICYCLE

The recent economic crisis is only the peak of a process that has its roots in the core structure of modern societies. The growth model itself, on which modern capitalistic societies are based, has hit its limits. The idea of limits to growth is not new—already in the early 1970s the Club of Rome sent its alarming message that we would soon reach limits to growth due to the crisis of natural resources.[3] Technological development and aggressive globalization bought us the illusion that the prophecy of the Club of Rome had failed. We know better now.

Modern capitalistic societies are characterized by what sociologists call dynamic stabilization: they achieve social stability in a dynamic way by a continuing increase in economic volume and an ever-accelerating pace of innovation.[4] The mechanism of dynamic stabilization by means of growth can be compared to a bicycle[5] that has to keep moving forward so that it will not fall over. Indeed, with the logic of continuing growth it's even worse: this is a crazy bicycle that has to be constantly accelerating in order to keep its balance. As long as this process can carry on, stability is continuously, yet dynamically restored.

Given the existing conditions, which require economies to maintain growth in order to remain stable, to slow down in any way, and especially to stop, would lead to disaster. Societies that are dependent on growth will inevitably fall into recession and thus into crisis unless their basic institutions are radically changed.

However, we are currently faced with a fundamental crisis of the logic that underlies this particular dynamic. It has turned out to have dysfunctional effects with regard to the socio-economic, political, and cultural reproduction of modern capitalistic societies.[6]

On the one hand, after a certain threshold, the dynamic of continuing increase begins to undermine the very conditions that allow it to continue. For example, the growth rates that are still possible today do not necessarily lead to higher employment rates—a phenomenon known as *jobless growth*—nor to higher social mobility, nor to increased welfare for workers. Quite the opposite. The stabilization once associated with growth is fading away.

On the other hand, the so-called external limits of growth are becoming even more evident today than they were in the Club of Rome's report. These include social as well as ecological factors. The ecological limits concern our ability to continually boost access to important resources such as oil and phosphates in ways that are economically sustainable (this is why we talk about reaching "peaks"). They also include the ability of so-called "sinks" to absorb harmful pollutants from the atmosphere, ground, and water so that these crucial resources can be regenerated. The social limits of growth, by contrast, refer to the needs of consumers, which have to be artificially created and extended on a continuous basis in order to keep the machinery of growth oiled and functioning well. In addition to all this, individual workers are also reaching their own limits, because the demand on them to move faster and the pressure to achieve is continually increasing.

## LIMITS TO GROWTH OR THRESHOLDS OF JUSTICE?

The "limits to growth" debate, which in the early '70s was framed mainly in terms of external, ecological limits and resource scarcity, is reaching a new, momentous turning point. We are now facing a double economic-ecological crisis, in which measures to enhance economic growth inevitably increase the pressure on the ecological systems and in the long run compromise not only economic development, but also erode the basis of democracy. While promising a return to the golden age of growth, austerity politics instead foster recession by leading to a massive redistribution from bottom to top, with the consequence of dramatic cutbacks on basic liberties.

Moreover, the promise of growth as a condition for the improvement of quality of life for an increasing number of people has lost credibility. This is clear not only to experts looking at statistics and data that show an increase of poverty, precarious jobs, and struggles for survival, but also to most citizens, whose frustration is often channeled into hate against immigrants or desperate efforts to maintain their social status. An increasing number of people in Western countries are becoming aware that the promise of growth for a better life no longer holds. As several scholars have repeatedly shown in subsequent studies, after a certain threshold economic growth decouples from the individual feeling of well-being,[7] as well as from quality of life calculated on the basis of objective indicators such as the ISEW.[8] According to Binswanger, we are all somehow "trapped" within so-called treadmills, which while promising

happiness foster instead constant dissatisfaction. For example, innovative time-saving devices lead to an intensification of the workload
that requires even more time than before, rather than saving time
for other "free" activities.[9] (Think of the move from letters to email:
instead of buying us more free time, it has significantly increased
the pace of communication.)

In the meantime, capitalism is adapting to the crisis of economic
growth with even more dramatic consequences on people's lives. It is
not so much that we are running up against limits that will suddenly
and dramatically stop the capitalistic mode of accumulation. In fact,
the limits we have been considering are not so much *absolute limits*
that would make *any* further growth impossible. It's more accurate
to say instead that they are like thresholds; when they are reached,
the yields on capital investments begin to sink.[10] Limits of this kind
merely describe the end of "easy" growth and, as a consequence, the
failure of the promise of ever-rising prosperity. In order to generate
further growth in the face of these factors, the "capacity to exploit"[11]
has to be increased even further. This requires not only drawing more
intensely on natural resources, but also expanding many of the social
institutions that make it possible to accumulate capital: money, public
infrastructure, but also human creativity and the investment of time.

What results is a shifting of the boundaries in both a literal and
an extended sense. For example, private debts have to be encouraged
in order to create and cover new needs. Larger and larger investments
in infrastructures (transport, extraction, drilling technologies, etc.)
and logistics have to be made in order to extend and to process ever-
more limited resources. In the same vein we can consider the deregulation of international and domestic markets, increasing land-
grabbing around the planet, and an even greater commercial-
ization of natural processes and living things on which we depend,
such as photosynthesis and pollination. One already sees the readiness
to accept higher risks in obtaining resources and disposing of waste,
as we observe, for example, in fracking and in the arrangements for
storing atomic waste.

Generally, the ones who end up carrying the higher costs that stem from these changes are marginalized peoples, both in our own countries and in the countries of the Global South, which leads inevitably to a growing number of conflicts and wars. Indeed, when one looks at the results of a number of recent studies, one recognizes that the costs of these various developments are actually much higher than is usually estimated.

Growth has now turned from a preferred means for securing well-being into a goal of its own. As such, it is not only exacerbating the pressure on the environment, but also jeopardizing democratic stability and social cohesion, and ultimately impairing the quality of life. The "limits to growth" are not so much absolute barriers we run into, but thresholds of justice: we are reaching the limits of moral acceptability of societies that are based on economic growth for their own stabilization. An increasing number of people all over the world are becoming aware of this.

## SACRIFICE, INEQUALITY, AND HAPPY FRUGALITY: THE CONSERVATIVE CRITIQUE OF GROWTH

Aware of the "end of easy growth" and faced with the approaching fall of the crazy bicycle I mentioned earlier, conservative post-growth analysts, such as the German sociologist Meinhard Miegel, consider this to be an unavoidable destiny that will come upon us sooner or later. The only path left for them is developing coping strategies after the fall of the bicycle. Conservative thinkers envision a post-growth society under *Business-As-Usual* conditions, i.e., without a radical change of the basic structures of societies. The crisis will inevitably lead to impoverishment, recession, inequality, and more social conflicts.

Miegel presupposes that in the future the economy will necessarily continue to contract, which means that the amount of time that one can work will continue to shorten, though without compensation for the reduced income. In order to be able to cover the basic costs of life, people will become dependent on holding several different jobs, and in general they will become poorer. In addition, Miegel claims that, with the end of growth, the amount of taxes that the country receives will decrease, which will lead inevitably to a shrinking of the state's contribution to the well-being of its citizens. He thus proposes to privatize what have been government-supported services, particularly in the areas of education and healthcare. Moreover, he expects philanthropic donations to reduce misery, thus replacing redistribution policies.

As part of the solution, Miegel advocates a change of consciousness, so that people can learn to adapt to this new condition of economic contraction. The loss of prosperity and the growing poverty caused by the reduction of work hours, he thinks, will be transformed into a net gain. He proposes a cultural shift toward non-material values, including more family relations, cultural recreations, spiritual and community values. In his elitist perspective, people will rediscover the kind of leisure that brings meaning to life, and they will come to appreciate cultural and spiritual values more deeply.[12]

Instead of recognizing the necessity of a redistribution of resources and a transformation of society as a whole, conservative thinkers like Miegel demand sacrifice and happy frugality in order to cope with the crisis. His concern above all is for humans to adapt to the new conditions, which he sees as a kind of unavoidable fate, rather than to change them.

The transformation of consciousness that Miegel envisions will however only be satisfying for those who possess sufficient education, time, and material resources. Without income redistribution and public services, the option of enjoying cultural and non-material values, obviously, remains open only to those who do not have to work all day to make a living and take care of family members in their spare time. For the large majority of the people, the promise of well-being without growth does not imply an overall improvement in either their material or their psychological condition. Quite the opposite: they simply won't have any time left over for leisure activities and the joys of life but will be crushed by a new, highly unequal, and ultimately unjust society.

Such a vision of economic contraction represents nothing more than the well-known neoliberal program of the destruction of the welfare state, presented under the cover of a post-growth economy. Miegel's critique of growth thus amounts to a program for returning to a kind of feudal system, in which existing differences of social status and hierarchies will only be deepened, including the traditional division of labor among the genders and oppressive patriarchal relations. The inequalities will be massively increased, further strengthening traditional forms of discrimination.

## DEGROWTH: A VISION FOR A RADICAL TRANSFORMATION OF SOCIETY

One finds a completely different approach in the movement known as *décroissance* or Degrowth.[13] This movement, characterized by its critique of ongoing growth, has its roots in France and the other countries of southern Europe. Instead of expecting societies to simply adapt to economic contraction, the Degrowth movement works toward a radical transformation of the core conditions of society, in order to free social institutions from this fixation on growth. The goal of the Degrowth movement is to bring about a just, democratic, solidarity-based society in the post-growth era, a society that is no longer dependent on growth in order to remain stable and legitimate.

Due to its fruitful heterogeneity, it is difficult to speak of a "single" social movement in any strict sense.[14] Some common elements can be identified, however. Degrowth envisions a transition to a quantitatively smaller and qualitatively different economy that implies a gradual and equitable downscaling of production and consumption.[15] In a wider sense, it is also "an attempt to re-politicise the debate on the much needed socio-ecological transformation."[16] Starting from the recognition that in the countries of the Global North the end of easy growth is approaching and that further growth will come at dramatic social, ecological, and economic costs, Degrowth claims that it is possible for people to have a better quality of life working less and having less under the conditions of redistribution, solidarity, and self-management.

The Degrowth movement does not represent a political program as much as a call to battle; it's what Paul Ariés called a *mot obus*, a missile word, that like an arrow aims directly at the heart of modern capitalist societies. As such, it radically questions not only their economic structures, but also the cultural infrastructure that justifies them. Degrowth offers a fruitful foundation for new synergies, as well as for the experience of fighting side by side for a transformation of the basic conditions of society today. It can play a crucial role in uniting different groups, approaches, forms of resistance, and fights against the capitalistic mode of production and its logic of exploitation and expansion.

For example, Degrowth proved to be successful in bridging more antagonistic and more constructive forms of resistance. One thinks of post-carbon initiatives like the Transition Towns Movement, in which citizens work together to render their town or neighborhood independent from fossil fuels, and climate activism to block the extraction and transport of fossil fuels, like the Break Free initiative that successfully took place all over the world in May 2016 (see breakfree2016.org).

One can understand Degrowth in this sense as a guiding political concept that seeks to mediate between different groups, forms of resistance, social struggles, and alternative proposals for society.[17] One should count the global farmers movement as a part of this struggle, as well as the various groups that are critical of the Western models of development and globalization. Also, the Degrowth movement is actively supporting the proposals of feminists, who challenge the capitalistic division of labor and the obliteration of care activities from the so-called "productive" sphere of society.

The idea of Degrowth thus bears the chance of fostering a radical transformation of society. When talking about societal transformation we have to consider at least three dimensions, all of them essential and linked to the other two by a relation of interdependence.

The first one, the *structural and institutional* dimension, encompasses economic relations, relations of power and domination, and institutions. As we can learn from Whitehead, institutions and social structures are not an unchangeable reality that we have to face, even if this is often the way we experience them. They result — to use an image — from the coagulation and sedimentation of long-term, repeated patterns of belief, actions, and collective practices that over time became established habits and in the long run ossified structures.[18] Over time, repeated patterns of collective behavior grow into material structures that become increasingly powerful in determining the present and the future. After a while we forget how they originated and take them for granted as something unchangeable.

Take the very idea that debts have to be paid back with increasing interest and no cancellation: this is a great example of the ossification of a relatively recent practice that nonetheless for most of us has now become almost obvious. The expectation of paying back debts with interest is inscribed in collective values and sanctioning systems that are very strong in our societies. (We are ashamed if we cannot keep up with this expectation and teach our children to conform to this collective norm.) However, we know about alternative institutions in the history of humanity in which, for example, canceling all debts was a great institutional moment that played an essential role in creating peace and stability in the community. Potlucks and jubilees embody a different pattern that strengthens social relations, reduces inequality, and enables a radical renewal of the social fabric. Similarly, the idea of a collective access to health care was implemented by the collective, repeated actions of factory workers, who in the nineteenth century were struggling for their survival against capitalistic exploitation, and who created a solidarity network of mutual help and support.[19] On this ground, public health care institutions were later founded. We can create new institutions or radically change the existing ones by establishing, repeating, and sustaining alternative collective practices. For Whitehead, reality is not something given once and for all, but the result of endless processes of actualization; whatever is, has to be re-enacted in order to keep being. Even a stone is what it is because its endless components keep repeating the same pattern over and over again.[20] In this re-enaction novelty can emerge.

The second dimension encompasses both collective and individual *practices* and refers to the action and behavior of the people. On the one hand, practices are rendered possible and supported by institutions: think of the possibility of education and of political assemblies. On the other hand, as I have just explained, they contribute to establishing new institutions in the long run. We can decide to buy organic produce rather than conventional vegetables within the scheme of the market distribution of goods; we can cycle instead of using a car. These are important individual practices that are rendered possible by infrastructures and institutions (like bike lanes and organic markets). More radical practices, which would lead to a transformation of institutions, would aim instead at creating collective, alternative forms of self-managed production and distribution, or at re-appropriating one's own neighborhood and transforming it into a pedestrian area. In practices, possible alternative modes of living, ideals and creative experiments, gain materiality, as they are embodied into something that goes beyond the mere idea of possible alternatives.

The third dimension is the cultural and psychic dimension of social transformation, what some scholars have called the imaginary dimension of society, or *social imaginary*. In contrast to Miegel, the social imaginary has less to do with individual values, and more to do with the foundations for our deepest convictions and with the kind of fundamental self-understanding of a society that holds it together. It legitimates reciprocal expectations and is the repository of collectively shared values, meanings, images, fears, hopes, feelings, and so on. In this way, the social imaginary also constitutes the background that legitimates and justifies practices, actions, and institutions in the broadest sense.

While in a traditional Marxist perspective the cultural dimension results from the social structure and the economic relations, for non-orthodox Marxists like the French philosopher Cornelius Castoriadis (and for Whitehead) the dimension of the imaginary and the power of imagination are creative; they transform social relations. Ideas are efficacious in the world, i.e., they have the effectual power of transforming reality, which is, as I said before, in a constant process of becoming. Insofar as they are embodied and enacted in practices, they can challenge existing social structures.[21]

For Castoriadis, each society constitutes itself as a more or less coherent whole of institutions by creating a comprehensive universe of meaning, which is not just determined by its history.[22] In other words, each society is a system for interpreting the world. Far from being simply immersed in a given set of values that are justified by ideology, a society can become aware that it explicitly creates its own imaginary and that its institutions are its own creation. When a society becomes aware of its self-instituting character it has the chance to become truly *autonomous*, i.e., it follows the rules and conditions (*nomoi*) that it has given to itself (*autós*) without any external influence or determination. Ideology veils this process of self-instituting and feeds the illusion of some indisputable facts or principles (often framed as TINA = There Is No Alternative) that legitimize social institutions on the basis of something "other" to it, such as God or the so-called "law" of the market or, more recently, the necessity imposed by globalization. This leads to what Castoriadis calls *heteronomy*, which is the very opposite of autonomy; it is following the laws given by those who are in power. For Whitehead, ideologies are overly one-sided and survive only by obliterating diversity and hindering novelty.[23]

The Social Imaginary of modern, capitalistic societies has been colonized by the ideology of growth. As a result, questions about the conceptual conditions for social life together have fallen again and again into the background. After all, the promise of ever-increasing prosperity supposedly did not require any common vision in order to navigate toward a better future. Quite the opposite: as long as economic growth could be continued, hardly anyone wanted to cast doubt on the conditions and consequences of growth-based ways of living together. Growth thus has turned into what the German sociologist Harald Welzer calls a "mental infrastructure," a very powerful mode of thinking and acting that seems so obvious that we even fail to notice it.[24] Therefore, as Serge Latouche, a leading figure in the French Degrowth movement, claims, the first step toward a post-growth society lies in the decolonization of the social imaginary.[25]

## DEGROWTH: WITH MILITANT OPTIMISM TOWARDS A CONCRETE UTOPIA

In each of these respects, the radical social critique advanced by the Degrowth movement embodies what Ernst Bloch referred to as *concrete utopia*. Whereas abstract utopias are more similar to a mere daydream, the concept of a concrete utopia initiates a process of actualization. Here the first requirements for a just future are brought into the present, at least in a tentative and experimental fashion.

Abstract utopias might very well play a merely compensatory role under oppression. In this case, instead of mobilizing people for a transformation of the status quo, they work as a relief from suffering while at the same time sheltering people from reality and suffocating any attempt at resistance and subversion.

Instead, the transformative potential of a concrete utopia lies in its ability to anticipate the real-possible, i.e., what is possible not only in general terms, but on the ground of existing tendencies. A concrete utopia brings to light the potentials for development that already lie dormant in the folds and meanderings of the present. It helps unfold them, making them real in the future.[26] It is possible to achieve this goal because what is real is open and in a constant process of change, as we can learn from Whitehead as well. The influence of the past on future possibilities never amounts to a total determination, no matter how powerful it might be.

The process that underlies what we call reality is complex and multi-dimensional, like a woven carpet in which countless threads are woven together into visible patterns. We are used to seeing only the dominant pattern because everybody calls attention to it. The myth of TINA-narratives feeds on the belief that this is the only possible pattern that can be woven with what we have at our disposal. Yet when we focus on the main pattern, we neglect the threads that constitute it. Some of them are less visible and hidden under the surface, and yet they are part of the actual world and await to be discovered, lifted, and woven into new patterns. A concrete utopia detects tendencies that are really possible and puts them to work, guided by what Whitehead would call the lure of new possibilities for actualization.

To succeed at this project, one needs to develop an attitude that Bloch labeled "militant optimism." This attitude is not the same as merely naïve optimism, which is blind to relations of power and awaits the contradictions within society to automatically bring about transformation (as in some Marxist perspectives). By contrast, militant optimism identifies the hidden social potentials and useful tendencies; it actively grasps them, works upon them as a sort of amplifier, and thereby makes them visible.

In this way, concrete utopias challenge the established social imaginary and the ruling ideologies. Even the most influential ideologies remain dependent on ongoing legitimation. This is why they have somehow to embody a promise for a better life by at least addressing the expectations, needs, and hopes of citizens, *including* those who in fact have no place in the promises that these ideologies offer. Manipulation and false consciousness (i.e., blinding people to the exploitation and oppression they are exposed to) alone are not sufficient to keep them in power.

Yet this is precisely the weak point of the dominant ideologies, including the ideology of continuous growth, which seems to be omnipresent in our day. As Bloch realized, these ideologies contain an excess of meaning that goes beyond the way in which their principles are actually interpreted and implemented. The core of a concrete utopia can begin with these promises, unfolding its potential for subversion from this point outward. No completely new values and images are required for such a transformation. Instead, concrete utopias feed upon the wishes and value judgments that are already laid down in the social contradictions of contemporary society and through subversive practices transform them. At the same time, they awaken the longing for radical change. Concrete utopias thus possess not only a *pre-figurative* but also a *performative* power; they open a space for alternatives. Moreover, they already embody these alternatives *here and now,* in the form of a multitude of projects, social experiments, and protected spaces. In all of these, the outlines of a possible future are not only communicated but also tried out and developed further, even if the development is provisional and linked to a particular niche or location.

Finally, by grasping and enhancing the contradictions in the legitimation of dominant systems, concrete utopias can address and appeal to different people who share a similar discontent and a desire for a better way of living. Such a discontent might take the explicit form of critique and resistance against structural forms of oppression, discrimination, and deprivation (as is the case with antagonistic protest, boycotting, social conflicts). But it may also be a rather vague sense of frustration. The recent economic crisis that has been continuing for years now opens up the opportunity for a radical transformation of society, one that also encompasses the social imaginary.

Degrowth as *mot obus*—as missile word—has the power to catalyze different forms of discontent by offering a narrative for alternatives: where people already feel like being sacrificed for the sake of securing economic growth, which is supposed to eventually enhance the standard of life. Degrowth brings together people concerned about the environment, people concerned about social injustice and environmental racism, and people fed up with the constant acceleration of the rhythm of life and the increasing pressure for performance and improvement.

For example, for about ten years, in communities and cities, the globally active "Transition Town" movement has been experimenting with a carefully planned transition toward an age without fossil fuels. Transition Town communities are decoupling themselves from energy sources derived from fossil fuels, with the goal of strengthening their autonomy and their ability to survive crises. The model is so successful because it combines a multitude of diverse initiatives, each of which is particularly well adapted to a particular set of local conditions. In the numerous, if also small-scale activities of the Transition Towns, people can for example experience what it is like to live well without a car, or they can develop the ability to repair technical appliances and to use them in their particular social contexts. In this way, they are creating new spaces of freedom, liberating themselves from needs that they once felt were indispensable.

However, these various social experiments are particularly effective when they are networked together with more antagonistic forms of resistance, for example, with protest movements that fight back against coal mining and against massive and pointless infrastructure projects.

## THE YEARNING FOR ALTERNATIVES

How can the transformation of the social imaginary be experienced in a practical way? Social experiments contribute to the transformation of social imaginary insofar as they do not only anticipate the possibilities of a utopian future, but also embody them here and now, by creating the space in which these possibilities can be experienced, lived, and tested.

The Commons Movement is a good example of alternative forms of production, which at the same time also make possible other types of relationships among people. When a commons-based economy is fostered, even complex machines can be built by people using a decentralized approach, placing cooperation above competition. The plans for such machines are available to all the participants, and all can change and improve them. The ideal behind the movement is not hard to express: creativity increases when it is shared. "Commoners" draw on important values from modern society, such as innovation, technological development, and a creative re-forming of their common life. As they do this in their experiments, they anticipate future possibilities. They have been able to demonstrate that there are alternatives to mass production, that competition does not need to be the main motivation for commitment and performance, and that innovations don't have to be kept as secrets among experts. Innovation is a process that belongs to everyone instead of excluding those who cannot afford or access it, as it is under the logic of competition in a capitalistic market.

In bringing this example of the Commons Movement, I do not claim that the goal is to upscale individual social experiments. Instead, I am emphasizing that transformative potential usually requires that experiments be embedded in highly specific ways; they must be locally rooted. This embeddedness triggers a yearning for alternatives. The experiments thus make it possible to achieve social innovations and to test out new forms of living together, which in turn help to create new relationships and new ways of reciprocal recognition. Above all else, however, such experiments are places where participants can find the power and the motivation for resisting, and for building alliances. When they achieve this, they are able then to transfer the transformations that they envision into other realms of life.

## WORKSHOPS FOR LIBERATION

Concrete utopias do not only envision alternatives; they also embody alternative practices in the numerous laboratories in which new spaces are created and protected for actual experimentation. Without concrete spaces for new kinds of experience, our ability to imagine alternatives is limited.

The Degrowth movement can learn from the feminist movement what it means to fight against structural discrimination and mental infrastructures that are deeply inscribed also in those who are struggling for liberation. The ideology of growth, like patriarchy, works like a default-option in habitual practices, interactions, and even hopes for alternatives. Feminism made clear that awareness-raising groups were indispensable spaces in which the "obviousness" of dominant narratives could be addressed, discussed, and challenged not only at the abstract level of social analysis and critique (as is typical in Marxist antagonist groups), but also with respect to emotions, daily experiences, and internalized expectations. Patriarchal structures are not somewhere in front of us; they are literally embodied in our daily actions and thoughts. Creating spaces in which alternative modes of living could not only be envisioned, but felt, was the fundamental condition for the success of feminist struggles against patriarchy. This is not in and of itself anti-political, as some critics have claimed. At most it is pre-political; it expresses a critique of existing forms of relationship. The experiences that arise out of the awareness-raising groups showed that the spheres where new kinds of political and practical experience are made can actually provide the seeds for political resistance. Here people have the possibility of escaping from pressures imposed on them from outside. When they do so, they begin to create alternate types of everyday experience; they find new forms of empowerment.

Because this drive for growth is written into people at a deep level, just as patriarchal structures are, we need such workshops for liberation. Here people can directly experience how allegedly indispensable needs and pseudo-desires turn out to be merely the expression of a set of established and inherited values, which have been forced upon individuals in the interest of preserving the social relationships that keep the growth-machine going. Concrete utopias thereby take over the function of the "education of desire."[27] Instead of pushing back against desires, which expresses a one-sided notion of voluntary simplicity, these alternative spheres of experience open the door to significant social experiments, in which participants can collectively learn about their desires and what it means to live well together. This can ignite a process of liberation from drives that limit their autonomy, so that they are then able to articulate political demands that go beyond the usual assumptions.

Such political demands aim, above all else, for a new form of collective autonomy. When the neoliberal logic is made sovereign, freedom is understood as a mere plurality of options. It then means nothing more than the choice within a given set of possibilities and the individual arbitrariness in shaping one's own personal lifestyle. However, the concept of freedom bears in itself the potential for the idea of *collective autonomy*; it can be re-interpreted as involving a collective self-determination, enabling people to determine the basic conditions of their life together and not merely their individual lifestyles.

Of course, we are currently very far away from such an achievement. As the philosopher Ivan Illich reminds us, "prisoners in rich countries often have access to more things and services than members of their families, but they have no say in how things are to be made and cannot decide what to do with them. They are degraded to the status of mere consumers."[28]

Similarly, the plurality of options that consumers are given is actually limited to the choice between different brands; in their consumer-roles they cannot decide about the basic conditions under which products are manufactured and services are provided. Under the regime of growth, the consumer thus has hardly more scope for action than a prisoner in a jail; he or she is not able to make democratic and autonomous decisions about economic structures and the means of production, nor about the basic social conditions that determine such structures.

It is exactly this autonomy that the concrete utopia of the Degrowth movement seeks collectively to relearn. Here our autonomy also means self-limitation, living in the present and being embedded within a particular social and ecological fabric, which we ourselves knit together. Understood in this sense, autonomy is only possible in a society that offers democratic processes for making decisions and that allows people to specify forms of production based on the solidarity of the people. Such a society guarantees that economic activities remain oriented toward felt and publicly articulated needs, rather than that new needs are constantly being produced. The Degrowth movement, as perhaps no other contemporary political movement, stands not only for a radical departure from the ideology of growth, but also for a newly learned collective freedom.

## NOTES

1   First published in German in *Blaetter fur deutsche und international Politik* 2 (2015): 101–09. Republished in modified form by kind permission of the editor. This chapter is based on a lecture given by the author at the fourth international degrowth conference in Leipzig, September 2014. Translation by Philip Clayton.

2   Output legitimation means that democracies are not legitimized by the fact that the people actively participate in political decision making — this would be input legitimation — but rather by the kind of promise the governments can keep in terms of well-being.

3   See D. H. Meadows and Club of Rome, *The Limits to Growth: A Report for the Club of Rome's Project X on the Predicament of Mankind* (New York: Universe Books, 1972).

4   See Hartmut Rosa, *Beschleunigung. Zur Veränderung der Zeitstrukturen in der Moderne* (Frankfurt am Main, Suhrkamp, 2005).

5   I am grateful to Kate Farrell for suggesting this metaphor.

6   See Klaus Dörre, et al., *Sociology, Capitalism, Critique* (London: Verso, 2015).

7   See Richard A. Easterlin et al., "The Happiness-Income Paradox Revisited," *Proceedings of the National Academy of Sciences of the United States of America* 107, no. 52 (2010).

8   See Manfred Max-Neef, "Economic Growth and Quality of Life: A Threshold Hypothesis," *Ecological Economics* 15 (1995): 115–18.

9   See Mathias Binswanger, "Why Does Income Growth Fail to Make us Happier? Searching for the Treadmills behind the Paradox of Happiness," *The Journal of Socio-Economics* 35, no. 2 (2006): 366–81.

10   See Birgit Mahnkopf, "Peak Everything—Peak Capitalism? Folgen der sozialökologischen Krise für die Dynamik des historischen Kapitalismus," Working Paper der DFG-KollegforscherInnengruppe Postwachstumsgesellschaften (2013).

11   See Francois Schneider, "Macroscopic Rebound Effects as Argument for Economic Degrowth," in *Proceedings of the First International Conference on Economic Degrowth for Ecological Sustainability and Social Equita*, ed. Fabrice Flipo und Francois Schneider (Paris: Research & Development, INT 2008), 29–36.

12   Meinhard Miegel, *Exit: Wohlstand ohne Wachstum* (Berlin: Propyläen, 2010).

13   For a history of Degrowth in its various versions, see Barbara Muraca, *Gut Leben: Eine Gesellschaft jenseits des Wachstums* (Berlin: Verlag, 2014).

14   See Panos Petridis et al., "Degrowth: Between a Scientific Concept and a Slogan for a Social Movement," in *Handbook of Ecological Economics*, ed. Joan Martinez-Alier and Roldan Muradian (Cheltenham: Edward Elgar, 2015), 176–200.

15   See François Schneider et al., "Crisis or Opportunity? Economic Degrowth for Social Equity and Ecological Sustainability," *Journal of Cleaner Production* 18 (2010): 511–18.

16   See Federico Demaria, et al., "What is Degrowth? From an Activist Slogan to a Social Movement," *Environmental Values* 22, no. 2 (2013): 191–215.

17   This is precisely the program that one could observe at the Fourth International Degrowth Conference in Leipzig in September 2014. See Ulrich Brand, "Degrowth: Der Beginn einer Bewegung," *Blätter* 10 (2014): 29–32.

18   See Barbara Muraca, "Care for our Common Home and the Degrowth Movement: A Message of Radical Transformation," in *For Our Common Home: Process-relational Responses to Laudato Si,* ed. John B. Cobb, Jr. and Ignacio Castuera (Anoka, MN: Process Century Press, 2015), 139–49.

19   In Italy the public health care system is still today commonly called "mutua," a reminder of the mutual help networks created by the workers.

20  For Whitehead it is not so much the components of the stone, but the events that constitute it that repeat its structure with no significant modification over time. Living beings have to continuously keep their balance by interacting with their environment and regenerating their structures. Human institutions are even more fragile in their endurance. See Barbara Muraca, *Denken im Grenzgebiet: Prozessphilosophische Grundlagen einer Theorie starker Nachhaltigkeit* (Freiburg im Breisgau: Verlag, 2010).

21  See for example Alfred North Whitehead, *Adventure of Ideas* (New York: Free Press, 1967).

22  See Cornelius Castoriadis, *A Society Adrift: Interviews and Debates, 1974-1997* (New York: Fordham University Press, 2010).

23  Seem, for example, Alfred North Whitehead, *The Function of Reason* (Boston: Beacon Press, 1971), 43, where with reference to the modern scientific method he introduces the term 'obscurantism': "Obscurantism is the inertial resistance of the practical Reason, with its millions of years behind it, to the interference with its fixed methods arising from recent habits of speculation." With a little leap of thought we can consider the ideology of growth as obscurantist against any novel practices and alternatives visions for a better future.

24  See Harald Welzer, *Mental Infrastructures: How Growth Entered the World and Our Souls* (Berlin: Heinrich Böll Stiftung, 2011).

25  See Serge Latouche, *La Scommessa della Decrescita* (Milan: Feltrinelli, 2007).

26  See Ernst Bloch, *Das Prinzip Hoffnung* (Frankfurt am Main: Suhrkamp, 1976).

27  See Ruth Levitas, *The Concept of Utopia* (Bern, 2010).

28  See Ivan Illich, *Tools for Conviviality* (New York, 1973).

# ❧ 10 ❧

## MARIÁTEGUI AND WHITEHEAD:

### THE METAPHYSICS OF LOCAL MARXISMS

*Justin Heinzekehr*

IN 1928, THE SAME YEAR THAT WHITEHEAD gave the Gifford lectures that would become *Process and Reality*, a young Peruvian journalist was writing a collection of essays on the economic history of his country. José Carlos Mariátegui's *Seven Interpretive Essays on Peruvian Reality* would eventually become one of the foundational texts for the young Latin American Marxist movement. Looking back now, one can trace Mariátegui's influence in nearly all Latin American leftist thought, from dependency theory to liberation theology. But in order to apply Marxism to Peru, Mariátegui felt the need to make several adjustments to Marx's own theories. The types of economic structures that had emerged in Peru were quite different from the ones that Marx knew in Europe. Mariátegui also realized that these differences between Europe and Latin America were the result of global economic relationships. He therefore developed a "local" interpretation of Marxism that criticized colonial influences on Peru's economy and drew on indigenous wisdom traditions to suggest an alternative to global capitalism.

As a good Marxist, Mariátegui always considered material factors to be the real drivers of history, and he was reluctant to talk about the more abstract principles that lay behind his economic philosophy. After all, as he once said in an interview, "metaphysics is not in style."[1] And yet all of Mariátegui's innovations in Marxist theory suggest certain metaphysical commitments. As an attempt to make metaphysics fashionable again, this chapter draws out some of the metaphysical implications of Mariátegui's local Marxism and hopefully some implications for local socialisms that might be emerging in the United States and elsewhere. My argument here will be that Mariátegui's Marxism depends on metaphysical commitments that line up very well with those of process philosophy.

Mariátegui began his short career as a journalist, first writing literary reviews and short stories, then political satire and finally serious social criticism. His opposition to Augusto Leguia's presidency earned him an unofficial exile in 1919. Mariátegui spent the majority of his time in France and Italy, where he encountered the work of Antonio Gramsci, Benedetto Croce, Georges Sorel, and other leaders in the European Marxist tradition. He returned to Peru in 1923 firmly committed to Marxism, but also aware of the diversity and creativity that could be contained under the Marxist umbrella. He never occupied an academic post, but gave numerous lectures at universities in Lima, which allowed him to develop his own indigenous version of Marxism. He founded the journal *Amauta*, which means "wise teacher" in the Quechua language, and served as the first secretary-general of the Peruvian Socialist Party until his early death in 1930.

Mariátegui was convinced that Marxist economic analysis provided the best framework to understand the problems that Peru was facing. When discussing the indigenous peoples of Peru, for example, he says, "Any treatment of the problem of the Indian—written or verbal—that fails or refuses to recognize it as a socioeconomic problem is but a sterile, theoretical exercise destined to be completely discredited."[2] In other words, no amount of education, moral improvement or humanitarianism would make any difference as long as existing economic structures were left in place.[3]

The main problem, he thought, was that Peru had never been able to develop beyond a feudal agricultural system. Mariátegui says:

> Within European feudalism, the elements of growth — the factors of town life — were, in spite of the rural economy, much greater than within criollo semi-feudalism. The countryside, however secluded, needed the town. It had, above all, a surplus of food crops to dispose of. Instead, the coastal hacienda grows cotton or sugar cane for distant markets. Assured of the transport of these products, it has little interest with relations with its surroundings.[4]

Essentially, Mariátegui believed, Western capitalism had alienated the Latin American economy from its environment, both the natural and the social. It destroyed the original Incan economy, which was a relatively efficient communalism, and replaced it with a very inefficient semi-feudalism that benefited Western capitalists and large landholders. "The result," as Hosam Aboul-Ela summarizes, "[is] a region full of economies run by a class that [is] most often aligned with powerful foreign interests. The structure of Latin American economies... [is] such that the elite class, in simply pursuing its own self-interest, operate[s] against the interests of popular national constituencies."[5] The dynamics are different enough that they warrant a new class category, that of the *comprador*. The *comprador* owns the means of production in a peripheral economy but identifies with and invests in a location distant from his or her economic base.[6]

Because of the relationship between Latin American and Western economies, Mariátegui realized that Marxism would have to be applied differently in Peru than in other contexts. For instance, one could not expect an organic development from feudalism through capitalism to a socialist revolution, since Peru lacked both a bourgeoisie and a proletariat. Instead, Mariátegui suggested that indigenous communalism could provide the basis for a Peruvian socialism that would bypass the feudal colonial structures altogether. Of course, there could be no return to Incan communalism in its original form, but Mariátegui suggested building on those elements of Incan culture that remain intact in modern Peru. He says, for example, that indigenous communities have been able to organize collectively while simultaneously motivating their workers in a spirit of friendly competition, which is very difficult to achieve.[7] In indigenous economies, in distinction from those imposed on Peru from without, there is also a much stronger relationship to the land. "The principle that life springs from the soil was truer in the Peru of the Incas than in any other country," Mariátegui claims.[8] So in Peru, as opposed to Europe, "communal property does not represent a primitive economy that has gradually been replaced by a progressive economy founded on individual property. No; the 'communities' have been despoiled of their land for the benefit of the feudal... latifundium [landed, agricultural estates], which is constitutionally incapable of technical progress."[9]

The task of a Peruvian Marxist activist, then, is not to develop a socialist economy out of a capitalist one, but to encourage indigenous resistance to economies and legislation that attempt to expropriate or individualize their existing communities. Mariátegui uses the example of indigenous workers who sign collective rather than individual contracts.[10] In contemporary Latin America, one could cite various indigenous groups who have developed communal farms and are currently resisting the expropriation of land by large corporations, either through legal means or through nonviolent action.[11]

Though Peru has changed since 1928, Mariátegui's Marxism continues to be very influential throughout Latin America. His ability to contextualize Marx's original theories has inspired others to do the same, even if the details of their theories continue to evolve. But this very contextualization depends on innovations at the deepest level of Marx's theory, even the metaphysical level. Specifically, Mariátegui emphasized Marxism as voluntaristic rather than deterministic, local rather than universal, and holistic rather than reductionist. Each of these three is crucial to the success of the

Mariátegui tradition in Latin America. First, given the context of Peru, it is clear to Mariátegui that socialism will not naturally emerge from existing economic conditions. It requires a conscious effort on the part of an engaged group of people, and it is certainly not an inevitable outcome of history. He says, "Marxism, where it has shown itself to be revolutionary—that is, where it has been Marxist—has never obeyed a passive and rigid determinism."[12] Drawing on Sorel, Mariátegui saw Marxism not only as a sociology or a science, but also as a mobilizing cultural force.

Second, Mariátegui was the first Latin American to recognize Marx's Eurocentrism. He says, "Socialism was an international theory, but its internationalism ended at the borders of the West, at the boundaries of Western civilization."[13] Because of his position as a Latin American theorist, he anticipated the postmodern critique of universalism, which allowed him to incorporate indigenous resources into his own interpretation of Marx.

And third, although he certainly believed that material causes were the most basic forces of history, he appreciated the relevance of cultural, ideological, and even religious factors. In fact, he tended to think in holistic terms, with cultural and material realities interwoven. Again, this meant that he was sensitive to specific pieces of Peruvian culture that could be used as leverage against global capitalism. He considered it a false dichotomy to suppose "that a materialist conception of the universe is not suitable for producing great spiritual values"[14] or that socialist movements could be sustained without such values. If any of these three aspects of his interpretation was missing, Marxism would not have been nearly as compelling an alternative for Peru or, by extension, other Latin American nations.

So far, I have not mentioned Whitehead at all, and obviously, given Mariátegui's work, it is possible to develop local Marxisms—that is, interpretations of Marx that emerge organically from a specific context—without reference to process philosophy. But it is interesting to me that the very ingredients that make Mariátegui's Marxism different from traditional Marxism are the same ingredients that make Whitehead's metaphysics so unique in contrast with the Western metaphysical tradition.

In one passage of *Process and Reality*, Whitehead describes his own system in comparison to that of Spinoza:

> The philosophy of organism is closely allied to Spinoza's scheme of thought. But it differs by the abandonment of the subject-predicate forms of thought, so far as concerns the presupposition that this form is a direct embodiment of the most ultimate characterization of fact. The result is that the "substance-quality" concept is avoided; and that morphological description is replaced by description of dynamic processes. Also Spinoza's "modes" now become sheer actualities; so that, though analysis of them increases our understanding, it does not lead us to the discovery of any higher grade of reality. The coherence, which the system seeks to preserve, is the discovery that the process, or concrescence, of any one actual entity involves the other actual entities among its components.[15]

Whitehead makes two basic metaphysical statements here: (1) there is no higher reality beyond or above material events, and (2) reality is coherent because all of the events are intimately related to one another. In the next paragraph, he says that there is an ultimate principle in his philosophy, but this is the principle of creativity rather than God, as in Spinoza's philosophy. For Whitehead, God is the "primordial, non-temporal accident" of creativity.[16] And creativity itself is not a thing, not something that could be identified apart from its physical manifestations.

If we use Whitehead's relationship to Spinoza as an analogy for Mariátegui's relationship to Marx, there are many striking similarities. Again, we can see the three major shifts at work here: nondeterminism, localism and holism.

Nondeterminism is one of the hallmarks of Whiteheadian philosophy. The actual event is always situated within a historical context that constrains its existence, and yet there is always a spark of creativity which allows the event some freedom within those constraints. In the same way, Mariátegui thinks of socialism as requiring a creative, even heroic, working class—not in a romantic, utopian sense that ultimately withdraws from reality, but as a class that is conscious of the practical necessity of a new social order. For Whitehead, then, reality is constituted by the same dynamic of materialism and creativity that defines the working class in Mariátegui's thought.

Whitehead's localism is even more relevant to Latin American Marxism. Here again, Whitehead walks a line between the inescapable particularity of an event and its universal relevance. He says, for instance, that "no two actual entities originate from an identical universe," but also that "it belongs to the nature of a 'being' that it is a potential for every 'becoming.'"[17] The Whiteheadian universe is therefore made up of events that emerge within unique contexts but that nonetheless become at least potentially relevant for all other events. Whitehead's ontology bleeds right into his epistemology; for Whitehead, metaphysics is a discipline that uses empirical data as a starting point. This necessarily means that a metaphysician begins from a specific, and therefore limited, context and then makes speculative interpretations about these data. This means that metaphysics is always a collection of "metaphors mutely appealing for an imaginative leap."[18] And yet Whitehead has faith in the relevance of metaphysics: "At the very least, men do what they can in the way of systematization, and in the event achieve something. The proper test is not that of finality, but of progress."[19] We might say, then, that Mariátegui is a Whiteheadian Marxist, in the sense that he uses empirical evidence to tweak existing systems of thought and, in the process, uncovers truths about global economic relationships that might have otherwise gone unrecognized. The locality of Mariátegui's Marxism is precisely what makes it relevant to Marxist thought in general. In fact, finality or universality would be the real sign of failure both for Whitehead and for Mariátegui because it would signify a refusal to incorporate data that don't fit one's own abstractions (what Whitehead calls "the fallacy of misplaced concreteness").[20]

The best analogy to the holism in Mariátegui's work is Whitehead's integration of the material and the ideal. Whereas philosophers like Descartes and Spinoza had separated the two in some way (Descartes in a complete dualism, and Spinoza by defining them as separate, parallel attributes), Whitehead integrates the two in a single metaphysical scheme. So for Whitehead, the indeterminism at the bottom of reality is evidence for at least a modicum of subjectivity, and he defines matter as a process of subjective decision. This is important because, with the possible exception of the eternal objects, one could define Whitehead as a materialist, since he offers a way of integrating ideas, cultures, religions, etc. as important aspects of material reality with concrete effects. Mariátegui never explains how he can call himself a materialist while still arguing for the mutual influence of culture and economics, and Whitehead's metaphysics provides a possible justification for a more holistic Marxism.

It would be antithetical to finalize any particular combination of process philosophy and Marxism, and yet it does seem that, in order to apply Marxism to new contexts (such as the United States), one would require certain basic metaphysical commitments similar to the ones that Whitehead articulated so fully. Whether or not these commitments are explicit, they help move Marxism toward creative new applications. Especially at a time when ecological crisis makes the limitations of capitalism very clear, it is important that Marxism is able to make a global impact — not as a monolithic philosophy, but as a network of communities that share with each other their particular experiences of alienation and discovery. The metaphysics implicit in Mariátegui's work made it possible for Marxism to unfold in creative ways across an entire hemisphere. Therefore, as we think about possible forms of socialism that might emerge in the United States, our best hope might lie in an explicit partnership between Whiteheadian metaphysics, Marxist theory, and local experience.

## NOTES

1   José Carlos Mariátegui, *Seven Interpretive Essays on Peruvian Reality,* trans. Marjory Urquidi (Austin: University of Texas Press, 1971), xv.

2   Ibid., 22.

3   Ibid., 25.

4   Ibid., 19.

5   Hosam M. Aboul-Ela, *Other South: Faulkner, Coloniality, and the Mariátegui Tradition* (Pittsburgh: University of Pittsburgh Press, 2007), 73.

6   Ibid., 70.

7   Mariátegui, *Seven Interpretive Essays on Peruvian Reality,* 61.

8   Ibid., 35.

9   Ibid., 58.

10  Ibid.

11  For example, see the struggle of farmers in Las Pavas, Colombia, to retain their land rights against the efforts of the Daabon palm oil company. Christian Peacemaker Teams has been helpful in making this struggle more visible (http://www.ecapcolombia.org/en/category/las-pavas/).

12  José Carlos Mariátegui, *Mariategui: An Anthology,* ed. Harry E. Vanden and Marc Becker (New York: Monthly Review Press, 2011), 188.

13  José Carlos Mariátegui, *The Heroic and Creative Meaning of Socialism,* trans. Michael Pearlman (Atlantic Highlands, NJ: Humanities Press, 1996), 36.

14  Ibid., 159.

15  Alfred North Whitehead, *Process and Reality,* corr. ed. (New York: Free Press, 1978), 7.

16  Ibid.

17  Ibid., 22.

18  Ibid., 4.

19   Ibid., 14.

20   Ibid., 7–8.

꒰ 11 ꒱

# RESPONDING TO CLIMATE CHANGE:

## LOCAL KNOWLEDGE IN AFRICAN AMERICAN
## COMMUNITIES ON MARYLAND'S EASTERN SHORE[1]

*Christine D. Miller Hesed*

A NTHROPOGENIC CLIMATE CHANGE is arguably the biggest challenge facing the world today. Though capitalism and the free market are generally discussed as a solution to climate change by those working on global climate policy, a more populist discourse has begun to blame capitalism for being the root cause of the greenhouse gas emissions that accumulate and alter our global climate.[2] More specifically, this alternative discourse contends that the capitalist philosophy of neoliberalism, which argues that a growing free market will solve all social problems (a view often expressed by the aphorism "a rising tide lifts all boats"), has spurred on the emission of greenhouse gases with its requirement that the economy grow ever larger. The resulting anthropogenic climate change already affects communities and ecosystems around the world.[3]

While climate change will impact everyone, some are more vulnerable to those impacts than others.[4] Just as neoliberal economic policies have contributed to the changing climate, so also they bear some responsibility for the unequal distribution of vulnerability to climate change impacts. The neoliberal promise that all people would benefit from a growing economy has proven false; despite astounding economic growth over the past several hundred years, poverty remains a reality for millions in the United States and around the world, with the gap between the rich and the poor growing ever wider.[5] Unfortunately, it is those who are least responsible for causing climate change—those who have benefited least from neoliberal economic policies—that are positioned to bear the brunt of climate change impacts.[6]

Recognizing that climate change will now impact communities around the world regardless of mitigation measures taken in the future, many policymakers, from the international to the local level, are working on developing effective adaptation strategies. There are many different ways to adapt to climate change impacts,[7] but adaptation options are limited by previous adaptation decisions and the availability of resources.[8] Given that adaptation options are constrained, the development of climate change adaptation policies and programs at all levels will require trade-offs.[9] Determining how best to allocate limited adaptation resources between present and future needs, social and environmental goals, and among geographic areas, communities, and individuals is a daunting problem.

One way policymakers are approaching this problem is by identifying and prioritizing the regions and groups that are most vulnerable to climate change impacts.[10] In its most general sense, vulnerability can be defined as susceptibility to damage or harm from a disturbance.[11] It is often conceptualized as being composed of the risk of exposure to a disturbance, the sensitivity of the system to that disturbance, and the capacity of the system to adapt to the disturbance in such a way that the negative effects will be limited.[12]

Typically, measures of vulnerability involve the aggregation of already existing demographic data, such as income and race, which are then combined with spatial projections of risk to a given impact.[13] For example, the Social Vulnerability Index (SoVI) that is being used by the United States National Oceanic and Atmospheric

Administration (NOAA) to consider vulnerability to flooding in coastal areas is a metric based on thirty socioeconomic variables drawn from national data sets, primarily the United States Census.[14] Indices such as these are useful for facilitating general comparisons of the differential vulnerability between geographic units of various scales. However, their general reliance on available datasets limits the selection of input variables and makes it difficult to capture subtle, complex, or unique aspects of local vulnerability that are crucial for coping and survival.[15]

A more integrated approach that includes qualitative data is required to more fully understand these subtle and complex dimensions of local vulnerability.[16] Specifically, community attributes such as social networks, trust in the government, institutional capacity, access to resources, systems of meaning, and disaster readiness are difficult to quantify yet may strongly influence communities' susceptibility to loss and ability to adapt.[17] The form and dynamics of these community attributes will vary from community to community because they are significantly influenced by historical experiences and cultural knowledge.

Cultural knowledge is comprised of systems of beliefs and values that are shared by a group. These systems consist of both explicit statements about topics as well as underlying schemas, which are generic categories that are built up from cumulative experience and the application of language and cognition to produce explanations of phenomena and associated meanings and values.[18] These schemas are stored in memory[19] and may be filled with various specifics.[20] As such, cultural knowledge directly influences behavior and decision-making. Historical ecologist Carole Crumley explains:

> Each disturbance parameter [such as a given climate change impact] has a threshold or crisis level that, if reached, triggers some cultural response. Thresholds are determined by, transmitted through, and vary with the corpus of cultural knowledge possessed by a given society. Determining both the threshold at which a response will be generated and also

the particular response itself, cultural knowledge frames a society's resilience in the face of environmental (and other) disturbances.[21]

Applied to environmental issues, cultural knowledge is comprised of the explicit and implicit beliefs and values that a social group applies to understand nature and ecology.[22] All social groups (e.g., environmentalists, farmers, scientists, and African American church communities) apply their cultural knowledge to understand and value environmental changes, including climate change, which in turn affects how they respond to those changes.

The aggregate, quantitative, and top-down nature of typical vulnerability measures suggests that the cultural knowledge of those communities most vulnerable to climate change is being excluded from vulnerability assessment. We can characterize the excluded cultural knowledge as local ecological knowledge (LEK), and that which is being employed in the vulnerability indices as scientific ecological knowledge (SEK). Policymakers overwhelmingly value and employ SEK because it is perceived to be objective and apart from culture. Using SEK, policymakers derive environmental management practices from broad, general principles that are derived from scientific experimental studies. In contrast, LEK is knowledge that is rooted in direct experience with local ecosystems and is an integral part of local culture.[23] LEK helps to shape both the assessment of vulnerabilities and the behavioral responses of communities. LEK offers important insights about the local environment that may be overlooked by those considering only SEK. Especially in considering the impacts of climate change, it is important to incorporate LEK because locals are often able to notice changes in the local environment before scientists.[24] In addition, locals may also have knowledge of those aspects of vulnerability not easily captured by quantitative vulnerability indices.

There has been very little study of local vulnerability using systematic and formal qualitative research methods.[25] Here I present the results of a study that integrates qualitative and quantitative methods to elicit local cultural knowledge on climate change and vulnerability. Fieldwork (including participant observation, interviews, a questionnaire, workshops, and cognitive methods) was carried out from September 2012 through August 2014.[26] This study took place among African American communities on the Eastern Shore of the Chesapeake Bay that are particularly prone to flooding from sea-level rise.

## THE EASTERN SHORE OF THE CHESAPEAKE BAY

Due to the shifting of tectonic plates after the last glacial period,[27] the Eastern Shore of the Chesapeake Bay is sinking as sea level rises and is the fourth largest region vulnerable to sea-level rise along the Atlantic and Gulf Coasts of the United States.[28] This region has seen about 30 centimeters of sea-level rise over the past century[29] and is expected to see an additional 110 centimeters of sea-level rise this century,[30] which will cause the shores along the central portion of the Eastern Shore to move inland by at least five to ten kilometers.[31]

Recognizing the threat of climate change, the State of Maryland has developed a comprehensive mitigation and adaptation strategy that includes plans for addressing sea-level rise and corresponding flooding and storm surges. In 2007, Governor Martin O'Malley signed Executive Order 01.01.2007.07 to establish the Maryland Commission on Climate Change. In 2008 the commission presented its climate action plan, which describes how climate change will affect Maryland's citizens and natural resources, what Maryland can do to reduce greenhouse gas emissions, and what Maryland can do to adapt to climate change.[32] The Maryland Commission on Climate Change benefited from the input from environmentalist organizations and area ecologists. It did not, however, employ a process which solicited input or feedback from the communities most vulnerable to the impact of sea-level rise. Indeed, in four climate change response meetings I attended during the course of my fieldwork—a national conference on disaster preparedness (in January 2013), a Maryland Governor's meeting on greenhouse gas reduction (September 2013), a meeting of the Maryland Climate Communication Consortium on climate change education (October 2013), and a meeting of regional scholars and nonprofit organizations working together to protect marshes from climate change (April 2014) — I was both impressed by how well policymakers were working together with environmental conservation organizations and ecologists, as well as disappointed at the lack of representation of those most vulnerable to climate change and sea-level rise impacts.

Dispersed throughout the Eastern Shore are African American communities, many of which have existed since Emancipation. Established at a time of intense racial discrimination and with few resources, many of these communities are on marginal and flood-prone land.[33] The members of these communities have historically depended on their local ecosystems for their livelihoods. While some worked in agriculture, many more — including men, women, and children — were involved in seafood harvest and processing.[34] Such work allowed these communities to get by, but many remain resource poor. The dependence on local resources combined with their close proximity to wetland systems makes these communities particularly vulnerable to the impacts of sea-level rise. This vulnerability is further exacerbated by their relative lack of economic, social, and political resources.

## AFRICAN AMERICAN STUDY COMMUNITIES

To examine the local ecological knowledge about climate change, three communities were selected for inclusion in the study: the African American community in St. Michaels; the community composed of Smithville, Aireys, Fork Neck, and Liner's Road in Dorchester County; and the African American community in Crisfield. These communities share much in common, with histories that include slavery, struggles during Jim Crow, work in seafood processing, recent outmigration and unemployment due to lack of jobs, and the continued centrality of the local African American churches in community life. These communities also share a designation of "high vulnerability" as measured by SoVI.[35] Though these communities have successfully coped with periodic flooding in the past, recent socio-economic changes and demographic shifts suggest that these communities will face considerable hardship confronting the more frequent flooding caused by climate change in the future.

St. Michaels was founded on a narrow neck of land in Talbot County in 1677. With a single road connecting the town to the main peninsula, it is at risk of being cut off from the rest of the Eastern Shore during a flood.[36] After Maryland outlawed slavery in 1864, the vast majority of African Americans in St. Michaels worked catching and processing seafood or in the tomato packing houses.[37] Overharvesting of seafood and stricter government regulations by the mid-1960s led to the closing of the African American-owned Coulbourne and Jewett Seafood Packing Company. A maritime museum now stands where the packing house once stood.[38] The museum and a number of retail stores have brought a good deal of tourism to St. Michaels in recent years; however, the African American community receives little benefit from this industry. Rather, they are struggling to keep up with the increases in the cost of living, and many can no longer afford to eat or shop at the local businesses. The African American church, Union United Methodist Church (UMC), which was established in 1852, continues to serve as the spiritual and communal center for African Americans living in St. Michaels. Union UMC currently has between 40 and 50 active members who live in St. Michaels and the surrounding communities.

The four communities in Dorchester County are rural, located among the protected tidal wetlands of Blackwater National Wildlife Refuge, and already have standing water on roads and in their yards during high tides. These communities are unincorporated and too small to even be designated as villages. They therefore lack any form of local government; rather, the local churches serve as both the organizational and spiritual centers for these communities. The population of these communities has diminished from what it was in the past. In the 1960s, they may have had hundreds of residents, whereas today only a handful of homes remain occupied. Those who have left are dispersed as far as Baltimore, Maryland's Western Shore, and beyond, though many are living in nearby Cambridge. Despite the significant out-migration, those who remain in the area continue to travel back to their churches each Sunday, and those who have left the area continue to visit and provide some monetary contributions. Because the congregations are now quite elderly, the monetary contributions from those who have left to find employment is important for keeping the churches open. For example, at New Revived UMC in Smithville, only five of about twenty-five regular attendees are employed while the rest are retired or semi-retired.

The third community is the African American community in Crisfield, in Somerset County, which was flooded by Hurricane Sandy in October of 2012. Crisfield was founded in 1666 off of the Tangier Sound, which had an abundance of oysters. By the late nineteenth century, Crisfield was known as the "seafood capital of the world" because of the massive amounts of oysters that were harvested, packed, and sold from the town.[39] During the oyster boom, African Americans were employed in seafood packing houses and other local industries. The oyster boom was not to last, however. The seafood industry began to decline in the 1970s and the late 80s and early 90s saw the shutdown of two other local industries.[40] In interviews, African American community elders described how their parents had to travel as far away as Baltimore to earn money to send back to their family. Younger families in the community have doubts about whether they will be able to remain in the area. These economic challenges are exacerbated by tense race relations. In Crisfield, African American interviewees lowered their voices when describing the injustices and discrimination they continue to face. As in the other communities, local African American churches serve as the community center, though in Crisfield one has closed and others have greatly diminished attendance as a result of outmigration.

## THE IMPORTANCE OF LOCAL ECOLOGICAL KNOWLEDGE

Despite the hardship endured by these African American communities, they have persevered and even thrived. Discrimination in the past meant that these communities had to be largely self-sufficient in facing whatever challenges came their way, whether economic hardship or flooding. Thus, these communities have accumulated a wealth of knowledge about adapting to changes in their local environment—including the social, economic, and ecological changes. Based on my years of research among these communities, in this section I offer three arguments for why their local ecological knowledge should be included in vulnerability assessment and adaptation planning for the region. In short, these communities have additional information about their local vulnerability, have more experience living in and adapting to their particular landscape, and have different perspectives and values that need to be included in any decision-making that involves the distribution of limited resources.

### ADDITIONAL INFORMATION ON LOCAL VULNERABILITY

While quantitative vulnerability indices are useful for identifying vulnerable regions, local ecological knowledge is needed to understand the way social and ecological factors interact to affect vulnerability at the local level. At a workshop in each of the three study communities in 2013, participants were each given a stack of thirty climate change words (which were previously generated by a similar African American communities on the Eastern Shore) and instructed to sort those words into two or more piles such that words that were more similar would be together in a pile, while words that were different would be in different piles. After the workshops, the individual pile-sorts were aggregated for each community, which transformed individual cognitive knowledge to community cultural knowledge. The aggregated pile-sorts for each community were analyzed quantitatively with multidimensional scaling (MDS) and cluster analysis and interpreted qualitatively with assistance from the community members.[41]

Exploring cultural knowledge with this mixed-methods approach yielded some striking results. First, we found that in all three communities the climate change words were organized in three main groups that corresponded with the scientific vulnerability components of risk, sensitivity, and adaptive capacity. This finding was somewhat surprising; since study participants have had very little to no science training, we did not expect their thinking to align so well with the scientific model of vulnerability. Even more interesting and important, however, was a second main finding: the communities differed in the way in which they categorized specific social and ecological factors among the risk, sensitivity, and adaptive capacity groups. For example, St. Michaels and Crisfield included the term "roads" in the risk category, while Dorchester County categorized "roads" with other terms for adaptive capacity. While participants in Dorchester County know which local roads will flood under different conditions and view use of alternative routes for temporary relocation as a key adaptive response, St. Michaels views roads primarily as a risk because they could be cut off if their main road were to flood. Likewise, Crisfield included roads in the risk category because, following Hurricane Sandy, roads in predominantly African American neighborhoods remained flooded for days longer than other streets because the city had failed to maintain floodgates in those areas. The three study communities also categorized the terms communication, family members, food, God, knowledge, self-preservation, and shelters differently. Whether or not each of these terms was viewed primarily as a risk, sensitivity, or adaptive capacity in a community depended on the accumulated experience of the community in adapting to their local environment. Such information is highly relevant for understanding local vulnerability, but impossible to capture with top-down, quantitative vulnerability indices alone.

EXPERIENCE ADAPTING TO THE SOCIAL-ECOLOGICAL LANDSCAPE

The results of a questionnaire conducted in the spring of 2014 suggest that those in a position to make decisions about how resources will be allocated for climate change adaptation on the Eastern Shore have far less experience with its social and ecological landscape than the vulnerable African American communities. This questionnaire was designed to compare experiences with flooding and views on vulnerability, adaptation, and justice. It was then distributed to two groups: 260 questionnaires were distributed by postal mail to 24 African American church communities that are at risk of flooding with a rise in sea-level of 10 feet or less, and 345 questionnaires were emailed to local, county, and state policymakers and to environmentalists who work on climate change issues on the Eastern Shore.[42] Responses to the questionnaire indicated that while 100% of the African American church respondents live on the Eastern Shore, only 57% of policymaker and environmentalist questionnaire respondents do. Of those that live on the Eastern Shore, the mean number of years policymakers and environmentalists have resided there is 33, while African American community members have resided on the Eastern Shore for an average of 56 years.

Granted, it is important to note that the above numbers are not based on a random sample; while surveys were sent to all the African American churches on the Eastern Shore that are at risk of flooding (with the exception of one church that elected not to participate), distribution to policymakers and environmentalists was based on a purposive sample.[43] Nevertheless, ethnographic data suggests that the results of the survey are representative of African American church communities and policymakers and environmentalists working on climate change adaptation on the Eastern Shore. Nearly all of the African American community members interviewed reported having lived the majority of their lives on the Eastern Shore, often having spent only a couple years working elsewhere before returning. In contrast, many of the environmentalists and policymakers I talked with grew up in a different part of Maryland or in a different state. Some had moved to the Eastern Shore quite recently, and some did not live on the Eastern Shore at all, though their work pertained to it.

Experiential knowledge of the local social and ecological land-scape in the African American communities has accumulated over the generations. Living in flood-prone areas, these communities have been dealing with flooding for decades and possess a store of practical wisdom about preparing for, coping with, and recovering after a local flooding event. For example, community members in Dorchester County as well as Crisfield know what can be salvaged and what has to be thrown out after a flood, and members of all three communities know where to find resources (food, water, and shelter) in their community. Study participants at all three sites also have a detailed knowledge about the strengths and limitations of members of their communities. They know, for example, who can be counted on for a ride or accurate emergency information, as well as who will need to be alerted to an oncoming storm or given assistance during a flood.

Key to the adaptive capacity of these communities is their local churches. In addition to serving the spiritual and social needs of the community, the church attends to material needs. For example, Union UMC in St. Michaels helps to support an area food bank and pays the rent, electricity, or medicine bills up to twice a year for those who call requesting assistance. The churches also serve as shelters during hurricanes, and if a storm damages a church community, other churches will often send them aid. For example, Union UMC sent boxes of supplies to Crisfield after Hurricane Sandy hit in 2012, and members of New Revived UMC remember receiving bleach and other recovery supplies from other congregations after their church was flooded by Hurricane Isabel in 2003. The churches also provide meals after special services on Sundays, sending boxes of leftover food home with parishioners and taking meals to those who were unable to attend because of ill health or immobility. Such meals are undoubtedly helpful in these communities where many are elderly and on a fixed income.

Policymakers and environmentalists who have little to no experience adapting to flooding or other disturbances on the Eastern Shore will not be aware of the importance of various local resources—such as the local churches—for adaptation. Lacking a nuanced understanding of local networks and resources, these policymakers and environmentalists may enact top-down adaptation policies that, at best, fail to utilize local resources to their full potential and, at worst, are maladaptive.

DIFFERENT PERSPECTIVES AND VALUES

In addition to possessing knowledge and experience to complement that of the policymakers, African American study communities have different perspectives and values and should, therefore, be included in the decision-making process for the distribution of limited adaptation resources. When asked about their level of concern for their current home flooding in the questionnaire described above, 72% of the policymakers and environmentalists responded that they were "not concerned." In contrast, only 18% of the African American church community members reported being "not concerned," while 33% reported being "somewhat concerned" and 49% reported being "very concerned." This remarkable difference in the degree to which policymakers and African American community members are concerned for their own homes will likely affect the way in which each group would prioritize climate change adaptation strategies.

Furthermore, while those trained in policymaking generally utilize some sort of cost-benefit analysis when making decisions (a practice that aligns well with neoliberal capitalism), local communities may have alternative valuation systems that would rank monetarily inefficient options higher because of some other criteria. Indeed, in her book exploring the role of community and culture in economic development, Meredith Ramsay argues that the predominant local values in Crisfield were shaped by the requirements of a subsistence economy, a poor population, paternalistic social structures, and historical experience. These values led the majority of the town to disapprove of profit maximization and to refuse to allow Crisfield to be transformed into a growth machine despite intense economic distress in the 1980s.[44]

Negotiating a resilient adaptation strategy will involve decisions on how to distribute costs and benefits in the present. Communities will have to balance management for adapting to known risks with the maintenance of flexibility for responding to unknown future risks. Even if highly robust and repeatable methods were developed to determine individual and community vulnerability to disturbance, making decisions about who should bear the costs and reap the benefits of adaptation strategies would still not be a straightforward process. Stakeholders will differ in their perspectives, values, and adaptation priorities; therefore, even if vulnerable community members did not have useful and relevant knowledge and experience, it would still be important to employ inclusive, democratic processes for climate adaptation decision-making.

## THE ROLE OF SCIENCE AND NUMBERS

Of course, arguing that local knowledge should be included and given a larger role in vulnerability assessment and adaptation planning does not preclude the application of the generalized scientific and technical knowledge that policymakers and environmentalists have to offer. Often these professionals have had access to more education and training, as well as exposure to a greater diversity of ideas. Scientific and statistical data is important for understanding the probabilities of risk and the trade-offs involved in various adaptation scenarios. Such data needs to be communicated clearly to the public so that they can incorporate that information into their judgments. Cass R. Sunstein argues that people's intuitions about risks are highly unreliable because they rely on mental shortcuts, are subject to social influences, and neglect to consider trade-offs.[45] Thus Sunstein argues that science, and particularly quantitative measures such as cost-benefit analysis, can help to correct mistaken judgments by providing information about general trends and highlighting the trade-offs inherent in various policy decisions.

Despite the usefulness of quantitative measures, they are not sufficient for resolving policy issues, which ultimately come down to what outcomes are most valued. Cost-benefit analysis attempts to objectively compare policy options by putting all outcomes in dollar amounts. While useful for making comparisons, this method is problematic because it requires putting a dollar amount on things like lives and environmental health. The value of such things is subjective, and it is therefore important to include local communities in adaptation decision-making so that they can voice their values and preferences, which may differ considerably from those of policymakers, as discussed above. Thus, the top-down modeling of vulnerability is useful for bringing in statistical and regional factors relevant for vulnerability, while tapping into cultural knowledge is useful for identifying things that are highly relevant at the local level, but which the models cannot capture. They are complementary.

## RECOMMENDATIONS

The international community has recognized that not all countries will be affected to the same extent by climate change, with those who have contributed least to emissions bearing the brunt of climate change impacts. Similarly, within the United States, those who have contributed least to emissions are most vulnerable to its impacts. Creating environmentally minded economic policies that are responsive to the unique and dynamic conditions in different communities is a difficult yet necessary task. We have seen how the uniform application of Marxist ideas under the communist reigns of Stalin and Mao resulted in human suffering, environmental degradation, and cultural loss. The current emphasis on SEK in assessing vulnerability is also problematic because it excludes some stakeholders and forms of knowledge from the decision-making process,[46] thereby perpetuating the structures of injustice that contribute to disparate vulnerability. Homi Bhabha theorizes that dominant ideology can be transcended in a "third space" where dichotomous classifications do not apply. He writes that:

> The language of critique is effective... to the extent to which
> it overcomes the given grounds of opposition and opens up a
> space of translation: a place of hybridity, figuratively speak-
> ing, where the construction of a political object that is new,
> *neither the one nor the other*, properly alienates our political
> expectations, and changes, as it must, the very forms of our
> recognition of the moment of politics.[47]

Thus, it is in moving beyond the opposition between SEK and LEK
that decision-makers and those most vulnerable to climate change
will be able to come together to co-construct adaptation policies that
will result in a more just distribution of environmental costs and
benefits and an overall decrease in vulnerability.

As I am writing this chapter, the Maryland Commission on
Climate Change released its final report for 2015, which calls on the
state to reduce its greenhouse gas emissions by 40% by 2030, while
also developing the economy and creating jobs.[48] The report also
recommends that the action goals for 2030 be expanded to include
increasing the resilience of the most vulnerable communities. The
specific process to be used in addressing the needs of the most vulnerable communities is not laid out in the report. Based on my work
on the Eastern Shore, I would recommend that they make use of local
knowledge in their adaptation planning, and I offer three suggestions.

First, democratic processes of decision-making need to be
enhanced to incorporate the concerns of the most vulnerable communities. Just as environmental advocates and business interests have
been included in meetings to plan for adaptation to climate change,
so, too, the particular needs and values of vulnerable communities
need to be represented at adaptation planning meetings. This representation could take various forms. In some cases, members of vulnerable communities could be invited to attend adaptation planning
meetings; however, for such participation to be meaningful those
community members should be informally briefed on the issues to
be discussed ahead of time so that they have a chance to consider the
implications for their particular community. In addition, informal

briefings ahead of meetings may help prepare community members to follow the technocratic jargon at the meeting itself, though policymakers should seek to avoid such jargon as much as possible.

Second, it may not always be possible to include members of vulnerable communities in adaptation planning meetings, so it is important that policymakers themselves are educated about the needs of vulnerable communities. While some information can be gained from reports, policymakers would gain a much better understanding of local situations from fieldtrips and the establishments of sustained relationships with members of vulnerable communities. Again, the form of these fieldtrips and relationships may vary according to particular circumstances, but the local churches provide a number of promising possibilities. For example, policymakers could coordinate with local pastors to arrange informal meetings with community members. Gathering over food is a time-tested way of building relationships, and perhaps in some cases a sort of pen pal correspondence could be established so that policymakers and vulnerable community members could keep each other informed of what is happening in their respective spheres. Building relationships between policymakers and vulnerable community members will result in better-informed policymaking and strengthen the adaptive capacity of the local communities by giving them direct access to someone with additional information and tools.

Finally, policymakers should seek to empower local, non-governmental community organizations. State-wide policy should be crafted so as to support greater autonomy at the local level, while still providing technical and scientific information in a consultancy capacity.

In this chapter I have used a case study with African American communities on the Eastern Shore to illustrate what can be gained by including local knowledge in vulnerability assessment and adaptation planning. In essence, evidence I presented here suggests that enhancing democratic processes and actively engaging underserved communities in grassroots efforts for adaptation planning is key for reducing vulnerability among those who are most vulnerable. In addition, adaptation policy at the regional level should seek to support greater autonomy at the level of the local community, while still providing technical and scientific information in an advisory role.

## NOTES

1    This research was financially supported in part by a grant from the NOAA Climate and Societal Interactions — Coasts Program (NA11OAR4310113). While conducting this research I was supported by an EPA STAR Fellowship (FP—91749201-0). I would like to thank Michael Paolisso for his role in project development and data analysis, Kyle Miller Hesed for his assistance in the field, and the African American communities of St. Michaels, Dorchester County, and Crisfield for their participation in this study.

2    W. Neil Adger et al., "Advancing a Political Ecology of Global Environmental Discourses. Development and Change," 32, no. 4 (2001): 681–715; Hans Baer, "Global Warming as a By-product of the Capitalist Treadmill of Production and Consumption — The Need for an Alternative Global System," *Australian Journal of Anthropology* 19, no. 1 (2008): 58–62.

3    IPCC, *Climate Change 2007: Impacts, Adaptation and Vulnerability. Contribution of Working Group II to the Fourth Assessment Report of the Intergovernmental Panel on Climate Change,* ed. M. L. Parry, et al. (Cambridge: Cambridge University Press, 2007).

4    IPCC, "Summary for Policymakers," in *Climate Change 2014: Impacts, Adaptation, and Vulnerability,* ed. C. B. Field et al. (Cambridge and New York: Cambridge University Press, 2014), 1-32.

5    Carmen DeNavas-Walt and Bernadette D. Proctor, *Income and Poverty in the United States: 2014, Current Population Reports, U.S. Census Bureau* (Washington, DC: U.S. Government Printing Office, 2015) 60-252; OECD, *In It Together: Why Less Inequality Benefits All* (Paris: OECD Publishing, 2015); United Nations, *The Millennium Development Goals Report* (New York: United Nations, 2015).

6    Shirley J. Fiske et al., *Changing the Atmosphere: Anthropology and Climate Change: Final report of the AAA Global Climate Change Task Force* (Arlington, VA: American Anthropological Association,

2014); IPCC, "Summary for Policymakers"; Jason Samson et al., "Geographic disparities and moral hazards in the predicted impacts of climate change on human populations," *Global Ecology and Biogeography* 20, no. 4 (2011): 532–44.

7   Thomas F. Thornton and Nadia Manasfi, "Adaptation—Genuine and Spurious: Demystifying Adaptation Processes in Relation to Climate Change," *Environment and Society: Advances in Research* 1 (2010): 132-55.

8   IPCC, "Summary for Policymakers."

9   Jouni Paavola, "Science and Social Justice in the Governance of Adaptation to Climate Change," *Environmental Politics* 17, no. 4 (2008): 644–59.

10  Nick Brooks et al., "The determinants of vulnerability and adaptive capacity at the national level and the implications for adaptation," *JGEC Global Environmental Change* 15, no. 2 (2005): 151–63; Samson et al., "Geographic disparities."

11  Donald R. Nelson, et al., "Adaptation to Environmental Change: Contributions to a Resilience Framework," *Annual Review of Environment and Resources* 32 (2007): 395–419.

12  W. Neil Adger, "Vulnerability," *Global Environmental Change—Human and Policy Dimensions* 16, no. 3 (2006): 268–81; Jörn Birkmann, "Risk and vulnerability indicators at different scales: Applicability, usefulness and policy implications," *Environmental Hazards* 7, no. 1 (2007): 20–31; Susan L. Cutter et al., "A place-based model for understanding community resilience to natural disasters," *JGEC Global Environmental Change* 18, no. 4 (2008): 598–606.

13  W. Neil Adger et al., *New Indicators of Vulnerability and Adaptive Capacity* (Norwich, UK: Tyndall Centre for Climate Change Research, 2004); Md. Nasif Ahsan and Jeroen Warner, "The socio-economic vulnerability index: A pragmatic approach for assessing climate change led risks—A case study in the south-western coastal Bangladesh," *International Journal of Disaster Risk Reduction* 8 (2014): 32–49; Brooks et al., "Determinants of vulnerability"; Omar D. Cardona, *Indicators of Disaster Risk and Risk Management: Summary Report* (Washington, DC: Inter-American Development Bank, 2005); Natainia Lummen and Fumihiko Yamada, "Implementation

of an integrated vulnerability and risk assessment model," *Natural Hazards* 73, no. 2 (2014): 1085–1117; South Pacific Applied Geoscience Commission and United Nations Environment Programme, *Building Resilience in SIDS: The Environmental Vulnerability Index* (Suva, Fiji: South Pacific Applied Geoscience Commission, 2005).

14    Susan L. Cutter and Daniel P. Morath, "The evolution of the Social Vulnerability Index (SoVI)," in *Measuring Vulnerability to Natural Hazards*, 2nd ed., ed. Jörn Birkmann (Bonn: United Nations University Press, 2013), 304–21; Susan L. Cutter, "The Vulnerability of Science and the Science of Vulnerability," *Annals of the Association of American Geographers* 93, no. 1 (2003): 1–12; "Social Vulnerability Index (SOVI)," *National Oceanic and Atmospheric Association* (http://coast.noaa.gov/digitalcoast/data/sovi).

15    Birkmann, "Risk and vulnerability factors"; Susan L. Cutter et al., *Social Vulnerability to Climate Variability Hazards: A Review of the Literature* (Columbia, SC: University of South Carolina, 2009); Hallie Eakin and Amy Lynd Luers, "Assessing the Vulnerability of Social-Environmental Systems," *Annual Review of Environment and Resources* 31 (2006): 365–94.

16    Birkmann, "Risk and vulnerability factors"; Cutter, "The Vulnerability of Science"; Eakin and Luers, "Assessing the Vulnerability"; Carrie Furman et al., "Social justice in climate services: Engaging African American farmers in the American South," *Climate Risk Management* 2 (2014): 11–25.

17    Cutter et al., *Social Vulnerability.*

18    Dorothy Holland and Naomi Quinn, *Cultural Models in Language and Thought* (New York: Cambridge University Press, 1987).

19    Claudia Strauss and Naomi Quinn, *A Cognitive Theory of Cultural Meaning* (Cambridge, UK: Cambridge University Press, 1997).

20    Roy D'Andrade, *The Development of Cognitive Anthropology* (New York: Cambridge University Press, 1995).

21    Carole L. Crumley, "Historical Ecology: A Multidimensional Ecological Orientation," in *Historical Ecology: Cultural Knowledge and Changing Landscapes,* ed. C. L. Crumley (Santa Fe: School of American Research Press, 1994), 10.

22    William Cronon, ed., *Uncommon Ground: Rethinking the Human*

*Place in Nature* (New York: W.W. Norton & Co., 1996).

23 David Craig Griffith, *The Estuary's Gift: An Atlantic Coast Cultural Biography* (University Park, PA: Pennsylvania State University Press, 1999).

24 Larry Merculieff, "Linking Traditional Knowledge and Wisdom to Ecosystem Based Approaches in Research and Management: Supporting a Marginalized Way of Knowing," in *Ethnobiology and Biocultural Diversity*, ed. J.R. Stepp et al. (Athens, GA: International Society of Ethnobiology and University of Georgia Press, 2002), 523–31.

25 Fiske et al.; Carla Roncoli et al., "Fielding Climate Change in Cultural Anthropology," in *Anthropology and Climate Change: From Encounters to Actions*, ed. S.A. Crate and M. Nuttall (Walnut Creek, CA: Left Coast Press, 2009), 87–115.

26 Christine D. Miller Hesed and Michael Paolisso, "Cultural knowledge and local vulnerability in African American communities," *Nature Climate Change* 5, no. 7 (2015): 683–87.

27 Carl H. Hobbs III, "Geological history of Chesapeake Bay, USA," *Quaternary Science Reviews* 23, no. 5-6 (2004): 641–61; George F. Oertel and Anthony M. Foyle, "Drainage Displacement by Sea-Level Fluctuation at the Outer Margin of the Chesapeake Seaway," *Journal of Coastal Research* 11, no. 3 (1995): 583.

28 James G. Titus and Charlie Richman, "Maps of Lands Vulnerable to Sea Level Rise: Modeled Elevations Along the US Atlantic and Gulf Coasts," *Climate Research* 18 (2001): 205–28.

29 James G. Titus and Elizabeth M. Strange, *Background Documents Supporting Climate Change Science Program Synthesis and Assessment Product 4.1: Coastal Elevations and Sensitivity to Sea Level Rise* (Washington, DC: U.S. EPA, 2008).

30 Donald F. Boesch et al., *Updating Maryland's Sea-Level Rise Projections* (Cambridge, MD: University of Maryland Center for Environmental Science, 2013).

31 Titus and Richman, "Maps of Lands."

32 Maryland Commission on Climate Change, "Climate Action Plan," *State of Maryland*, 2008 (http://www.mde.maryland.gov/programs/ Air/ClimateChange/Documents/www.mde.state.md.us/assets/

document/Air/ClimateChange/News/2007_Interim_Report.pdf).

33 Margaret L. Andersen, "Discovering the Past/Considering the Future: Lessons from the Eastern Shore," in *A History of African Americans of Delaware and Maryland's Eastern Shore*, ed. C. C. Marks (Wilmington, DE: Delaware Heritage Commission, 1998), 101-21; Roland C. McConnell, "The Black Experience in Maryland: 1634–1900," in *The Old Line State: A History of Maryland*, ed. M.L. Radoff (Annapolis: Maryland Hall of Records Commission, 1971), 405–32.

34 John R. Wennersten, *Maryland's Eastern Shore: A Journey in Time and Place* (Centreville, MD: Tidewater Publishers, 1992).

35 "Sea Level Rise and Coastal Flooding Impacts," *National Oceanic and Atmospheric Association*, 2014 (http://coast.noaa.gov/slr/).

36 Bernard Demczuk, "Unionville: Race, Time, Place and Memory in Talbot County, Maryland, 1634-1892," (Ph.D dissertation, George Washington University, 2008).

37 Natalie Tyler, ed., *Lift Every Voice: Echoes from the Black Community on Maryland's Eastern Shore* (Wye Mills, MD: Chesapeake College Press, 1999).

38 Bill Robinson and Eric Jodlbauer, "Elwood Small Jewett," 2011 (http://www.umes.edu/125/Content.aspx?id=38154).

39 John R. Wennersten, *The Oyster Wars of Chesapeake Bay* (Centreville, Md.: Tidewater Publishers, 1981); Woodrow T. Wilson, *History of Crisfield and Surrounding Areas on Maryland's Eastern Shore* (Baltimore: Gateway Press, 1973).

40 Jason Rhodes, *Crisfield: The First Century* (Charleston, SC: Arcadia, 2006).

41 For more details on these methods, see Miller Hesed and Paolisso, "Cultural knowledge."

42 The policymakers and environmentalists group includes responses from those working in an environmental research or advocacy organization, government employees, and elected representatives. More specifically, 27% of the policymakers and environmentalists group conduct environmental research or work for a non-governmental environmental advocacy organization, 49% are government employees, and 21% are elected representatives. The response rate

was 39% for African American church communities and 22% for policymakers and environmentalists.

43  Greg Guest, "Sampling and Selecting Participants in Field Research," in *Handbook of Methods in Cultural Anthropology*, ed. H.R. Bernard and C. C. Gravlee (Lanham, MD: Rowman & Littlefield, 2015), 185–214.

44  Meredith Ramsay, *Community, Culture, and Economic Development: Continuity and Change in Two Small Southern Towns* (Albany: State University of New York Press, 2013).

45  Cass R. Sunstein, *Risk and Reason: Safety, Law, and the Environment* (Cambridge, UK; New York: Cambridge University Press, 2002).

46  Michael Paolisso et al., "Climate Change, Justice, and Adaptation among African American Communities in the Chesapeake Bay Region," *Weather, Climate, and Society* 4, no. 1 (2012): 34–47.

47  Homi Bhabha, *The Location of Culture* (New York: Routledge, 1994), 25.

48  Maryland Commission on Climate Change, "Final Report," *State of Maryland*, 2015 (http://www.mde.state.md.us/programs/Marylander/Documents/MCCC/Publications/Reports/MCCC2015FinalReport.pdf).

## ᚦ 12 ᚦ

# WHY MOVEMENTS MATTER MOST:

## A CONVERSATION WITH THE NEW MATERIALISM[1]

## *Joerg Rieger*

BOTH PROCESS THINKERS AND NEW MATERIALISTS understand the limits of philosophical idealism and the need to focus on material reality in non-deterministic ways. As new appreciation for the transformative potential of material reality is emerging in various fields, this chapter will focus on the contributions made by material reality as shaped in the worlds of social and religious movements.

The matters of religion and religious experience are made up of multiple components. In the study of religion, and even in some theological approaches, it is increasingly becoming clear that religious experience is never merely a matter of ideas and doctrines, nor is it merely a matter of disembodied individual experiences or mindless practices. Crude idealism, which focuses on abstract ideas, is insufficient for the study of religion, if not misguided. The same can be said of crude materialism, which focuses on matter in a deterministic way, although religion and theology have less frequently been studied from this perspective.

Nevertheless, these approaches still have plenty of followers. At one extreme are those who seek to explain religion and religious experience in terms of certain versions of the history of ideas. It is not only graduate students of religious studies who talk as if modern religion, for instance, and indeed modernity itself, had been invented singlehandedly by the ideas of philosophers like Immanuel Kant or theologians like Friedrich Schleiermacher. On the whole, variations of idealism are still prominent not only in the study of theology, where anti-materialism has found one of its homes, but also in various approaches to religion and religious experience.

At the other extreme are those who seek to explain religion and religious experience in crude materialist terms. In newly emerging fields like neurotheology, for instance, religion and religious experience are explained in terms of the function of the temporal lobes of the brain.[2] Crude political or economic materialism, seeking to explain religion and religious experiences in terms of political or economic structures, also has a few remaining adherents, but those approaches are mostly conjured up as ghosts of the past by anti-materialists who are keen to deny any impact of politics or economics on religion and religious experience.

In this context, new materialist approaches broadly conceived are helpful because they reclaim elements of the long-suppressed dialectical legacy of certain forms of materialism (and in some cases certain kinds of Hegelian idealism) for the study of religion and religious experience. At stake is not the abortive discussion of whether material or ideal factors are all-determinative, but how these factors influence and shape each other. While such approaches seem reasonable enough — even commonsensical — it is surprising that they still face substantial opposition, particularly in the realm of religious studies and theology. The so-called new materialisms are not the only approaches that reclaim the dialectic, but they are original proposals that deserve a closer look at a time when dialectics has faded from view in much of the study of religion and theology.

The way mental illness is being discussed helps exemplify the various positions. For the purposes of the following discussion, depression may serve as our example. Crude materialists argue that depression is best understood as chemical imbalances of the brain. As a result, it is treated with medications that help regulate these imbalances. The multi-billion dollar pharmaceutical industry profits from the prominence of this approach. Idealists, on the other hand, identify depression as located in the realm of ideas. For them, the treatment has to do with therapies that help depressed people think differently. The so-called power of positive thinking that is promoted by certain therapists as well as by a myriad of self-help books exemplifies a set of approaches that have proven to be quite lucrative as well. Each of these approaches has some benefits. Medication has done a lot of good for people suffering from depression, and positive thinking has saved others from self-destructive behavior.[3] Nevertheless, something is still missing here.

Better results are often achieved when there are overlaps between the various approaches. If they can afford it, people suffering from depression are often treated with both medication and the tools of psychological counseling. Moreover, the latter is not always based on pure idealism. A psychoanalyst, for instance, tries to figure out some of the material causes of depression. A behavioral therapist, to give another example, pays close attention to the effects of simple verbal instructions. Nevertheless, from a dialectical materialist position, a deeper analysis of the relation of material and ideal factors is required.

In order to get to the core of the problem of depression and to understand it from a dialectical materialist perspective, it is not sufficient to analyze what ideas are at work in a person's mind or what chemical imbalances are at work in the brain, although these things are important. Depression needs to be understood in terms of the intersection of mind, chemistry, and outside factors, reflecting on how these things mutually influence each other. The new materialisms in particular would insist that we cannot expect to find a simple determinism either way. Yet these reflections, which exemplify some of the concerns addressed by new materialists, are still too narrow because they often fail to consider broader structures and flows of power.

A very promising new approach to depression, developed from the perspective of pastoral counseling, exemplifies the broader perspective that is required. Here, depression is analyzed in terms of its occurrence under the conditions of neoliberal capitalism. This means that depression needs to be understood not only in terms of personal and social developments—both ideal and material—but also in terms of broader flows of power in a capitalist world. Large-scale economic factors, for instance, make a difference not only in politics and finance but also in the world of culture, religion, and ideas, as well as at the emotional level of individuals. Emphasizing these connections does not need to imply determinism. This kind of analysis, which exemplifies some of the implications of new materialist thinking even if it has not adopted that name, leads to different conclusions and to a different kind of therapy. As Bruce Rogers-Vaughn, a pioneer of this approach, has pointed out, depression is not only linked to capitalism, it can also help subvert it.[4] In other words, the concern of approaches that take material reality more seriously in dialectical fashion is never merely to analyze, but also to change, conditions. This is what Marx realized early on, in his famous *Theses on Feuerbach*.[5]

Based on these observations, I seek to explore three questions in this chapter: What might be the roadblocks that prevent materialist approaches from taking a hold in the study of religion and religious experience? What is the contribution of the new materialisms in this context? And where might we need to go beyond the discussions presented by the new materialists?

## FIRST, WHAT MIGHT BE THE ROADBLOCKS FOR MATERIALIST APPROACHES?

It is both the benefit and the burden of materialist approaches that they introduce a certain complexity or even messiness into our understanding of religion and religious experience. Complexity can be a burden because it implies more work for the scholar and, at times, a certain inconclusiveness that some people may find frustrating. By comparison, definitions of religion and religious experience in terms of ideas tend to be relatively succinct and orderly. In addition, defining religion and religious experience in terms of ideas allows for relatively clear-cut identifications of certain kinds of religious orthodoxy, which seek to determine what (or who) is legitimate and what (or who) is not. In the still predominantly conservative cultural and political climate in the United States, such orthodoxy continues to enjoy high currency, although the situation seems to be changing slowly. However, the world of ideas also tends to be preferred in more liberal systematic theologies, as it allows greater orderliness and control over the subject matter.[6]

It is interesting to note that crude and deterministic materialisms tend to display characteristics similar to idealism, in that they appear to be succinct and orderly. If religious experience can be explained in terms of certain functions of the brain, for instance, the complexity and the messiness that is characteristic of religious experiences can be held at bay. Likewise, if religious experience is merely a function of politics or economics, there is no need to spend much time contemplating the complex realities of religion; one can then either reject it or embrace it for what it is. The attractiveness of non-dialectical methods endures for good reasons.

Perhaps the most misguided roadblock for materialism, which finds expression in popular discourse but is not "off-limits" in academic discourse, is the common complaint that people are "too materialistic." This appears to be a valid critique of life under the conditions of capitalism, but it is ultimately just another version of idealism, as the implication is that people are unduly driven by certain material concerns. Desires for a bigger house or for a new car and more money seem to come at the expense of spiritual concerns like ideals or beliefs. Here, whatever is considered to be material is bad and whatever is considered to be spiritual is good, and there is a simple choice that can be made by individuals as to whether they want to care about material or spiritual things. Several issues are overlooked: What if the desire for a new car is not merely a desire for material but also for spiritual matters, in that it promises safety, love, and comfort? The advertising industry has long figured this out. Moreover, what if religion is not the antithesis to what is material in general but provides a different way of being material and engaging material reality? In the Abrahamic religious traditions, for instance, there are strands that embody precisely this insight, teaching us that the problem is not material reality as such, but the kind of material reality that is embraced: is it that of the prophets and of Jesus or that of the successive empires of history?

To be sure, in many of the more recent approaches to the study of religion complexity is acknowledged to some degree when scholars deal with multiple layers of ideas and texts or when scholars come to think of religion in terms of material embodiments, practices, or historical and cultural dynamics. This is a welcome development. Even the various postmodern turns to language and to culture have integrated some understanding of the material qualities of linguistic and cultural phenomena, informed by thinkers like Michel Foucault and his notion of discourse, which combines both ideal and material components.

What is still missing for the most part, however, are the kinds of complexities that include the broader structural power dynamics that have been the subject of dialectical materialisms since Karl Marx. The study of material embodiments and practices is often engaged without wondering where the tensions are and what drives these things. Moreover, Foucaultian discourse analysis is frequently performed without taking a look at who benefits from the flows of power and who does not. In some cases, even class identities are studied without an analysis of power, for instance when scholars investigate practices of working class religion without considering the influences of the ruling class and of capitalism.[7]

The benefit of overcoming the various roadblocks mentioned above is that dialectical materialisms are better equipped to take seriously the complexity of religion and religious experience, as they are receptive to a range of both ideal and material forces in the formation of religious experience. In this way, they are addressing the many criticisms made of the "tunnel-vision" of crude materialisms.

Nevertheless, this is not the end of our problems, as the challenge is bigger yet. Additional roadblocks emerge when any of these materialisms raise the question of power in the formation of religion and religious experience. Naming the dominant powers invariably leads to tensions and pushback, as these powers usually prefer to operate unconsciously and resist being analyzed for good reasons. If corporate advertising, for instance, is seen not only as spreading information or enticement to buy certain products but also as shaping people's most intimate sensitivities and preferences, new questions emerge that raise some concern. Those kinds of questions are not commonly addressed when religious experience is discussed. In my own work, I have encountered some of the fiercest resistance whenever I argue that religious experiences are shaped by various influences and forces, including monetary and political interests.

The benefit of dialectical materialisms is that they remind us that religious experience is not only complex and shaped by various ideal and material influences; it is also shaped by particular interests and powers whose effectiveness increases the more they operate underground and out of sight. This is what both crude materialists and idealists are missing. The most interesting materialisms insist on naming these powers, and this is where the resistance against materialism is most pronounced. In most (if not all) historical periods, the dominant powers that shape religious experience seek to ensure that they are not found out, pushing back against any approach that would question the pristine nature of religious experience.

For the Romans in the imperial period, for instance, it was more advantageous to believe in the gods sustaining the empire than in the empire sustaining belief in the gods. As a result, questioning these gods by pointing out their constructed nature amounted to treason. The early Christians who raised such questions and talked openly about idolatry, like the apostle Paul,[8] were persecuted and killed. In capitalism, it is more advantageous to believe in an invisible hand sustaining the neoliberal free market than in the neoliberal market sustaining the belief in an invisible hand, and, thus, those who raise questions about the genuine nature of this belief are quickly ostracized or simply ignored. To be sure, being ignored may be preferable to being persecuted and killed, but the end result is the erasure of opposition and thus the phenomena are not completely dissimilar.

## SECOND, WHAT IS THE CONTRIBUTION OF THE NEW MATERIALISMS TO THE STUDY OF RELIGION AND THEOLOGY?

The new materialisms are of interest because they take up the dialectical heritage and thus help us broaden our investigations both in religious studies and in theology. They analyze how certain material factors (other than the ideal and crude material ones commonly studied) shape religious experience. This critical perspective leads to a constructive one that has often been overlooked, as religion can now also be examined in terms of the difference it makes to material reality. In addition, this perspective also allows for an awareness of the existence of alternative religious experiences that do not conform to the dominant powers and provides a deeper understanding of the nature and the promise of such experiences.

At the level of religious beliefs, philosopher William Connolly distinguishes between epistemic beliefs, which can be addressed and altered through reason and arguments, and beliefs that are linked to stronger identities "in which creed and affect mix together." When such beliefs are challenged, people experience "the tightening of the gut, coldness of the skin, contraction of the pupils, and hunching of the back." At the same time, these beliefs are also linked to feelings of abundance and joy.[9] Connolly, following Gilles Deleuze, calls this a "surplus," a term that complements my own earlier use of the notion of "theological surplus."[10] Such an understanding of religion allows for a two-way street between ideal and material realities.

In a recent book, religion scholars Clayton Crockett and Jeffrey Robbins reclaim Ludwig Feuerbach's materialist critique of religious experience with a positive twist: that human concerns play a major role in the formation of religious experience, they note, is not reason for rejecting religion but for reclaiming it.[11] Religious experience, in the account of the new materialists (via Karl Marx, G. W. F. Hegel, and Slavoj Žižek), is not merely false consciousness (keep in mind that no consciousness escapes falsehood altogether); it can become a force for empowerment and social change. Based on this insight, these new materialist scholars of religion invite us to take seriously material and physical realities and to reconceive the roles of economics, ecology, and energy in the production of religious experience.

This proposal merits closer attention, as it introduces new aspects into the study of religion and religious experience. In many conventional religious and theological discourses that are concerned with matters of social justice, for instance, religious experience is often discussed as affecting economics and ecology in straightforward fashion, but rarely as being affected by it and affecting it in dialectical fashion. Crockett and Robbins provide various examples for a dialectical relation of religious experience and material dynamics, keeping a close eye on broader material developments tied to ecology and the Earth. In their work, the material perspective is broadened to include developments in the natural sciences, including the topic of energy. In a push beyond traditional physical concepts, Crockett and Robbins introduce new models of nuclear energy, with the conclusion that "the Earth [capitalized] becomes who it is through us if we have the energy and the foresight and courage to realize it."[12] Energy is thus both an external and an internal concept, as it passes between the natural sciences and the humanities, including the study of religion.

Such broadening of the dialectical materialist traditions is promising for various reasons. First, it includes a wealth of new insights produced in the natural sciences, from quantum physics to genetics and neurobiology. The natural sciences have come a long way from the days of Newtonian physics where cause and effect, subject and object, were easily distinguished and every question had a straightforward answer. This does not mean, however, that the natural sciences are now followed uncritically, as if their materialism would trump all other considerations. As the sciences are taken more seriously in the humanities and religious studies, we need to keep in mind that "sciences (and technologies) and their societies co-constitute each other," as Sandra Harding has pointed out from a feminist and postcolonial perspective.[13]

Second, new materialisms reshape and broaden our understanding of agency, as agency is not primarily rooted in terms of ideas and good intentions. Realizing a "mismatch between actions, intentions, and consequences," new materialists Diana Coole and Samantha Frost advocate an open systems approach to the interactions between socioeconomic and environmental conditions, combining biological, physiological, and physical processes. It is not necessary, of course, to argue that actions and intentions do not matter at all, but scholars of religion and theology in particular can benefit from seeing them in a broader perspective. If the way to hell is paved with good intentions, as the adage goes, we need to take another look at the problem of intentions, which is not merely a matter of good intentions that are not carried out. By the same token, matter needs to be considered as having agency in its own right, as new materialists emphasize "the productivity and resilience of matter."[14] These insights resonate with scientific thinking as developed in various fields, including quantum physics and molecular biology, resulting in a challenge of conventional ways of thinking about cause and effect. Matter, we are beginning to realize, is always in a process of becoming rather than merely being. One of the great advantages of these approaches is that the weight of having to produce transformation no longer rests on the shoulders of individuals alone.

Much of what we take for granted can be rethought from new materialist perspectives, even death itself. As Rosi Braidotti puts it, "death is overrated"[15] because our individual lives need to be seen in the larger context in which they affect and are affected by others, both human and nonhuman. This insight, which has parallels with the work of thinkers in the process theology and philosophy traditions, is comforting especially for progressives who, as Braidotti notes, are "just as human as others, only considerably more mortal."[16] Indeed, too many progressives have paid with their lives for the cause, from Jesus to Mahatma Gandhi and Martin Luther King. Braidotti is not a religious thinker, but her proposal to think "a Life [capitalized] that may not have 'me' or any 'human' at the center"[17] has profound parallels to various religious traditions, not the least of which is Christianity. In the words of the apostle Paul: "It is no longer I who live, but it is Christ who lives in me" (Gal. 2:20).

There is some potential here, although we need to gain further clarity about who the agents are in this model and how such agency can be realized under the conditions of capitalism, which seeks to harness every agency, human as well as nonhuman, for its own purposes. Crockett and Robbins, for instance, envision what they call a "postcapitalist world,"[18] but how do we deal with the capitalist world in which we now live? We cannot just step outside of it. While it is commendable that in the new materialisms "the capitalist system is not understood in any narrowly economistic way but rather is treated as a detotalized totality that includes a multitude of interconnected phenomena and processes,"[19] we still need a clearer understanding of how capitalism works and how it shapes our reality as a whole, including religion. A start might be Coole and Frost's awareness of the "immense and immediate material hardship for real individuals" who lost their savings, their pensions, their houses, and their jobs in the meltdown of the economy after 2007.[20] Unfortunately the two authors fail to mention work and workers — one of the most crucial insights of dialectical materialism after Marx — and thus the exploitation of those who still have jobs and who therefore have no choice but to function within the parameters of the neoliberal capitalist society.

Elsewhere in their book, Crockett and Robbins are clearer about capitalist reality, for instance, when they talk about "corporate control," which assures that even the immaterial (like digital reality) matters and takes on material force.[21] This is a crucial insight, because not even material reality itself escapes the flows of power in capitalism, a fact that is often overlooked. Nevertheless, these kinds of comments appear to be relatively infrequent in new materialist discussions and need to be deepened and expanded.

## THIRD, WHERE MIGHT WE NEED TO GO BEYOND THE NEW MATERIALISMS?

In addition to the need to develop a stronger and more dialectical assessment of capitalist reality, many of the new materialisms are moving too fast when they look past some of the fundamental tensions traditionally addressed by dialectical materialism — namely, tensions that arise in the world of *labor*. It may come as a surprise, but this matter is highly relevant to the study of religion and religious experience, as we shall see soon.

In one collection of essays that is representative of the spectrum of thought in new materialism because it brings together significant representatives, there is hardly any mention of labor or work at all. When labor is mentioned, this is done mostly in order to note that the new materialisms need to go beyond the focus on labor that has been characteristic of materialisms in the past. Braidotti, who helped us see that even death can be relativized, develops her proposal as if labor were not even an issue, proposing instead a "biocentered egalitarianism" that "breaks the expectation of mutual reciprocity." She links this sort of egalitarianism to giving up ideas of retaliation and compensation.[22] Yet while retaliation and "tit-for-tat" may indeed not be the most productive ways of relating to others and certainly not to the powers further up on the food chain, giving up notions of compensation and reciprocity altogether is not a real-life option for working people.

In order to go one step further, we need to go one step back. Where Crockett and Robbins "posit earth as subject"[23]—a factor that is indeed too often overlooked in religious discourse—what if we were to add working people who are doing most of the work that sustains humanity and its progress as subjects as well? This move does not have to exclude the earth, to be sure, but a dialectical materialism cannot afford to forget particular groups of people or, to use a term rarely heard in religious studies these days, certain *classes* of people that are not usually featured in religious discourse. In order to understand religion and religious experience more comprehensively, it needs to be taken into account that religion and religious experience shape up differently depending on who or what are their subjects, that is, who or what is involved in producing them. The problem is that, at present, not only are the contributions of the earth and of working people overlooked, they are systematically repressed. A broader understanding of religion and religious experience, and particularly of the various alternative forms, is not possible here.

It is no accident that among the most substantial roadblocks for materialist interpretations of religion in recent history have been efforts to downplay the role of oppressed people as authoritative sources of religious experience. This matches what is happening in the world of labor: workers' contributions are increasingly devalued by cutting salaries, benefits, and even hours at work—particularly for the lowest-paid workers, but also for many others. The workers of the Walmart corporation, the world's largest private employer, bear witness to this process.[24] If it is true that Walmart sets the pace for the rest of the economy (including white collar workers and professionals, if only by default), it is not inconceivable that Walmart's actions also have implications for the study of religion and what is considered appropriate. Large amounts of money certainly have implications for the practice of religion in communities where they are located.

I suspect that some contemporary forces would rather acknowledge the earth as subject than oppressed people as subjects.

We can identify examples of efforts to downplay the role of oppressed people as authoritative sources of religious experience in the highly organized backlash against Latin American liberation theology, feminist theologies, and other theologies from the margins that keep demanding more than mere inclusion within the dominant system.[25] At the same time, the study of popular religion, which has become a hot topic, is not subject to similar backlashes, quite possibly because popular religious experience is usually studied in isolation from dominant religious experience and is therefore not perceived as threat. In other words, popular religion is not studied in terms of power and thus the question whether popular religious experiences might conflict with or challenge dominant religious experiences is rarely raised.

Here, remembering Marx's critique of Ludwig Feuerbach's materialism might be helpful. Going beyond Feuerbach, Marx observes that material objects and matter itself are not mere givens, but are produced by labor and commerce. Materialism needs to take into account the produced nature of matter, which means it needs to take into account not only the natural world but also the labor that is involved in producing matter. Matter, in other words, is never a static entity, as it is constantly produced and reproduced. This is true even for the natural world itself, a fact which did not escape Marx. Both nature and workers are constantly engaged in "changing the form of matter." Material wealth is always generated from the interplay of labor and nature.[26] While the new materialisms have done an excellent job deepening our understanding of the productive capacities of the "natural" world, far beyond what Marx and his contemporaries could have known, we must still provide a deeper analysis of the productive contributions of labor in the current economic situation. The dominant economic system is built on the exploitation of both nature and work, and one cannot be understood without the other.

For religious experience, this means that we need to study it in terms of material relations that are not universal — this is the mistake that many theists and atheists alike are making — but that are produced in the context of particular relations of power. Unless the materialist study of religious experience takes into account the history of how power is shaped and reshaped in particular social relations and in relation to social movements, paying attention to who benefits and who does not in a given system (including both people and earth), it will be unable to take seriously alternative forms of religious experience. That is precisely what was missing in Feuerbach, and that is what a contemporary materialist study of religion still needs to investigate.

A start is made by Jason Edwards in his conclusion to an important collection of essays on the new materialisms, when he argues for a return "to a kind of historical materialism that focuses on the reproduction of capitalist societies and the system of states, both in everyday practices of production and consumption and in the ideological and coercive power of states and the international system."[27] Edwards' focus on "material practices" is right on target, but this proposal could still benefit by addressing the realities of labor.

What difference would taking a closer look at labor and the reality of work make to new materialism and the study of religion and religious experience? First, nothing exists apart from production — production is a central fact of life, and we would not be able to exist without it. Taking a closer look at labor will help us to become more aware of the produced nature of all that surrounds us, religious experience included. This does not imply a negative judgment, as production is not a negative thing in itself, but it reminds us of the fact that nothing ever just "fell from heaven" and that there may be a few options involving alternative mechanisms of production.

Second, there is an odd sort of transcendence that occurs when produced objects are commodified. Marx uses the example of a table. In terms of its use value, there is nothing mysterious about a table. Wood, produced by nature, is altered by labor in order to produce a common thing to be used for particular purposes: a dining-room table, a desk, a kitchen table, etc. A strange transcendence, however, enters in terms of the exchange value of the table. In economic exchanges, the table becomes a commodity, and what matters is no longer the labor, the materials, or the use value but the profit that can be made when it is sold. Because profit is usually thought of as a relationship between things, what is concealed is that it is produced in a relationship between people.[28] In Marx's words, "A commodity is therefore a mysterious thing, simply because in it the social character of men's labour appears to them as an objective character stamped upon the product of that labour; because the relation of the producers to the sum total of their own labour is presented to them as a social relation, existing not between themselves, but between the products of their labour."[29] Marx compares this to religious ideas, where "the productions of the human brain appear as independent beings endowed with life."[30]

While the significance of labor and of human relationships is covered up in this process of commodification (this is what Marx means when he talks about "commodity fetishism"), it does not disappear. One of the new materialist thinkers, Sara Ahmed, makes a similar case.[31] Moreover, as Ahmed has argued, the example of the table also reminds us of other divisions of labor, manifest for instance in the division between who usually works at a desk and who usually works at a kitchen table. In this example, the kitchen table represents the racial and class-based divisions of labor, as work at the desk is supported by the domestic labor of black and working-class women.[32]

These reminders of labor and material relations can help us rethink our options when it comes to religion and religious experience. What Marx calls religion in the above example is how idealism views religion, as "independent things endowed with life"; but there is no reason why religion cannot also be viewed from a more materialist perspective that takes the relation of life to material realities into account. The same is true for the notion of transcendence: transcendence does not have to be an idealist notion. There are other ways to conceive of transcendence than as a dangerous abstraction from real life, for instance when it is defined not in opposition to immanence but as transcending one kind of immanence in favor of another.[33] While capitalism covers up the contributions of work, the study of religion can resist the cover up and thus benefit from taking work into account.[34]

Earlier, I welcomed the reference to material practices as crucial to any new materialism. There is nothing wrong with broadening this notion beyond activities that are immediately related to processes of production to include, as Edwards suggests, "all those practices involving material bodies — organic and nonorganic — that . . . can be seen as a totality of practices that reproduce the relations of production over time."[35] At a time when the nature of labor is shifting and more and more people are pushed into the informal sector where they might hold down casual jobs, so-called temp jobs, or no jobs at all, this is an important reminder. It also reminds us of the importance of the kind of work that is done without compensation, like housework or volunteer work, and other productive activities that people are doing off the clock. What Edwards calls "the constitution of experience through the manifold forms of material practice outside the immediate space of production,"[36] is valuable, especially when thinking about religious experience. This is what *mujerista* theologian Ada María Isasi-Díaz has called "*lo cotidiano*," the "everyday" that is at the heart of life for most common people and for Latinas in particular.[37]

At the same time, in the current cultural climate in the United States there is very little reflection on how experience, religious experience included, is constituted through the regular processes of production at work, as labor is not a phenomenon that is commonly considered in the various fields of study, with few exceptions like the so-called "New Working Class Studies." Moreover, there has been hardly any work done on how class as a relational category shapes religion and religious experiences.[38] As a result, one of the most interesting questions yet to be investigated is how regular processes of production shape religious experiences of people. Without relating back to these very basic processes that occupy most of the waking hours of most people, despite the changes in labor just mentioned, we may not be able to develop a clear enough understanding of the importance of material practices more broadly conceived. Merely talking about the material practices of "everyday life" can also be misleading if it is not acknowledged that everyday life invariably is shaped by labor. Even leisure time is not off the hook, because it is designed for the reproduction of our productive labor capacities and shaped by the trends and interests of the capitalist economy. That economy rests on the foundations of labor — that it constantly seeks to cover up.

The most important point is that the approach being suggested is not merely a matter of analyzing the impact of material practices on our lives, including religious experience. This approach is also a matter of identifying alternative ways of life and religious experiences that grow out of these material practices and the potential that reshaping processes of production might have for reshaping religious experience. To be sure, this is not a romantic dream about life far away from or above the dominant system. As Edwards correctly notes, "the material practices constitutive of modern life are the only grounds from which we could hope and expect to bring about important political and social transformations."[39] While material practices can make us compliant to the status quo, they also harbor the potential for resistance and for producing alternatives. The challenge for us is to find out which material practices are the most fertile ground for producing alternatives. In Marx's time, he identified industrial labor, which helped spawn the labor movement of his time. Today, that question is more complex, although I do not believe that it can be answered without the labor movement.[40]

Alternative religious experience is, therefore, closely linked to material practices and the alternative ways of life that grow out of them. Once again, this is where labor is important, as it has produced powerful movements that have not only kept some of the worst abuses of capitalism in check but also built communities at the local, national, and international level that have made positive contributions to the world. As scholars of religion we need to investigate more thoroughly how alternative religious experiences shape up in the history of particular movements of exploited working people, in touch with the exploited earth, and what difference these experiences are making in the context of dominant religion. Neither scholars of religion nor theologians can produce such alternative religious experiences synthetically. They will have to study them while involving themselves in the resistance movements of our time, exploring what it all means for religion as a whole, including its practices, its doctrines and beliefs, and its ways of life. That was one of the concerns of the book *Occupy Religion*, co-authored with Kwok Pui-lan.[41] To bring it down to a formula: Materialism needs movements.

## CONCLUSIONS

Some may wonder whether materialism ultimately threatens the work of scholars of religion and theology. This would be the case if religion and theology were understood as reflections on disembodied ideas and doctrines whose only connection to the world is that they need to be "put into practice." While that is indeed a widespread assumption, and the premise of many Sunday sermons, it is quickly becoming clearer that there are other options.

Dialectical thinking in the materialist tradition asks questions of power: What are we up against, where are the contradictions, what are the alternatives? Among the basic contradictions in capitalism are still the tensions between the ruling class and the working class. Knowing that we cannot escape these tensions — no matter how much we would prefer to hide behind scholarly objectivity — we need to decide what to do with them and how to rethink them in the present.[42] The question for politics and economics is clear: what side are we on, where do we hang our hat? The same question applies to matters of culture and religion. If we fail to answer these questions, the dominant status quo will answer them for us.

This awareness is surprisingly underdeveloped in the various discussions of the new materialism. For example, Crockett and Robbins write, "The political crisis we face today is that no one or nothing decides. The people have been rendered the object of market forces. The market... follows its own self-annihilating logic where only the few stand to benefit but none hold the power to control."[43] I am not so sure that is the case. The proverbial 1 percent is making decisions, and the rest of us had better realize this in order to organize and to exercise our options in the decision-making process. Unfortunately, class is rarely mentioned in these discussions. When it is referenced by Edwards, who is one of the few exceptions, it is only in order to note that class is not everything.[44] While is this true, of course, one wonders how many voices are left today who would seriously argue that class is everything.

In this regard, it seems to me that the Occupy Wall Street movement has done more for us than any other movement in recent history. The proverbial tension between the 1 percent and the 99 percent, while not expressing a mathematically correct equation and while not claiming to be a full-fledged theory of class, may be more crucial than ever; not only for an understanding of politics and economics but also for an understanding of culture and, ultimately, of religious experience as well. As religion comes to life again in the discussion of new and dialectical materialisms, we grasp its alternative forms only when we grasp the larger structures of power that are at work in, around, and underneath neoliberal capitalism.

## NOTES

1    An earlier version of this chapter appeared as "Rethinking the New Materialism for Religion and Theology: Why Movements Matter Most," in *Religious Experience and the New Materialism: Movements Matter,* ed. Joerg Rieger and Edward Waggoner (New York: Palgrave Macmillan, 2015), reproduced with permission of Palgrave Macmillan.

2    http://science.howstuffworks.com/life/inside-the-mind/

human-brain/brain-religion.htm.

3 Chemical dependencies, for instance, are common and medical drugs often merely cover up the deeper causes and problems of depression, providing a quick fix that does not resolve anything. Positive thinking can create a make-believe world that does not change reality and that misleads people into believing that they have power when they really do not. For a broader critique of positive thinking see Barbara Ehrenreich, *Brightsided: How the Relentless Promotion of Positive Thinking Has Undermined America* (New York: Metropolitan Books, 2009).

4 Bruce Rogers-Vaughn, "Blessed Are Those Who Mourn: Depression as Political Resistance," *Pastoral Psychology* 63, no. 4 (2014): 503–22, doi: 10.1007/s11089-013-0576-y.

5 "The Philosophers Have Only Interpreted the World, in Various Ways; the Point is to Change It." https://www.marxists.org/archive/marx/works/1845/theses/theses.htm.

6 In response to this problem, several theologians, myself included, have preferred to classify their work as constructive theology rather than systematic theology.

7 Sean McCloud, *Divine Hierarchies: Class in American Religion and Religious Studies* (Chapel Hill: University of North Carolina Press, 2007).

8 Romans 1:25: "They exchanged the truth for a lie and worshiped and served the creature rather than the Creator."

9 William E. Connolly, "Materialities of Experience," in *New Materialisms: Ontology, Agency, Politics,* ed. Diana Coole and Samantha Frost (Durham, NC: Duke University Press, 2010), 196.

10 Joerg Rieger, *Christ and Empire: From Paul to Postcolonial Times* (Minneapolis: Fortress Press, 2007).

11 Clayton Crockett and Jeffrey Robbins, *Religion, Politics, and the Earth: The New Materialism* (New York: Palgrave Macmillan, 2012).

12 Crockett and Robbins, *Religion, Politics, and the Earth,* 110.

13 Sandra Harding, "Beyond Postcolonial Theory: Two Undertheorized Perspectives on Science and Technology," in *The Postcolonial Science and Technology Studies Reader,* ed. Sandra Harding (Durham, NC: Duke University Press, 2011), 21.

14   Diana Coole and Samantha Frost, "Introducing the New Materialisms," in *New Materialisms: Ontology, Agency, Politics,* ed. Diana Coole and Samantha Frost (Durham, NC: Duke University Press, 2010), 7.

15   Rosi Braidotti, "The Politics of 'Life Itself' and New Ways of Dying," in *New Materialisms: Ontology, Agency, Politics,* ed. Diana Coole and Samantha Frost (Durham, NC: Duke University Press, 2010), 212.

16   Ibid., 209.

17   Ibid., 210 talks about "a profound love for Life as a cosmic force and the desire to depersonalize subjective life-and-death. This is just one life, not my life. The life in 'me' does not answer to my name: 'I' is just passing."

18   Crockett and Robbins, *Religion, Politics, and the Earth,* 145.

19   Coole and Frost, "Introducing the New Materialisms," 29.

20   Ibid., 31. I talk about this in terms of the "logic of downturn." See Joerg Rieger, *No Rising Tide: Theology, Economics, and the Future* (Minneapolis: Fortress Press, 2009).

21   Crockett and Robbins, *Religion, Politics, and the Earth,* 16.

22   Braidotti, "The Politics of 'Life Itself,'" 214.

23   Crockett and Robbins, *Religion, Politics, and the Earth,* xx.

24   See, for instance, the testimonies of Walmart workers who are organizing through OUR Walmart: http://forrespect.org/category/associate-voices/why-i-joined-our-walmart/.

25   By backlash, I do not mean legitimate debate, which is normal and healthy, but a wall of opposition that included ridicule, defamation, and other methods to discredit valid arguments. This organized opposition is not limited to the world of scholarship. In the 1980s, the Reagan administration, in its Santa Fe Document, identified Latin American liberation theology as a phenomenon that had to be held in check. See also the work of the so-called "Institute for Religion and Democracy."

26   "[Humans] can work only as Nature does, that is by changing the form of matter. Nay more, in this work of changing the form he [or she] is constantly helped by natural forces." Karl Marx, *Capital:*

*A Critique of Political Economy,* vol. i, trans. Samuel Moore and Edward Aveling; ed. Frederick Engels (Moscow: Progress Publishers, 1887; https://www.marxists.org/archive/marx/works/download/pdf/Capital-Volume-I.pdf).

27  Jason Edwards, "The Materialism of New Materialism," in *New Materialisms: Ontology, Agency, Politics,* ed. Diana Coole and Samantha Frost (Durham, NC: Duke University Press, 2010), 283.

28  Marx talks about these issues in *Capital,* 46–47, but since he does not mention the terms exchange value and profit in this section, it is difficult to follow.

29  Ibid., 46–47.

30  Ibid., 47.

31  Sara Ahmed, "Orientations Matter," in *New Materialisms: Ontology, Agency,* Politics, ed. Diana Coole and Samantha Frost (Durham, NC: Duke University Press, 2010), 243.

32  Ahmed, "Orientations Matter," 248–254.

33  See our comments on transcendence in Joerg Rieger and Kwok Pui-Lan, *Occupy Religion: Theology of the Multitude, Religion in the Modern World* (Lanham, MD: Rowman & Littlefield, 2012), 71–76.

34  One of the fundamental shifts that I am suggesting in my book *No Rising Tide* is the move from a focus on redistribution to production.

35  Edwards, "The Materialism of New Materialism," 283.

36  Ibid., 288.

37  See, for instance, Ada María Isasi-Díaz, *Mujerista Theology: A Theology for the Twenty-First Century* (Maryknoll, NY: Orbis Books, 1996).

38  To my knowledge, the notion of class as relationship has only been picked up lately in religious studies. *See Religion, Theology, and Class: Fresh Conversations after Long Silence,* ed. Joerg Rieger (New York: Palgrave Macmillan, 2013). Class, when discussed at all, is often described in terms of stratification rather than in terms of relationship.

39  Edwards, "The Materialism of New Materialism," 292.

40  See also the use of the term "multitude" in Rieger and Kwok,

*Occupy Religion.*

41   Rieger and Kwok, *Occupy Religion.*

42   See Rieger, *Religion, Theology, and Class.*

43   Crockett and Robbins, *Religion, Politics, and the Earth,* 38–39.

44   See, for instance, Edwards, "The Materialism of New Materialism," 296.

## ᔛ 13 ᔛ

## SOCIALISM FOR THE COMMON GOOD

### *Philip Clayton*

It has become more and more evident that these pressing problems — climate change and environmental degradation, growing disparity of wealth, unemployment and underemployment — do not have capitalist solutions and in fact are caused by capitalist assumptions about human relationships and our relationship with the environment. *-from Chapter 1 above*

IT'S BEEN SAID THAT SOCIALISM IS DOA (dead on arrival) as a serious political option in American discourse. Socialism, the critics continue, is linked to Communism and Marxism, both of which are completely destructive. Socialism would make the United States like Venezuela, where the economy and society are collapsing. "Venezuela is burning — and we're overlooking the root cause of its crisis," writes Andres Malavew in his "Socialism Is Devastating Venezuela and Americans Don't Seem to Notice" in the *U.S. News & World Report.*[1]

This book, and this chapter in particular, ask the reader to set aside these stereotypes. The matter would not be so urgent if we were not now faced with the worst crisis of the twenty-first century, and perhaps beyond: the human-induced disruption of the global climate and the exhaustion of essential natural resources such as clean water, clean air, and healthy soil. Because the current system is causing this cycle of destruction, we *must* consider alternatives. To do this, we have to look closely at social and political options that were earlier dismissed within our society.

## PROCESS SOCIALISM

In the broadest sense of the word, everything that exists in the world around us is in process: every person, every species, stars and galaxies, and certainly societies as well. But there is also a technical sense of the term. Rigorous process philosophies have been developed in each of the world's major philosophical traditions, with similar understandings of process. In the West, the process insight was worked out most deeply by Alfred North Whitehead and, among his publications, in its most sophisticated form in *Process and Reality*. There one finds an entire metaphysics of process, including all the fundamental categories that underlie a process-relational worldview.

Socialists have usually been more interested in *changing* the world than in spelling out the metaphysical foundations for societal transformation. I agree: pragmatically driven ideas of process and change are generally more useful for addressing immediate concerns. For example, socialism has always been in process. Especially today, in this explosive, postmodern, twenty-first-century world, it's crucial to unmoor socialist thought from the ropes of its nineteenth-century origins, allowing it to move into new contexts in new ways.

Still, *part* of that task involves also freeing socialism from the conceptual frameworks that defined it in the past, frameworks that (we believe) led to mistakes and misapplications. Together with the other authors in this volume, I believe that process thought offers the new framework that we need. In the Claremont School of process philosophy, we often use the phrase "a process-relational worldview for the common good." That idea, far more than concepts like materialism and the historical dialectic, will guide socialist thinking and action in an increasingly divided world. Here, we believe, socialist reformers will find the worldview that we need.

## AMERICAN DNA AND THE NEED FOR CHANGE

Some say that Korea is the most Confucian culture in the world today; others say China. Although in the end Koreans and Chinese will have to decide the issue, most agree that traditionally these have been highly Confucian cultures.

And what's most distinctive about American culture? At home and abroad, people offer similar lists: individuality, ingenuity, the dream of upward mobility ("Anyone who works hard will succeed"), creativity, technological innovation... Hollywood, and Disneyland. Most Americans would add *individualism* as one of our most positive qualities. Socialists view this differently, as we will see in a moment.

Individualism is always bonded with its twin, capitalism. I suggest that the United States, over its brief history, has been and remains the most capitalist nation the world has ever seen. Capitalism has been built into American DNA from the beginning. Later, Americans exported capitalism around the world and fought, sometimes violently, to make sure that it came to dominate in every nation. No country is free, Americans often argue, if it is not capitalist.

Why does this unlikely assertion seem so obvious to the majority of Americans: that capitalism and freedom are Siamese twins?

We have prided ourselves on being rugged individualists, as our folk wisdom suggests: "every man for himself"... "may the best man win"... "he who works hardest will get the farthest"... "the sky's the limit." Somehow we have molded four ideas—individualism, capitalism, freedom, and happiness—into a single ball of wax, melding them together so thoroughly that we can no longer tell them apart.

## THE ANTECEDENTS OF AMERICAN CAPITALISM

The mix-up can be traced back to the U.S. Declaration of Independence. In this founding document, in which the founding fathers declared their independence from England, Thomas Jefferson proclaimed that among a human's "unalienable Rights" are "Life, Liberty and the pursuit of Happiness." By Liberty he meant first of all Americans' freedom from England and, by implication, also their freedom from any unnecessary form of government control. Henceforth the individual man (it *was* man back then) and his family would be free to make his own decisions, to go his own way. Freedom and individualism thereby became "unalienably" linked.

What about happiness and capitalism? We often forget that when Jefferson used the word "happiness," he was actually paraphrasing a famous sentence that the English political theorist John Locke had used in his *Second Treatise*. Locke's text read differently, however. Instead of "life, liberty and happiness," he had proclaimed that the core rights of the individual are "life, liberty and *property*."

This word substitution is highly significant. It was not a mistake on Jefferson's part; it was intentional. Jefferson and his fellows did not leave the idea of property behind, as we know well from other sources. Instead, they assumed that acquiring property *was* the key to happiness. It's almost as if they believed that property *just is* happiness.

However one interprets this crucial question about the genesis of the independent United States, it's clear that Jefferson — and through him, the founding fathers — accepted the central contention from John Locke: the purpose of government is to protect the property of its citizens. In the pre-industrial age of Locke, property *was* the basis for wealth; wealth was created by owning land. In the centuries that followed, as Marx well understood, capital came to play the role that property once played. Because industrial expansion required huge investments, the acquisition of capital became the condition for success. If success means happiness, then amassing wealth was now the key to happiness.

Perhaps it's no surprise, then, that the American public continues to buy into this myth. The middle and lower classes self-medicate on handoffs from the wealthy, who increase their control as a result. Congress and the court system generally support the power of the corporations and their lobbying efforts, as in the Supreme Court's approval of Citizens United in 2010. From a socialist perspective, Citizens United is one of the strangest and most disturbing manifestations of the American DNA, as it is also a revealing symptom of the contemporary American situation. Because the Supreme Court's decision treats corporations as persons under the law, it effectively takes what were once the rights and guiding principles for treating *individual persons* and extends them on a wholesale basis to corporate business entities. This allows businesses greater power over their customers and the broader public. . . and hence a greater opportunity for affirming the interests of the wealthy over the needs of the poor.

Further examples are easy to list. We expect our political representatives to work for the common good. But because of the high cost of winning elections, candidates become beholden to special interests well before they take office. Political action committees (PACS) give their wealthy donors the ability to work around limits on contributions to political candidates, limitations that were originally put in place to prevent money from unduly influencing the outcome of elections. And the extraordinary effectiveness of lobbying at national and state levels assures that those who can pay for the best lobbyists can most influence policy. Our current systems allows for anonymous flows of wealth as big as the Mississippi.

So what are the prospects for change? The stranglehold of capital in the U.S. will not decrease on its own. In the history of economics one is hard-pressed to find serious examples of a wealthy class that voluntarily redistributes its riches to the poor. By itself, the dynamic of capital will not change. The rich will become richer, and they will continue to enjoy the rights and privileges pertaining thereunto. Inevitably, then, the poor will become poorer. That's business as usual.

## BUT IT IS NOT BUSINESS AS USUAL

There are a few occasions — very few, actually — when the U.S. government has acted significantly in the interests of the poor. The collapse of the stock market in 1929 led to economic collapse and vast unemployment. In response to the crisis, Roosevelt's "New Deal" for the first time restricted corporate abuses of the working class, regulated business practices, built federal employment programs, and vastly increased support for the needy. A few years later, in response to threats from the Second World War and the need for consolidated action, Americans accepted rationing, reoriented social norms, and (whether voluntarily or involuntarily) went to work as soldiers and factory workers.

Today we stand before another war, a war much more serious than any we have fought before, a war of our own making. Not only have we reached the limits of what the earth, air, and sea can bear; the science tells us that we have set in motion a series of cascading processes that will continue to snowball out of control for perhaps centuries to come. Global warming heats forests in Canada, weakening the trees' resistance to bugs; the infestations then kill the trees and release massive amounts of methane into the atmosphere. The melting polar icecap allows the dark-colored floor of the Arctic Ocean to be bathed in sunlight for the first time since human civilization began, likewise releasing clouds of methane into the air. These processes, like those that drive global climate change out of control, cannot be reversed within decades, and in some cases not within centuries. Whether or not people accept the strong consensus among scientific researchers does not change the facts of the matter. Global climate disruption is already causing deaths, extinctions, and mass migrations. In light of the best scientific models, what we will see in just the next few decades is almost beyond comprehension.

This changes everything.[2] Adding recycling programs or decreasing the miles we drive our cars will no longer suffice, nor will technological enhancements or more conferences such as the COP21 meetings in Paris in 2015. (An international summit conference that imposed *binding* requirements for greenhouse gas reduction would of course be another matter.) Even somewhat deeper changes within contemporary American society won't by themselves stem the tide. The science suggests that, without immediate and massive interventions on a global scale, the snowballing effects will push us beyond the conditions that have made modern society possible. Enduring droughts in some regions and floods in others, weather events more violent than anything Americans have seen before, and the need to relocate tens of millions from along American shores as ocean levels rise and begin to cover cities such as Miami — these are only a few of the expected consequences in North America. Climate disruptions in other parts of the world, which we are already beginning to see, will have immensely more serious consequences.

So what does all this mean? The most likely result of these radical changes to the climate is the end of the kind of civilization that has come to dominate the planet since the dawn of modernity about 400 years ago. Modern civilization was based on massive resource use (forests, coal, overgrazed and over-farmed land), unlimited economic growth, higher and higher per capital consumption and, above all, the magic power of fossil fuels.

Of course, civilizational change is nothing new to humanity. Edward Gibbon in *The Decline and Fall of the Roman Empire*, Oswald Spengler in *The Decline of the West*, Arnold Toynbee in his monumental *A Study of History*, and many other historians have chronicled the periodic rise and fall of civilizations.[3] Some scholars identify five civilizations over the last 5,000 years, counting only those of the Middle East and Europe; others, taking a more global perspective, tell the stories of many, many more. Forms of life change, no matter how permanent they may seem at the time. The unthinkable becomes quotidian. After the fall, the values and forms that structured society in one era come to appear hopelessly outdated and irrational, even immoral, to members of the civilization that follows. Why should things be any different for the civilizational structures of the so-called modern world?

Given what science tells us is headed our direction, the options are stark. Perhaps the human population will be reduced so radically — say, by 50% — that human activity will no longer disrupt planetary ecosystems even if the old practices are continued. Perhaps humanity will develop an ecological civilization, a sustainable form of life that works within nature's limits.[4] Perhaps the collapse of social structures will be so quick and massive that the survivors will live for a time with no identifiable civilization, say in the manner of hunter/gatherer societies. We don't know. What is beyond dispute, however, is that the form of civilization that has dominated since the Industrial Age is no longer sustainable.

The future may be unclear, but the most urgent question for humanity today is not. How will governments, businesses, and individuals respond as the climate change crisis grows more acute? Here's where socialism comes in. One possibility is that those who hold the most power will use it on behalf of the whole planet, leading the way to a sustainable society. Another is that nations, multinational corporations, and wealthy individuals will voluntarily share their power and possessions, creating an equitable and just world order. The third, and many would say the most likely scenario is that the nations, classes, and individuals who possess power will use it as a means to protect themselves, at whatever cost to the poor and powerless — "pulling a Trump," we might call it. If this happens, they will build larger and larger walls around themselves, will use more and more force to obtain the resources they need to stay alive, and will employ their armies and their technology to keep others out at whatever cost.

Will we as a species work together for the common good? Or will we devolve into the "war of all against all," as Thomas Hobbes put it, such that life becomes "nasty, brutish, and short"? Will unrestrained capitalism — maximizing profits and minimizing restraints on the rich — dominate even as societies are collapsing around us?

Recall the title of Naomi Klein's book, *This Changes Everything.* Because humanity has hit the limits of what the planet can sustain, the old debate between socialists and capitalists has been transformed.

Socialism is in process. To put it bluntly: we face an either/or that our species has never faced before, and the timer is ticking The far more probable option, it now appears, is that humanity will keep its foot on the capitalist accelerator until we hit the wall of planetary limits at full speed. But there *is* another option, however unlikely: *an ecological socialism for the common good.* When your choices are certain death or the slim possibility of escape, you pursue the latter, whatever the odds against you.

Let's pause briefly to clarify what socialism means and what roles it has played in American history, before concluding with a proposal for the future.

## SOCIALISM PAST AND PRESENT[5]

Socialism names "a range of economic and social systems characterized by social ownership and democratic control of the means of production"[6]; it includes "the political ideologies, theories, and movements" that seek to establish this shared ownership *by* the people and *for* the people. Socialism requires that political power be used for the good of society.

In the United States in the second half of the twentieth century, the Baby Boomer generation and their parents came to equate *socialism* with *Communism,* and the latter term with atheism, totalitarianism, censorship, and the denial of human rights. Both terms were dismissed by association with Stalinist Russia, the Cold War, the dark years of the Cultural Revolution in China, the East German state apparatus, and collapsing Latin American economies — in short, socialism was identified with an attack on mom, apple pie, and all that the Baby Boomers held dear. Colored in this way, it became the quintessence of all that Americans fear. Is it surprising, then, that associating any policy with socialism became the quickest and easiest way to refute it in their eyes?

Things were not always this way, however. By the first decade of the twentieth century, American historians could define *seven*

distinct socialist movements that had already played an important
role in American politics since the founding of the United States: the
Communistic ventures of the Shakers, Quakers, and other Radical
Reformation traditions; Utopian socialism; the period of (primarily) German immigration, which brought Marxist socialist ideals
to the U.S.; the founding of the Socialist Labor Party; the formation of a distinctive American socialism; the establishment of "the
Social Democracy of America" and the Socialist Labor Party; and
the founding and rapid growth of the Socialist Party.[7] In the years
between 1900 and 1950, socially oriented policies played an even
greater role. At the Socialist Party's high point in 1912, about 1,200
Socialist party members held public office. Some 340 cities were represented, including 79 mayors.[8]

Consider the example of Milwaukee, which emerged as a center
of socialism in the opening years of the twentieth century. The large
German and Polish immigrant population of the city brought with
them positive attitudes toward socialist principles: "the public ownership of utilities and transportation facilities; the expansion of parks,
libraries, playgrounds, and other services; a living wage for workers;
and a friendlier attitude toward unions, especially in time of strikes."[9]
By 1910 Milwaukee could boast a Socialist mayor, Socialist majorities
on the city council and county board, and Socialists serving in most of
the top municipal offices, including judgeships and the school board.[10]

The strongest socialist policies emerged during the Great
Depression, after the crash of the markets and the bankruptcy of
many financial institutions. The massive unemployment and poverty that followed the collapse of the American economy lasted for
almost a decade. In response to the excesses of capitalist speculation
that had caused the collapse and the almost complete lack of a safety
net for the poor and unemployed, President Franklin D. Roosevelt
launched a series of social reforms known collectively as the "New
Deal." For example, his Social Security programs offered the first
government-sponsored insurance programs for the elderly, sick, and
unemployed in American history. The Fair Labor Standards Act of

1938 set maximum hours and minimum wages for most categories of workers.

Although socialism played a transformative role in the United States through the 1930s, it has been almost 80 years since that time. Now the unexpected popularity of Bernie Sanders, an avowed socialist, in the presidential campaign leading up to the 2016 election has brought discussion of socialist principles back onto the national political stage.

Not surprisingly, the resurgence of socialism has been politically divisive, eliciting particularly sharp differences of opinion along racial, generational, socioeconomic, and political lines. Nine of out ten conservative Republicans (90%) view the term socialism negatively, while nearly six out of ten liberal Democrats (59%) view it positively. Low-income Americans are twice as likely as higher-income Americans to offer a positive assessment of socialism: 43% among those with incomes under $30,000, and 22% among those earning $75,000 or more. People under age 30 are divided in their views of both capitalism and socialism, as we will see in a moment. But to Americans age 65 and older (Baby Boomers and their parents), socialism is a sharply negative term (72%); only 13% of Americans in this demographic view it as positive.[11]

The "YouGov" polls provide similar data, although these polls are not independently conducted. In general, roughly twice as many Americans favor capitalism over socialism: 52% of Americans express a favorable view of capitalism, whereas only 26% favor socialism. Among Americans under 30, however, the responses to the two terms are almost equal: 36% have a positive view of socialism and 39% have a positive view of capitalism. Americans over 65, who came of age at the height of the Cold War, trend sharply in the opposite direction; 15% express favorable views of socialism, in contrast to the 59% who have favorable views of capitalism.[12]

Surveys taken during the 2016 election season likewise show that younger Americans tend significantly more to the liberal end of the spectrum — the region where socialism is most likely to be viewed positively. One study shows 45% of Millennials endorsing liberal views (29% mostly liberal and 16% consistently liberal), compared to just 15% who endorse conservative views. An additional 40% of Millennials hold a mix of conservative and liberal views.[13] The surveys of Donald Trump supporters, who tend to be significantly older (as well as white, male, and less educated), show exactly the opposite patterns. The strong shift to the left among younger American voters is already affecting the outcomes of elections, and this trend is expected to continue over the coming years.[14] Millennials are now the largest demographic group in the United States, recently overtaking Baby Boomers.

What explains the rebirth of socialism? The motivation of the New Socialists is not abstract or philosophical; many describe themselves as *pragmatic idealists*. The new face of younger American socialism was widely visible, for example, during the Occupy movement. The attempt to "occupy Wall Street" and other centers of power lasted only a short period of time. But the moral force of the Occupy movement has endured. In simplest terms, it is the distinction between the 99%, for whom conditions are steadily becoming worse, and the 1%, who are becoming richer and richer.

A close examination of the Bernie Sanders campaign and its message suggests that young Americans call themselves socialists because they are no longer willing for the "billionaire class" to dictate American social, economic, and political policies. They want decisions to be made on behalf of the 99% of the American population—which means that they want control of important policies to be wrested away from the rich and returned to the people. And they are willing to take active steps to make this happen. They are convinced that the deeper meaning of democracy is (in John Cobb's words) "that the people as a whole [should] inform the government's decisions."[15]

## SOCIALISM AND THE COMMON GOOD

Not all socialism is Marxist. Marx brought a sophisticated understanding of the history of economic systems, of the principles of socio-economic evolution, of class dynamics, and especially of the consequences of unrestrained capitalism. Although the core insights of Marx remain accurate, he was wrong about some of the details. He also failed to anticipate many of the social and technological changes that came after him. Theoretically, he presupposed a rigid materialism, a strict historical dialectic (partly under the influence of his co-author Engels), and an equation of ideas with ideology—all assumptions that have not stood the test of time.

None of these shortcomings refutes the critique of capitalism, however. Francis Fukuyama was clearly mistaken: our age has not seen the final victory of capitalism as a global economic system.[16] The comprehensive study by Thomas Piketty and his colleagues has shown that since the 1950s capitalism has increasingly added to the wealth of the already-wealthy while decreasing the resources of the middle and lower classes.[17]

In short, socialisms come in many different shapes and sizes. Some assist in the critique of unrestrained capitalism, while others flesh out the alternatives. If all socialisms had to be Marxist, it would be easy: any socialist philosophy would be judged by its faithfulness to Marx's original work. But given that Marxism is only one strand within the socialism as a whole, we will need to find some other criteria for selecting among the wide variety of options. In concluding this chapter, I will argue that *the common good* is the best available criterion, especially in light of the environmental crisis.

First, what is the common good? Clearly not wealth for the few. Nor is it just more possessions for the middle class in the developed nations. Instead, it challenges wealth disparity and calls for an "economics of the common good" of the sort that Nobel economist Jean Tirole has recently been advocating.[18]

Now one might object that the Common Good Criterion is too vague to serve as a guideline. It turns out, however, that it is not difficult to make it concrete enough to have teeth, that is, to guide policy formation at all levels, from local to international. I suggest that there are at least six such concrete implications:

(1) The Common Good Criterion (CGC) is only met when the motivation of the state is to ensure the greatest good for the greatest number of citizens, consistent with the long-term needs of life on this planet. Maximizing the wealth of one's own citizens at the expense of one's neighbors—say, by emptying a river to water golf courses, leaving the neighbor's farmers without water for irrigation (as Arizona is doing to Mexican farmers)—does not qualify. Similarly, maximizing the pleasure and comfort of all human beings living today is not consistent with the CGC. Only policies that explicitly consider, at minimum, the needs of our grandchildren will suffice. Remember the criterion used by some of the Native peoples in North America: act today such that the seventh generation after you (your great great great great great grandchildren) will prosper.

This criterion must then be turned into action at the executive, legislative, and judicial levels of government. It means that the large and influential bodies within society—both for-profit and non-profit—will exist for the purpose of increasing long-term goods for all. Because ordinary citizens don't just inhabit contiguous bits of land but are actually tied together into a single society by a common set of core values, it means that individual citizens also must work toward these shared values. Put all these criteria together, and you recognize that the CGC is actually a call for *global* citizens, people who make decisions in light of the interests of the planet and all its inhabitants.

(2) The CGC requires one to seek a broader perspective than the individual. The traditional term for this focus is *communitarianism*.[19] The Latin root is *communitas*: "community, society, fellowship, friendly intercourse; courtesy, condescension, affability." The Oxford English Dictionary notes that the Latin *communitatem* was "a noun of quality... meaning 'fellowship, community of relations or feelings.'"[20]

Communitarians have traditionally advocated for two major corrections to political philosophy. One is the focus on *community*—placing the needs of the community above the wishes and desires of the individual. The other focus is *to hold in common*—which is the stance most often associated with socialism.

(3) The CGC means that one must think and act not only for the good of his or her nation. In earlier eras one would have needed to emphasize here the transcending of other kinds of interests, such as clan, race, or religion. But one interest, one ideology, above all others has been the *bête noire* of the modern period: nationalism. Nationalism gave rise not only to continual warfare among nations (the Thirty Years War, the Napoleonic wars, the two World Wars), but also to expansionism, colonialization, xenophobia, Orientalism, and the like.

In the era of nationalism, economic policies and systems have been designed by powerful nations to serve their own national interests; for example, by keeping the prices of raw materials low and the prices of industrial products high. Many allegedly neutral practices are in fact bent to serve the economic interests of the powerful nations: international treaties and trade agreements, government subsidies and import taxes, and international development organizations such as the World Bank and the International Monetary Fund.

(4) The CGC thus implies moving beyond nationalism to what we might call a *post-nationalist worldview*. In the modern period it became difficult to conceive the good of society except in terms of the good of the nation. A society and a nation became indistinguishable: American society, Japanese society, Russian society. As a result, the more traditional defining factors of each society—its arts, literature, and distinctive cultural features—came to be subsumed under the economic and political interests of that particular nation. The cultural resources had to be put to work to support the leaders' interest in expansion and empire. Although Hitler's co-opting of the arts offers a particularly egregious example, he was by no means the only nationalist leader to employ such techniques. As I write these words, we are watching Recep Tayyip Erdoğan achieve a dictatorship in Turkey through calculated appeals to the Turkish people to protect their "national interests" at whatever cost.

In a post-nationalist world, by contrast, social principles come to replace nationalism as the guiding framework for forming and maintaining a healthy society. The difference is night and day. *Socialism* comes from *social*, which derives in turn from the Latin *socius,* "companion or ally."[21] *Society* has the same root: *societas,* also from *socius.*[22] In this framework we see ourselves as a group of friends and allies, working for the good of the whole community. To begin this transformation is to subordinate the nation or republic (*res politica*, literally the "political thing") to the community (*communis* = common, shared by all).[23] Good is therefore defined first in terms of the quality of life of the society: how each citizen lives, how the arts flourish, how these parts support the core values of a way of life (*ethos*) while it in turn supports all parts of the society.

(5) This reciprocity of part and whole applies not only to humanity. To support the long-term common good, the cycle has to be applied to other living systems as well. The first reason is clear: when the flourishing of society means the destroying of nature, it's doomed to be a short-term flourishing indeed!

But there's another reason. Consider an example: the antebellum South, which represents one of the most cultured and refined eras in U.S. history. But because the wealth of the plantations was built on the suffering of the majority of the people living there, because the very humanity of Africans had to be denied to make the system work, the system was not sustainable. The appearance of value was an illusion, a lie; you could only praise the Corinthian pillars and white mansions if you looked away from the slave quarters in which black men and women lived. When a building's foundation is rotten the whole structure is worthless, however beautiful it may appear on the outside. When the richest 1% of the world's population prospers on the basis of a system that deprives the remaining 99% of the fair fruit of their labors, the whole system is broken.

Likewise, it's not only true that human flourishing at the cost of the planet isn't sustainable; the value of such human flourishing is undercut as well. Socialism for the Common Good will be *ecological* in the original sense of the world: grounded on *oikos*, the household. Yet now the entire planet becomes the household, a single interlocking system. This way of thinking and living is environmental because it is biocentric or, as some prefer to say, "earthist." The well-known concept of Gaia exactly expresses this idea of a socialism expansive enough to include nature within the social community. Gaia, the earth goddess, stands for the overarching framework within which all the parts are combined. It is an interdependent living system, seeking to serve the shared good of all its members—universal socialism in the truest sense of the term.

(6) Put all these factors together and you get Organic Marxism. In *Organic Marxism: An Alternative to Capitalism and Ecological Catastrophe*,[24] Justin Heinzekehr and I argue that developments in the natural and social sciences, in ecology, and in cultural studies make socialism for the common good a serious contender in the current debate. Our conclusions are based on three realizations: capitalist justice is not just, the "free market" is not free, and the costs of global climate disruption will be most severe among the poor. We conclude that humanity has two choices. "We can begin now to turn away from the myth that it is best for the planet is to let wealthy people rule in their own interest. Or we can wait until the collapse of capital-based civilization in order to initiate structures that serve the common good. Now, not later, is the time to act."[25]

## CONCLUSION: SOCIALISM IN PROCESS

In these pages I have endeavored to work out a socialism for the common good. This project was inspired by the "process-relational worldview" that we associate with Whitehead's process philosophy and the work of his followers such as John B. Cobb, Jr. and his students. It rejects that idea that socialism is a fixed entity, canonized in the mid-nineteenth century and inviolate since then. It presupposes that socialism is always in process.

"The common good" is a broad idea; it ranks up with the greatest visions in the history of political philosophy: Aristotle's *eudaimonia* (happiness or human thriving), divine justice in the Middle Ages, the *humanum* (achieving ideal or essential human nature) in early modern philosophy, the Enlightenment idea of a state that would bring about a civilized existence for all of its citizens, and the utopias proposed by philosophers from Thomas More to Karl Marx to Ernest Callenbach's *Ecotopia*.[26] Turning to a new grand vision is appropriate, for we live in an era when the foundations of one civilization are crumbling and a new one is struggling to be born.[27]

The more concretely one can specify the particular situation, the more concrete are the entailments of the Common Good Criterion. The common good in Israel and Palestine requires finding an end to warfare and beginning to social and economic relations that benefit both. The common good in South Africa started with abolishing apartheid, but it now involves ending corruption, strengthening the economy, and improving basic social services such as medical assistance to AIDS victims. Similarly, Norway aided the common good by sharing oil revenues across the population; Switzerland supported it by establishing democratic procedures at the local and canton level; and the nation of Bhutan became a model by emphasizing not GDP but Gross Domestic Happiness (GDH).

Those are national examples. Within a single state or providence, the criteria for the common good can be made more precise; within a single city, yet more so; and for a single family or community, even more.

*This arrow downward* toward the increasingly concrete is balanced by an arrow upwards toward universal concern. Biological evolution programmed humans to fight on behalf of their relatives, who share their genetic material, and for members of their own clan, because the survival of their particular group depended on the survival of their clan. The result was an in-group versus out-group mentality, which has dominated human history ever since. The greater the fear, the stronger these tendencies become. *The arrow upward*, by contrast, extends the understanding of "good" from our clan to our region to our people group to our national or contingent, and finally to all life. In the end, the common good expresses the combination of both of these arrows.

The backdrop for this book on socialism is a dark scenario indeed. There are multiple reasons to give up. Oddsmakers would probably encourage bets for the dark side, and I do not disagree. Yet dark scenarios rightly give rise to their opposite, as in the ancient expression "the darkest hour is just before the dawn." Times of crisis call forth the greatest levels of human courage and readiness to sacrifice. When the most probable outcome is unthinkable, we have no option other than to seek another route.

## NOTES

1   Andres Malave, "Socialism Is Devastating Venezuela and Americans Don't Seem to Notice," *U.S. News & World Report,* June 6, 2016 (http://www.usnews.com/opinion/articles/2016-06-06/socialism-is-devastating-venezuela-and-americans-dont-seem-to-notice).

2   Naomi Klein, *This Changes Everything: Capitalism vs. the Climate* (New York: Simon & Schuster, 2014).

3   Oswald Spengler, *The Decline of the West* (New York: Oxford University Press, 1991); Arnold Toynbee, *A Study of History,* 2nd ed. (London: Oxford University Press, H. Milford, 1935-1961); Edward Gibbon, *The Decline and Fall of the Roman Empire* (New York: Harcourt, Brace, 1960).

4   See EcoCiv.org for an important project that works toward precisely this goal.

5   I wish to express my gratitude to my research associate, Jay Potter, who has conducted the research that underlies this section.

6   Definition appears at https://en.wikipedia.org/wiki/Socialism.

7   See *A Brief History of Socialism in America* (Debs Publishing Co, 1900), now available online at https://www.marxists.org/history/usa/parties/spusa/1900/0100-sdp-briefhistorysoc.pdf; *Encyclopedia of the American Left,* ed. Mari Jo Buhle, Paul Buhle, and

Dan Georgakas, 2nd ed. (New York: Oxford University Press, 1998), 646-48, 711–23; "Christian Socialism | Political Philosophy," https://www.britannica.com/topic/Christian-Socialism; "History of the Socialist Movement in the United States," Wikipedia, the Free Encyclopedia, June 13, 2016, https://en.wikipedia.org/w/index.php?title=History_of_the_socialist_movement_in_the_United_States&oldid=725108538; "A Time-Line of the Industrial Workers of the World," https://www.marxists.org/history/usa/unions/iww/timeline.htm; and "Espionage Act of 1917," Wikipedia, the Free Encyclopedia, https://en.wikipedia.org/w/index.php?title=Espionage_Act_of_1917&oldid=729557947.

8   "Bernie Sanders's Presidential Bid Represents a Long Tradition of American Socialism," *The American Prospect,* 4 May 2015 (http://prospect.org/article/bernie-sanderss-presidential-bid-represents-long-tradition-american-socialism).

9   Ibid.

10  Ibid.

11  Pew Research Center, "Little Change in Public's Response to Capitalism,' 'Socialism'," December 28, 2011, http://www.people-press.org/2011/12/28/little-change-in-publics-response-to-capitalism-socialism/.

12  "One Third of Millennials View Socialism Favorably," *YouGov: What the World Thinks,* 11 May 2015, https://today.yougov.com/news/2015/05/11/one-third-millennials-like-socialism/.

13  Pew Research Center, "A Wider Ideological Gap Between More and Less Educated Adults," 26 April 2016 (http://www.people-press.org/2016/04/26/a-wider-ideological-gap-between-more-and-less-educated-adults/).

14  Young people (ages 17–29) voted in remarkable numbers during the 2016 primaries. Voting by young Republicans broke records in almost every state for which data are available. Similarly, younger Democratic voters were the strongest base of support for the socialist candidate Senator Bernie Sanders. For more data on voting patterns in the 2016 primary season, see "Total Youth Votes in 2016 Primaries and Caucuses" (http://civicyouth.org/total-youth-votes-in-2016-primaries-and-caucuses/).

15  John B. Cobb, Jr., paper presented at the 11th International Congress

on Ecological Civilization, Claremont, CA, April 27, 2016, quoted with the kind permission of Prof. Cobb.

16 Francis Fukuyama, *The End of History and the Last Man* (New York: Free Press, 1992).

17 Thomas Piketty, *Capital in the Twenty-First Century* (Cambridge, MA: Belknap Press, 2014).

18 Jean Tirole, *Économie du bien commun* (Paris: PUF, 2016). For a summary of Tirole's book in English, see http://archyworldys.com/ where-is-the-common-good-asks-the-nobel-prize-in-economics/; see also https://www.kva.se/globalassets/priser/ekonomi/2014/ sciback_ek_en_14.pdf. For an entire website devoted to the economics of the common good, see https://www.ecogood.org/en/ what-economy-common-good.

19 Norman Arthur Fischer, *Marxist Ethics within Western Political Theory: A Dialogue with Republicanism, Communitarianism, and Liberalism* (New York: Palgrave Macmillan, 2015); Henry Tam, *Communitarianism: A New Agenda for Politics and Citizenship* (New York: New York University Press, 1998); Shlomo Avineri and Avner de-Shalit, ed., *Communitarianism and Individualism* (Oxford: Oxford University Press, 1992). For helpful historical comments, see also https://en.wikipedia.org/wiki/Communitarianism.

20 *Oxford English Dictionary,* loc. cit.

21 See Online Etymology Dictionary: http://www.etymonline.com/ index.php?term=social.

22 See *socius*—("associated, allied; partner, companion, ally") in Wiktionary, https://en.wiktionary.org/wiki/societas.

23 http://www.etymonline.com/index.php?term=community.

24 Philip Clayton and Justin Heinzekehr. *Organic Marxism: An Alternative to Capitalism and Ecological Catastrophe* (Claremont, CA: Process Century Press, 2014).

25 Ibid., 203.

26 Ernest Callenbach, *Ecotopia: The Notebooks and Reports of William Weston* (New York: Bantam Books, 1977).

27 See www.EcoCiv.org.

# CONTRIBUTORS

**Philip Clayton** is Ingraham Professor at Claremont School of Theology and an affiliated faculty member at Claremont Graduate University. Previous positions and guest professorships include Williams College, Sonoma State University, Harvard University, Cambridge University, and the University of Munich. Having published extensively on science and religion, Clayton has more recently focused on science and values, environmental ethics, and ecological socialism ("Organic Marxism").

**Mark Dibben** is Associate Professor of Management in the Tasmanian School of Business & Economics at the University of Tasmania and Visiting Professor of Applied Process Thought in the Center for Process Studies at the Claremont School of Theology. He is co-editor of *Philosophy of Management* (Springer) and an editorial board member of *Process Studies*. His work focuses on what he terms "Applied Process Thought," the serious minded, thoroughgoing, hard-core common-sense application of process philosophy to topics

in the sciences and social sciences, of which two important examples
are management and economics.

**Justin Heinzekehr** is Director of Institutional Research and
Assessment and Assistant Professor of Bible and Religion at
Goshen College. His research interests include process philosophy, Anabaptist-Mennonite theology, and political theology. Most
recently, he published *Organic Marxism: An Alternative to Capitalism
and Environmental Catastrophe* with Philip Clayton.

**Carol Frances Johnston** has taught environmental theology and
ethics at Christian Theological Seminary for twenty-five years, and
is now shifting to work full time for the Sustainability Revolution.
She is the author of *The Wealth or Health of Nations: Transforming
Capitalism from Within*.

**Ouyang Kang** is the former Vice President at the Huazhong
University of Science and Technology (HUST). He is now President
of the Institute of State Governance, Director of the Institute of
Philosophy, Chairman of the Center for Process Studies (HUST),
and Professor of Philosophy at HUST. He is a senior researcher in
Chinese Marxist philosophy.

**Christine D. Miller Hesed** is an environmental anthropologist and
conservation biologist. Her research interests include climate change,
justice, social-ecological systems, resilience, and adaptation.

**Barbara Muraca** is Assistant Professor of Environmental and
Social Philosophy at Oregon State University and co-director of
the International Association of Environmental Philosophy (IAEP).
Her research interests include social and environmental philosophy,
sustainability and degrowth research, process philosophy, feminist
philosophy, and ecological economics. In 2014 she participated in
the organization of the 4th International Degrowth Conference in
Leipzig. She has published several articles on Degrowth in English
and German.

**Leslie A. Muray** is Professor of Philosophy and Religious Studies at Curry College (MA) and Coordinator of the Philosophy and Religious Studies Area. He is the author of *An Introduction to the Process Understanding of Science, Society and the Self* and *Liberal Protestantism and Science* as well as eighty articles in five languages. He is an incorrigible fan of cats, especially his three-legged 17-year-old Sasha, rock 'n' roll, the blues, the Boston Red Sox, the Boston Celtics, and the New England Patriots.

**Timothy Murphy** works at the intersection of constructive theology, process thought, liberation theologies, and political theory. His forthcoming book is entitled *Counter-imperial Churching for a Planetary Gospel: Radical Discipleship for Today*. He has been an adjunct professor at Claremont School of Theology and served for three years as Executive Director at Progressive Christians Uniting in Los Angeles, California.

**Cristina Neesham** is a social philosopher and business ethicist and Senior Lecturer in Management at Swinburne University Business School. She has a PhD in Philosophy from the University of Melbourne exploring the relationship between human and social progress using Condorcet, Smith, and Marx. Her research interests focus on using philosophical methods to inform the strategic management of systemic social problems. In particular, she investigates interdependencies between individual and group behaviors, social norms and institutional-regulatory regimes, and their role in creating (as well as alleviating) social problems.

**Anne F. Pomeroy** is Professor of Philosophy at Stockton University. She has written numerous articles in the areas of Marx, Sartre, process and dialectical philosophies, and is author of *Marx and Whitehead: Process, Dialectics, and the Critique of Capitalism*.

**Joerg Rieger** is Cal Turner Chancellor's Chair of Wesleyan Studies and Distinguished Professor of Theology at Vanderbilt University Divinity School. His most recent books include *Unified We are a*

*Force: How Faith and Labor Can Overcome America's Inequalities* (with Rosemarie Henkel-Rieger, 2016), *Faith on the Road: A Short Theology of Travel and Justice* (2015); *Occupy Religion: Theology of the Multitude* (with Kwok Pui-lan, 2012); *Globalization and Theology* (2010); and *No Rising Tide: Theology, Economics, and the Future* (2009).

**Jung Mo Sung** was born in South Korea in 1957 and has been living in Brazil since 1966. He is a professor at Methodist University of São Paulo, Brazil. He has authored many books, among them, *Subject, Capitalism and Religion; Desire, Market and Religion; and Beyond the Spirit of Empire* (co-authored with Joerg Rieger and Néstor Miguez).

Made in the USA
Middletown, DE
23 March 2017